Bank Lending

Bank Lending

Bank Lending

The Hong Kong Institute of Bankers

WILEY

John Wiley & Sons Singapore Pte. Ltd.

Other Wiley Editorial Offices
John Wiley & Sons, 111 River Street, Hoboken, NJ 07030, USA
John Wiley & Sons, The Atrium, Southern Gate, Chichester, West Sussex, P019 8SQ, United Kingdom
John Wiley & Sons (Canada) Ltd., 5353 Dundas Street West, Suite 400, Toronto, Ontario, M9B 6HB, Canada
John Wiley & Sons Australia Ltd., 42 McDougall Street, Milton, Queensland 4064, Australia
Wiley-VCH, Boschstrasse 12, D-69469 Weinheim, Germany

ISBN 978-0-470-82745-1 (Paper)
ISBN 978-0-470-82747-5 (ePDF)
ISBN 978-0-470-82746-8 (Mobi)
ISBN 978-0-470-82748-2 (ePub)

Contents

Preface

Sophisticated and effective banking activities are vital for modern societies to prosper. These banking activities include, in a nutshell, deposits and lending. The latter, in particular, contributes significantly to the well-being of every banking institution and is instrumental to commercial and social development across the globe. As such, it is of vital importance that a bank, regardless of its scope and scale or geographic footprint, employ effective techniques and knowledgeable personnel to keep its risk exposure within established parameters and maintain, if not improve, its credit rating, credibility, and reputation. Banking professionals in turn must continuously develop and refresh their understanding of lending practices and procedures for the benefit of their employers, the banking system, and the economy.

Banks lend to individuals and corporations to generate profits through interest and fees. To do so, banks consider the risks inherent in the process of lending and use complex analytical tools to assess and mitigate them. The business of lending is intrinsically linked to the management of risk. Effective risk management is necessary for effective and profitable bank lending. This book looks at the process of lending, its risks, and how to assess them and tackle them. A second book in this series, *Credit Risk Management*, expands on the importance and the systems to manage risk effectively.

This book is primarily aimed at professionals with a solid grounding in the banking industry, but the layperson would also find considerable value in the discussion of bank processes and goals. Like the other books in this series, this work focuses on practices in Hong Kong, but does so with an international perspective. Ultimately, readers should find this work helpful in developing critical evaluation skills to perform the complex tasks of planning, design and supervisory or management functions necessary in a broad range of banking activities.

The first chapter in this book discusses the process of lending to personal customers, the types of loans that banks typically make available to them, and how banks can reduce risk. In the second chapter, the discussion shifts from personal customers to corporates, going through the important challenges of assessing and mitigating credit risks. Knowing the concepts of credit assessment and mitigation is only the first step towards understanding the practicalities behind these theoretical concepts. Chapter 3 starts down that route by discussing how to dig deep into financial statements and use ratios to fully understand the performance and risk associated with borrowers. The next chapter considers internal structures and how they can help banks lower lending risk. The last three chapters move on to the more practical realities of loan pricing, customer business needs, and the all-important processes of credit management.

This book includes detailed explanations, summaries, tables, and charts to help industry professionals develop a sound theoretical framework for their work in the field. Both students and working professionals can benefit from this detailed work produced in collaboration with some of Hong Kong's most prominent professionals. All efforts have been undertaken to ensure the information in this book is thoroughly up to date but it is worth noting that any changes to laws and regulations after June 30, 2011 are not included.

Aimed at banking practitioners and designed as an essential tool to achieve learning outcomes, this book includes recommendations for additional readings. A list of further readings at the end of each chapter will help readers expand their knowledge of each subject. Essential readings will occasionally be highlighted and these are important for students preparing for the Associates Examination of the Hong Kong Institute of Bankers (AHKIB) while students should also be familiar with supplementary readings that provide information that is necessary but not always spelled out in this book.

The preparation of this book and others in the series required generous input from various individuals from their respective expert areas. Those from Hong Kong's academia offered practical insights into the context for the ideas, concepts, and theories presented and discussed in this book. Subject experts and market practitioners helped ensure all information contained here is relevant and applicable to everyday practice. Stakeholders from the commercial sector and the banking industry in turn confirmed that the information provided here sufficiently reflects the reality of the banking sector, bridging the gap between theory and practice for banking professionals.

The preparation of this book would not have been possible without the help, advice, support and encouragement of dozens of people. In particular it is important to mention Eugene Iu, Simon Y C Lo, Wilson Lau, Kevin C.K. Lam and Candy Wan (Lui Mi Ping). We owe thanks to all of them.

The Hong Kong Institute of Bankers

1

PERSONAL AND CORPORATE LENDING

1

Lending to Personal Customers

After studying this chapter, you should be able to:

1 Discuss general lending principles in advances to personal customers

2 Explain the types and purposes of lending to individuals

3 Describe the characteristics of residential mortgage loans and how interest rates and other fees are computed

4 Explain the various home ownership schemes in Hong Kong and the role of the HKMA and HKMC in Hong Kong's mortgage loan market

5 Understand the process of evaluating personal credit applications

Introduction

Lending money is the business of banks. Banks lend to individuals and corporations on the condition that it will be returned after an agreed period, usually with interest and fees. But lending is inherently risky. Repayment of a loan and interest on it depends on the future cash flow of the borrowers, and that future cash flow can never be certain. To be successful, banks need to ensure that the risks they take are reasonable and controlled within defined limits.

In this chapter,[1] we discuss the process of lending to personal customers, the types of loans that banks typically make available to them, and how banks can reduce the risk that these advances to individuals will not be repaid. Let us first learn about the general lending principles in making loans to personal customers. To make these principles more memorable to practitioners, they are usually arranged into easy to remember mnemonic devices such as CAMPARI, 5Cs, PARTLAMPS and PARSER.

General Lending Principles

You may know Campari as an alcoholic drink obtained from the infusion of bitter herbs, aromatic plants, and fruit made by Italy's Campari Group. In banking, though, CAMPARI stands for the initial letters of the factors that banks consider when making a decision as to whether or not to extend a loan to a personal customer: Character, Ability, Margin, Purpose, Amount, Repayment, and Insurance.

- **Character.** Before extending credit, the bank must be certain of the borrower's character. How reliable is the borrower's word regarding the details of the application and the promises made to repay? Is the borrower making overly optimistic claims?
- **Ability.** An individual borrower's ability to repay can partly be gleaned from the manner with which he or she handles financial affairs. Is there adequate cash flow in present earnings? The bank should examine the borrower's proof of income against his or her bank account records (such as bank statements), credit card statements, and references from banks and credit agencies. It should watch out for red flags such as personal cheques being dishonoured for lack of funds, frequent requests of stop payment on issued cheques, excesses on agreed facilities, and loans not being repaid on schedule.
- **Margin.** The margin expected by the lender should never cause it to underestimate or set aside the risk. The interest rate and fees to be charged for each loan application need to be commensurate with the risk perceived. The bank should decline any loan application where repayment is in doubt.
- **Purpose.** The bank should know the customer and the reason for the application. It should lend only for good causes and not for illegal purposes such as smuggling.

---

[1] This chapter uses some material from *Commercial Banking* (2005) by Benton E. Gup and James W. Kolari, with permission from publisher John Wiley & Sons.

- **Amount.** The bank should ascertain if the amount of the loan requested is reasonable, if it matches the purpose, and if it is in proportion to the resources of the customer. In lending to personal customers, banks rely on the borrower's income. In general, the higher the income, the more prepared banks are to lend a greater proportion of the needed amount.
- **Repayment.** Does the borrower have sufficient capacity to pay whether through recurrent cash flows, disposition of a single asset, or anticipated income? If possible, the bank should arrange repayment through an automatic monthly debit from the borrower's salary. It should match the repayment period with the nature and purpose of the borrowing (e.g., a car loan does not usually exceed three to four years while a home mortgage loan may be granted for 25 years or even longer). The bank should be cautious of borrowers who change banks, particularly those who badmouth their previous banks. The bank should always be prepared to say "no" to any borrower who rushes it into a lending decision.
- **Insurance.** The bank should consider if some form of security is necessary, but should remember that security is not a substitute for repayment. The security must be measurable and stable in value, simple to take, easy to sell and liquidate, and must be legally enforceable. If in the form of real property, the title must be clean and transferable. The bank should be conscious of the difference in the market value and forced sale value of a security. It should always include a realistic margin to allow for the costs of realisation and the discount to be expected on a forced sale or a fall in the market.

    Another form of acceptable security is through a personal guarantee from a third party. Under the Code of Banking Practice, which is issued jointly by the Hong Kong Association of Banks and the DTC Association and endorsed by the Hong Kong Monetary Authority, the lender must apprise the personal guarantor of the risk by requiring him or her to take independent legal advice before signing any guarantee.

Besides CAMPARI, there are other easy-to-remember lending acronyms in use, such as 5Cs (character, capital, capacity, collateral, and condition); PARTLAMPS (purpose, amount, repayment, time, laws, accounts, management, profitability, and security); and PARSER (person, amount, repayment, security, expediency, and remuneration). All these acronyms deal more or less with the same elements and principles, and it is up to the individual bank to decide which ones are most useful for its own circumstances or to devise a lending acronym of its own.

Types of Personal Customers

To flesh out and apply the general lending principles, it is helpful for the banker to learn the types of personal customers that exist. Loan applicants can roughly be broken down into four categories, depending on how they earn their livelihood:

- **Salaried employees.** These applicants are permanent employees who typically receive a monthly salary, 13th month pay, overtime, allowances, and performance bonuses.

Among the key factors to examine when dealing with salaried employees are the total compensation package, length of employment, and the employer's industry and reputation.

- **Self-employed.** These borrowers own and run their own business, such as restaurants, hair salons, laundry services, or market stalls, or rely on freelance project-based work, such as journalists and editors. Because their living typically comes from a small enterprise, the risk of lending to self-employed persons is higher than for salaried workers. Banks need to closely examine assessments for profit tax by the Inland Revenue Department, financial statements, bank records, and other documents in lending to self-employed borrowers.

- **Professionals** (e.g., accountants, architects, doctors, engineers, and solicitors) can be self-employed with their own practice or salaried employees of companies, or a combination of the two. The risk of lending to professionals can be lower than that of lending to the self-employed, since professionals have specialised skills and qualifications and can charge substantial fees. Nevertheless, their income can be volatile depending on their reputation and the need for their services. Banks should take into account the stability of the profession—accountancy and medicine are typically seen as more stable professions than architecture and entertainment, for example.

- **Wage earners** or blue-collar workers are generally regarded as the most risky borrowers because they usually do not have job security and are paid by actual work done. If they are factory workers, they may not be entitled to wages if the factory is idle. If they are truck drivers, they may not be paid if there are no deliveries to be made.

- **Private investors** are those who invest in property, the stock market and other assets to make a living or supplement their income. They are typically retirees, housewives, or career people who gave up their jobs to focus on investing their money for profit.

The borrower's means of livelihood has a direct bearing on the two "As" in CAMPARI—ability to repay and the appropriate amount to be lent—as well as repayment and, especially for wage earners, insurance. Some banks may lend only to salaried workers and professionals as a matter of policy, but others may be willing to take on more risk and lend to the self-employed and wage earners as well, perhaps because the salaried/professionals market has become too crowded. Whatever the strategy, the borrower's generic and unique circumstances in terms of his or her means of livelihood must be taken into account in deciding whether or not to grant a loan.

General Purposes of Personal Advances

One key general principle in CAMPARI is the purpose of the personal loan. The most-cited reasons for asking the bank for a personal loan include the following:

- Buying a flat or house;
- Decorating a flat or house;
- Requesting bridge financing for a flat or house;
- Buying a car;
- Buying consumer products like computers and smart phones;
- Starting a new business or new practice;
- Investing or speculating in various financial products;
- Spending for a wedding;
- Paying for a vacation trip;
- School tuition;
- Paying salaries tax, inheritance tax and other taxes.

All of the above purposes are valid and legal, but banks also need to make sure their money will indeed be used as the borrower said it would be used. Knowing the purpose of the personal advance also has a direct bearing on the second "A" in CAMPARI—the amount to be lent obviously depends on how the loan will be used. It would be higher for buying a flat, for example, and lower to decorate that flat. The purpose of the loan will also help determine whether insurance is needed. Banks should ask for the title to the flat in a mortgage loan, but do not need to ask for a similar document when lending for the customer to buy a computer, which typically will be put on a credit card.

Types of Lending to Individuals

Individual clients can avail themselves of many personal loan products including the following:

- Home mortgages;
- Bridge loans;
- Probate advances;
- Investment loans and advances relating to consumer expenses;
- Personal loans and overdrafts;
- Tax loans;
- Credit cards.

Home Mortgages

A key product of Hong Kong banks is the home mortgage loan because these are generally more profitable and more secure with a lower delinquency ratio than other types of lending. The home borrower is called the "mortgagor" and the lender bank is the "mortgagee."

Residential mortgage loans differ from other types of loans in several respects. First, the loans are for relatively large amounts. Second, the loans tend to be long term. In Hong Kong, mortgagors usually have from five to 20 years to repay, but longer tenors have been offered due to heightened competition among banks. Third, the loans are usually secured, using the real estate to be purchased as collateral. However, real estate is illiquid, and its price can vary widely.

The two basic types of home mortgage loans are floating rate mortgages and fixed rate mortgages, in reference to the interest rates paid on the loan. Floating rate mortgages permit lenders to vary the interest rate charged on the mortgage loan, depending on the rise or fall of market interest rates. In fixed-rate mortgages, the interest rate charged does not change over the life of the loan. In Hong Kong, a variation to these two basic mortgages is the fixed adjustable rate mortgage (FARM), which locks in the interest rate on the loan for a certain period (say for 10 years), after which the borrower can re-fix the rate for another set period or convert the loan to a floating rate.

In Hong Kong, the wholly government-owned Hong Kong Mortgage Corporation (HKMC) buys mortgage loans from approved sellers, assuming the risk of those loans and

THE HONG KONG MORTGAGE CORPORATION'S MORTGAGE INSURANCE PROGRAMME

In 1999, a Mortgage Insurance Programme (MIP) was launched by the government-owned Hong Kong Mortgage Corporation (HKMC) to promote home ownership in Hong Kong. "Under the MIP programme, the HKMC is the insurer and the insured party is the bank, not the mortgage borrower," the company said. However, "banks have the full discretion to decide whether and to what extent the insurance premium will be passed on to the borrowers." In turn, the HKMC insures its exposure with a group of reinsurers and together they determine the mortgage premium.

The MIP enables banks to offer home buyers a higher loan-to-value (LTV) mortgage loan than the level recommended by the Hong Kong Monetary Authority (see "Prudential Measures for Property Mortgage Loans," page 13). As long as an application meets the eligibility criteria set by the HKMC, the bank can approve a mortgage of up to 90% LTV ratio. At this maximum ceiling, the home owner will need to pay a down payment of only 10% of the property price.

The MIP is periodically revised to reflect changes in the property market. On November 2010, the HKMC introduced a cap of HK$6.8 million on the value of property that can be covered by all MIP products. In June 2011, the HKMC further lowered the cap to HK$6 million. As a result, the maximum loan amount for mortgage loans with 70% loan-to-value threshold dropped to HK$5.4 million (from HK$6.12 million under the previous cap) and the maximum loan amount for mortgage loans with MIP cover at 60% loan-to-value threshold dropped to HK$5 million (from HK$6 million).

The rate of rejection under the MIP is historically low, and mainly due to the borrower showing insufficient proof of income, a debt-to-income ratio exceeding 50%, and a previous loan delinquency record.

thus helping maintain the stability of the banking sector. The HKMC also promotes home ownership through a Mortgage Insurance Programme (see "The Hong Kong Mortgage Corporation's Mortgage Insurance Programme" on page 8).

Floating Rate Mortgage

A floating rate mortgage, which is the predominant form of financing for home mortgages in Hong Kong, is one in which the interest rate changes over the life of the loan. The change can result in changes in monthly payments, the term of the loan, and/or the principal amount.

- **Index.** The idea behind floating rate mortgages is to permit lenders to maintain a positive spread between the returns on their mortgage loans (assets) and the cost of borrowed funds (liabilities) when benchmark interest rates change. This is accomplished by linking the mortgage rate to a standard benchmark rate. In Hong Kong, home mortgage rates are linked to the Hong Kong interbank offered rate (HIBOR), Hong Kong Prime Rate, Composite Interest Rate, or the prime rate quoted by mortgage loan sellers approved by the Hong Kong Mortgage Corporation.

  When an index such as the HIBOR changes, the lender can (1) make periodic changes in the borrower's monthly payments, (2) keep the monthly payment the same and change the principal amount of the loan, (3) change the maturity of the loan, or (4) any combination of the above. Some mortgage loans have fixed rates for three years, five years, seven years, or ten years, but may adjust one time, or annually after that.

  The best adjustment, from the lender's point of view, depends on whether interest rates are expected to rise or fall over the life of the mortgage loan. If they are expected to rise, increased monthly payments will increase the lender's cash flow. If they are expected to fall, the second option listed above will permit the lender to more or less maintain its spread between earning assets and costs of funds. The adjustment period may be monthly, annually, or any other time period, and changes are made according to the terms of the contract.

- **Caps.** Floating rate mortgages have caps that limit how much the interest rate or monthly payments can change yearly or over the term of the loan. For example, the interest rate change may be capped at 2 percentage points annually and 6 percentage points over the life of the loan. Alternatively, a $50 payment cap means that the monthly payment cannot increase more than $50 per year.

- **Margin.** Margin is the number of percentage points that the lender adds to the index rate to determine the rate charged on the floating rate mortgage in each adjustment period. The equation for the floating rate mortgage that is charged is:

$$\text{Floating interest rate} = \text{index rate} + \text{margin}$$

  Suppose the index rate is 6% and the margin is 2%. The interest rate that will be charged on the floating rate mortgage is 8% (6% + 2% = 8%). The margin usually remains constant over the life of the loan. However, the size of the margin can vary from lender to lender.

- **Rates.** Lenders may offer prospective home buyers a lower interest rate or lower payments for the first year of the mortgage loan to induce the buyer to use a floating rate mortgage. After the discount period, the interest rate on the floating rate mortgage is adjusted to reflect the current index rate.

  The lower rate is commonly called a *teaser rate,* because lenders expect it to increase in future years. Even without teaser rates, the initial interest rates charged on floating rate mortgages can be lower than the rates charged on fixed rate mortgages. The extent to which they are lower depends on the maturity of the loan, and varies widely.

- **Shifting the risk.** Using floating rate mortgages is one way lenders shift some of their interest rate risk when holding mortgage loans. However, lenders may end up trading reduced interest rate risk for increased default risk and lower income. First, floating rate mortgages are riskier than fixed rate mortgages because they generate less interest income during periods of declining interest.

  Second, floating rate mortgages have higher delinquency and default risk than fixed-rate mortgages in jurisdictions like the United States. One reason for this may be that loan-to-value ratios are higher for floating-rate mortgages than for fixed-rate mortgages, although this does not apply to Hong Kong, where the loan-to-value ratio for residential mortgage properties are subject to prudential caps.(see "Prudential Measures for Property Mortgage Loans," page 13). The delinquency rates may get worse if interest rates increase because the borrower's ability to repay the loan may be diminished. This is so because the borrower's disposable income may not increase as much during the same period to cover the higher interest payments.

Fixed Rate Mortgage

In fixed rate mortgages, the interest rate does not change throughout the repayment period and the debt is gradually extinguished through equal periodic payments on the principal balance. In other words, the borrower pays the same dollar amount each month until the mortgage loan is paid off.

There are several elements to consider in fixed rate mortgages.

- **Monthly mortgage payments.** The monthly payments depend on the size of the loan, the interest rate, and the maturity. To illustrate this, let us examine the monthly mortgage payments for a $1,000 mortgage loan.

  Table 1.1 shows the monthly mortgage payments for a $1,000 mortgage loan with selected annual interest rates and maturities. A close examination of the body of the table reveals two important facts. First, the dollar amount of the monthly mortgage payment increases as the interest rate increases. For example, the monthly mortgage payment for a loan with ten years to maturity ranges from $11.10 when the interest rate is 6%, to $16.76 when the interest rate is 16%. Second, the dollar amount of the monthly mortgage payment declines as the maturity of the loan is extended. When the interest rate is 6%, the monthly mortgage payment drops from $11.10 on the 10th year of maturity, to $6.00 on the 30th year of maturity.

TABLE 1.1 Monthly payment for a $1,000 mortgage loan[2]

Annual Interest Rate	Years to Maturity				
	10 Years	15 Years	20 Years	25 Years	30 Years
6%	$11.10	$ 8.44	$ 7.16	$ 6.44	$ 6.00
8	12.13	9.56	8.36	7.72	7.34
10	13.22	10.75	9.65	9.09	8.78
12	14.35	12.00	11.01	10.53	10.29
14	15.35	13.32	12.44	12.04	11.85
16	16.76	14.69	13.92	13.59	13.45

The monthly mortgage payments shown in Table 1.1 can be determined by using the equation below.

$$\text{PV of annuity} = PMT \left[\frac{1 - (1 + i)^{-n}}{i} \right]$$

$$\$1,000 = PMT \left[\frac{1 - (1 + 0.005)^{-120}}{0.005} \right]$$

$$PMT = \$11.10$$

By way of illustration, we will compute the monthly mortgage payment for a $1,000 mortgage loan at 6% interest for 10 years. Because we are solving for a monthly payment, the number of payments over 10 years is 120 (10 years $\times$ 12 months per year). Moreover, only 1/12th of the 6% annual interest rate $(0.06/12 = 0.005)$ is charged each month. The present value of the annuity is the $1,000 mortgage loan in this example. The monthly payment is $11.10.

To solve the problem on a financial calculator, such as a Hewlett-Packard 12C, clear the calculator then enter n = 10 years (multiplied by 12 monthly payments, blue key), i = 6 (divided by 12 monthly payments, blue key), and PV = $1,000 (also press END button, blue key), and then press PMT. The monthly payment PMT = $11.10. Each model and brand of calculator has unique features. Your operator's manual should explain how to compute loan payments for amortised loans. Online calculators are now also available. Many Hong Kong banks even feature on their websites an easy–to–use online calculator for home mortgages.

- **Maturity.** For a given interest rate and maturity, the *total* cost of the loan to the borrower is higher with longer maturities (smaller monthly payments) than shorter maturities

---

[2] Benton E. Gup and James W. Kolari, *Commercial Banking*, 3rd ed. (John Wiley & Sons, 2005), 287.

(higher monthly payments). The total cost is determined by multiplying the mortgage payment per $1,000 of loan for each interest rate by the dollar amount of the loan (in thousands) and the number of months.

By way of illustration, consider a $100,000 mortgage loan at 12% with a maturity of 10 years. The monthly payment is $1,435 ($14.35 × 100 = $1,435) and the total cost over the life of the loan is $172,200 ($1,435 × 120 months = $172,200). If the maturity were 25 years, the monthly payment would drop to $1,053, but the total cost to the borrower would be $315,900, which is $143,700 more than the cost of the 10-year loan.

- **Principal and interest.** Let's examine the monthly mortgage payment in greater detail and consider the amount that is allocated to principal and to interest. Table 1.2 shows the breakdown between principal and interest for the first year's payments of a $100,000 loan at 12% for 25 years.

The striking feature of this table is the disproportionate amount of the monthly payment that is applied to interest payments. Total mortgage payments amount to $12,636 ($1,053 × 12 = $12,636) during the first twelve months of the loan. Of that amount, $11,361.52 is applied to interest and only $1,274.48 is used to reduce the principal amount of the loan.

The implication of the data presented in Table 1.2 is that lenders earn most of their interest income during the early years of a mortgage loan. Therefore, all other things being

TABLE 1.2   Mortgage amortisation[3]

Month	Principal	Interest	Balance
1	$ 53.00	$ 1,000.00	$99,947.00
2	63.00	990.00	99,884.00
3	72.90	980.10	99,811.10
4	82.70	970.30	99,728.40
5	92.40	960.60	99,636.00
6	102.01	950.99	99,533.99
7	111.52	941.48	99,422.47
8	120.93	932.07	99,301.54
9	130.26	922.74	99,171.28
10	139.48	913.52	99,031.80
11	148.62	904.38	98,883.18
12	157.66	895.34	98,725.52
Totals	$1,274.48	$11,361.52	

[3] Benton E. Gup and James W. Kolari, *Commercial Banking*, 3rd ed. (John Wiley & Sons, 2005), 288.

equal, a high turnover of the mortgage loans contributes more interest income to earnings than having mortgage loans remain in their portfolio until they mature.

Fixed Adjustable Rate Mortgage (FARM)

The HKMC pioneered a Fixed Adjustable Rate Mortgage (FARM) Programme in 1998 to promote fixed-rate mortgage loans as an alternative choice of mortgage financing in Hong Kong. In a Hong Kong FARM loan, mortgage borrowers can lock in the interest rate on their mortgage for one year, two years, three years, five years, seven years, and 10 years. After the end of the contracted period, the borrower has the choice of re-fixing the interest rate for another term at the prevailing FARM rate or converting the loan to a floating rate mortgage at, for example, prime rate minus 3% per annum.

PRUDENTIAL MEASURES FOR PROPERTY MORTGAGE LOANS

The Hong Kong Monetary Authority (HKMA) has thought it prudent to issue guidelines from time to time to help protect the banking system.

In 1995, for example, the HKMA backed the industry-wide practice of lending home buyers only up to 70% of the market value of a residential property. In 1991, the banking sector had voluntarily adopted a 70% loan-to-value ratio for residential mortgage lending. This was subsequently endorsed by the government and incorporated in the HKMA's guidelines on property lending. Placing a 70% cap on the loanable amount or loan-to-value (LTV) ratio was "a long-term policy important for promoting stability in the banking system," the HKMA said in its 1995 Annual Report.

The cap could be adjusted downwards, as the HKMA did in January 1997, when it issued a guideline putting a 60% LTV or HK$8.4 million for luxury properties worth over HK$12 million. The HKMA withdrew this lower cap in October 2001.

Starting in 2009 and considering the increasing risk of an asset price bubble, the HKMA started issuing a series of guidelines that progressively lowered LTV on various classes of mortgages. The authority introduced countercyclical supervisory measures at least four times on October 23, 2009, August 13, 2010, November 19, 2010 and June 10, 2011 to ensure the stability of Hong Kong's banking system amid this increasing risk. These measures included standardising the limit on debt servicing ratios (DSRs) of borrowers to 50%, stress testing the debt servicing ability of borrowers assuming a rise in mortgage rates of at least two percentage points, and limiting the stressed DSR to a cap of 60%.

(Continued)

The process started in October 2009, when the HKMA issued a set of measures that included:

- Lowering the LTV ratio for mortgage loans for properties valued at HK$20 million or more to 60%.
- Capping the value of properties eligible for LTV ratios of 70% at HK$12 million, to avoid the anomaly of borrowers who purchased a property worth just under HK$20 million being able to borrow more than one whose property is worth just over that threshold.

Then, in November 2010, the HKMA issued a circular requiring AIs to follow additional guidelines in undertaking mortgage business, including:

- Lowering the maximum LTV for residential properties with a value of HK$12 million or above to 50%.
- Limiting the maximum LTV ratio for residential properties with a value of HK$8 million or above but below HK$12 million to 60%, subject to a maximum loan cap of HK$6 million.
- Maintaining the 70% maximum LTV ratio for residential properties valued at below HK$8 million, subject to a maximum loan cap of HK$4.8 million.
- Lowering the maximum LTV ratio to 50%, irrespective of value, for residential properties not intended to be occupied by the owners, properties held by companies, commercial and industrial properties, and properties with mortgage loans based on borrowers' net worth.

A few months later, in June 2011, the HKMA issued a new set of measures that further lowered LTV caps to both residential and non-residential property mortgages, including:

- Setting a maximum LTV ratio of 50% for owner-occupied residential properties worth HK$10 million or more, a maximum LTV ratio of 60% for properties valued between HK$7 million and HK$10 million to a maximum loan of HK$5 million, and a maximum LTV ratio of 70% for properties worth less than HK$7 million to a maximum of HK$4.2 million.
- Lowering the maximum LTV ratio by 10% for mortgages to borrowers whose income was derived from outside Hong Kong.
- Lowering the maximum LTV ratio for mortgage loans based on the borrower's net worth from 50% to 40%.

Alternative Mortgage Instruments

Alternative mortgage instruments is a generic term to denote a wide menu of mortgage instruments where the terms of the contract can change or where they differ from the traditional mortgage loan. Not all of the following are offered in Hong Kong, but they are included here in the interest of completeness.

- **Balloon mortgage.** Balloon mortgage loans are relatively short-term loans, such as five years. At the end of that period, the entire amount of the loan comes due and a new loan is negotiated.
- **Graduated payment mortgage (GPM).** Because of the high cost of housing, many young buyers cannot afford large monthly mortgage payments. Graduated payment mortgages (GPMs) address this problem by charging borrowers low monthly payments at first and then payments rise over a period of years.

    Because the monthly payments on GPMs are so low in the early years, there is negative amortisation—the monthly payments are insufficient to pay the interest on the loan. The unpaid interest accrues, and borrowers pay interest on the interest. If the borrowers decided to sell their residence in the early years, and it did not appreciate in value, the principal balance on the loan would have increased due to negative amortisation. In other words, they would owe more than they originally borrowed on the house, and the sale of the mortgaged property might not provide sufficient funds to pay off the loan.
- **Growing equity mortgage.** Growing equity mortgages are 15-year fully amortised home mortgage loans that provide for successively higher debt service payments over the life of the loan. They are made at a fixed rate and the initial payments are calculated on a 30-year schedule. However, they are paid off more rapidly because there is an annual increase in the monthly payments, all of which goes to reduce the principal balance of the loan. In addition, the interest rate is made below the prevailing rate for 30-year loans. Borrowers who can afford the increased payments can save thousands of dollars in interest payments over the term of the loan.
- **Interest-only mortgage.**[4] The interest-only mortgage lets the borrower pay only the interest portion of the loan for some predetermined period, and then the loan payments are adjusted to fully amortise over the remaining life of the loan. For example, on a 30-year mortgage loan the first 10 years is devoted to paying only the interest and then the loan payments are changed to amortise the loan over the remaining 20 years. One of the major advantages for the borrower is that monthly payments during the interest-only period are lower than they would be for a fully amortised mortgage. On the other side of the coin, the borrower may have little or no equity stake in the real estate during that period.
- **Shared appreciation mortgage (SAM).** A SAM is a mortgage loan arrangement where the borrower agrees to share in the increased value of the property (usually 30% to 50%) with the lender in return for a reduction in the fixed interest rate at the time the loan is made. The increased value of the property is determined at some specified date

---

[4] Per a circular letter issued by the HKMA on 20 March 2008, AIs should not offer residential mortgage loans (RMLs) with principal repayment holiday features to customers. Noting a growing trend among authorized institutions to provide residential mortgage loans (RMLs) with a principal repayment holiday of two to three years, during which borrowers are only required to service interest payments, the HKMA warned that lenders may be exposed to considerably higher risks in the event of loan default.

in the future when the loan can be refinanced or when the property is sold. Sharing a decline in value is not part of the loan agreement.

- **Reverse mortgage.** In the U.S., the reverse mortgage is designed for senior citizens, 62 and over, who own their houses free and clear of debt and want to increase their incomes by borrowing against the equity in their houses. In this case, the lender pays the property owner a fixed tax-free annuity based on a percentage value of the property. The owner would not be required to repay the loan until his or her demise, at which time the loan would be paid from the proceeds of the estate, or until the house is sold. The interest rate on the loan may be adjustable and the loan may have a refinancing option.
- **Second mortgage/home equity loan.** Many homeowners use a second mortgage when they need funds for business or as a substitute for consumer loans. Other than selling their homes, a home equity loan is the only way homeowners can convert their equity into funds they can spend.

Equity is the difference between the market value of the property and the mortgage debt. A traditional second mortgage is made in addition to the first mortgage and uses the same property as collateral. Second mortgages usually provide for a fixed dollar amount to be repaid over a specified period of time requiring monthly payment of principal and interest. Second mortgages have a subordinated claim to property in the event of foreclosure.

A home equity loan can be a traditional second mortgage or a revolving line of credit, in which case the line of credit has a second-mortgage status but would be the first lien if the borrower has no mortgage debt outstanding when the credit line was established. The line of credit has a more flexible repayment schedule than the traditional second mortgage. Under the home equity line of credit, the borrower with a fixed credit line can write checks up to that amount. In the case of a home equity loan, the loan is a lump sum that is paid off in instalments over time.

HOME OWNERSHIP SCHEMES IN HONG KONG

To enable lower-income families to acquire home ownership, the Housing Authority (HA) used to offer the following programmes: the Home Ownership Scheme, the Tenants Purchase Scheme, and the Home Assistance Loan Scheme. The schemes featured guaranteed buybacks and a loan-to-value (LTV) ratio of up to 90%–100% of the lower of the purchase price or assessed market value of the properties. All three schemes have since been suspended indefinitely.

The Home Ownership Scheme (HOS) targeted those buying HOS flats—subsidised public housing with certain restrictions set on their purchase, sale, and mortgages. The scheme was suspended in 2003, although the HA has been selling unsold and returned HOS flats in phases starting in 2007.

Under the Tenant Purchase Scheme (TPS), sitting tenants could buy public estate flats. The purchase, sale, and mortgage also came with certain restrictions. Being fully guaranteed by the HKHA, the loanable amount was set at 100% LTV and a lower interest rate could be charged compared with other private property buyers. TPS buyers had to show a debt-to-income ratio of 50% and produce a copy of a Letter of Offer from the HKHA.

The Home Assistance Loan Scheme (HALS) was first offered in 2003 with the aim of helping lower-income families afford their own homes. The programme gave three options: (1) an interest-free loan of $530,000 (repayable over 13 years); (2) $390,000, also interest free and repayable over 20 years); or (3) a monthly mortgage subsidy of $3,800 (payable for 48 months). Single persons could also avail of it but the loan and subsidy amount was halved. The scheme was terminated on 14 July 2004.

Besides the government, a non-profit non-government organisation called the Hong Kong Housing Society (HKHS) has been assisting in providing affordable housing. Since 1948, the HKHS has built around 67,000 residential units under such various schemes as Rental Estate, Rural Public Housing, Flat-For-Sale, Sandwich Class Housing, Urban Improvement, and Senior Citizen Residences.

Under the Flat-For-Sale Scheme, developed in the late 1980s, tenants were allowed to own their flats at concession rates. In the early 1990s, the Sandwich Class Housing Scheme was offered specifically for those who were not eligible to apply under the Government Home Ownership (GHOS) & Private Sector Participation (PSPS) programmes but could not afford to buy private flats. The LTV was set at 80%. Due to changing market needs, however, three of the Sandwich Class Housing developments were converted into private properties for sale at full market values after the year 2000.

VILLAGE HOUSES IN HONG KONG

Village houses are low-rise residential apartments that are much sought after but difficult to acquire using bank mortgages because of their unique features.

They are usually a cheaper choice for home buyers compared to residential flats. However, banks are generally cautious in lending against village houses because valuation is more difficult since comparable transactions are fewer than for the residential flats, the administrative control over quality is less strict and their management and maintenance may not be as professional as those for residential flats.

If the village houses are located on Tso land—meaning land owned by traditional organisations known as "Tso" or "Tong"—the transaction

(Continued)

becomes more complicated. In this instance, Chinese customary rights will prevail over English common law and equity concepts. This may substantially affect the value of the village house in question.

In September 1998, the Lands Department issued an extensive guide to buying and selling village houses located in the New Territories. This can be accessed on their website.

To make loans for the purchase of village houses less risky for banks, the Hong Kong Mortgage Corporation opened a separate window to provide mortgage insurance for up to 85% of the LTV ratio. Up to a maximum loan amount of $5 million can be covered but the borrower has to secure a floating rate mortgage, not a fixed adjustable rate mortgage. See the HKMC website for restrictions on the age and location of village houses that can be covered.

Resale of village houses is generally much more difficult in a receding property market. Still, banks do accept mortgages against village houses if the home buyer is able to prove a comfortable debt-to-income servicing ratio. But the LTV may have to be lower (e.g. 60%) and the loan tenor shorter due to higher risks involved.

Bridging Loans

Bridge loans "bridge a gap" in a borrower's financing until some specific event occurs. For example, a firm wants to acquire a new warehouse facility, but needs funds to finance the transaction until the old warehouse can be sold. Thus, a *bridge loan* is short-term financing that is made in anticipation of receiving longer-term financing on which an agreement has been reached.

In the case of home mortgage loans, a personal customer may put up his or her existing property for sale in order to use the proceeds to buy a new home. To assist such buyers, banks offer two types of bridging loans—the closed and open-ended.

In the closed bridge type of loan, the customer has signed a contract to sell his or her property and has a firm completion date. While the risk is low, problems can still arise if the sale of the existing property falls through.

With the open-ended bridge loan, the borrower approaches the bank for a mortgage to acquire a new property, on the premise that the sale proceeds of his existing property will go to the purchase. Lending risks are therefore high and banks will be wise not to consider this kind of bridging loan unless the property market is buoyant and potential buyers of the existing property have been identified. In addition, it is necessary for the lender to impose a substantial margin to cover all contingencies (e.g., the anticipated net sale proceeds can repay the loan as well as accrued interest for 12 months and allow for a 20% reduction in the asking price).

Both types of bridging loans require a professional valuation of both the existing and desired properties, full insurance cover, and status enquiries on the solicitors looking over the documents pertaining to the sale transaction in order to prevent mortgage fraud.

To calculate the amount of bridging finance needed, banks use the following formula:

	HKD
Purchase price of the new property	X
−) Mortgage on the new property	(X)
−) Any capital of the customer	(X)
+) Moving expenses	X
+) Amount to pay off the mortgage on existing property	X
= Bridging finance needed	X

Moving expenses include:
- Estate agency fees
- Solicitor fees
- Stamp duty

Probate Advances

Probate advances are a special type of loan to enable the personal representatives of a deceased person to settle debts of the estate or pay the inheritance tax prior to the grant of probate or administration.

A word of caution: Until the grant of probate is made, the personal representatives of the deceased have no effective power to borrow against the assets of the estate. They will therefore be personally liable for any borrowing. Such loans can still be granted, however, once the lender is able to satisfactorily ascertain the integrity of the personal representatives and their solicitor, the reasonableness of the inheritance tax amount, and the time required for the repayment of the advances from the realisation of the estate.

With the abolition of estate duty in Hong Kong from 2006, the need for probate advances has become rare.

Investment Loans and Advances Relating to Consumer Expenses

One usual type of investment loan is share financing, where personal customers borrow from the bank in order to purchase listed shares or place new share subscriptions. Lenders usually advance from 50% to 60% of the market value of the shares, which normally have to be blue chip to be deemed acceptable for bank financing. But some banks will advance loans to borrowers at a lower percentage of the shares' market value for stocks other than blue chips.

With initial public offerings and new share subscriptions, quality and marketability have to be checked by analysing the financial statements. Stock agents also have to be consulted to assess market demand and the likely percentage of over-subscription.

In addition, a memorandum of deposit and a charge form have to be signed by the borrower and the shares need to be transferred into the nominee name of the bank to establish legal charge.

Personal Loans and Overdrafts

The sum involved is usually small—up to four to six times the customer's monthly salary. The tenor or repayment period is short - between six months to three years. A minimum repayment ratio, e.g. 5% of the outstanding debit balance each month, is set for an overdraft and revolving loan facility.

This type of loan has a wide variety of uses (e.g., for credit card payments, purchase of cars or consumer durables, for education, tax payments, or even a wedding).

Because this loan is generally "unsecured"—it relies mainly on the borrower's word of promise to pay back—the risk is offset with a relatively high interest margin. But lower interest rates can be offered to professionals, civil servants, and homeowners, who are among the best regarded credit risks.

The bank should use credit scoring and bank references to evaluate customer risk. In general, those on a company payroll are preferred to daily wage and commission income earners, since the former have relatively stable income, more job security, and better track records in repaying personal loans.

While giving due regard to certain laws against discrimination in Hong Kong, the bank should exercise caution in lending to those employed by small or unknown companies or in industries or categories with high volatility and turnover (e.g., project-based, floating, or short-term contract staff, airline crew, speculative traders, salespersons, agents, brokers, as well as workers in casinos, bars, nightclubs, and other entertainment establishments).

Tax Loans

In Hong Kong, tax loans can be said to carry lower risks than many other types of lending to individuals because there is proof that the borrower really has a job and the bank has access to the salaries tax assessment issued by the Inland Revenue Department. The actual amount of tax to be paid is also a good indicator of the borrower's ability to repay. It is based on a maximum of 15% (standard tax rate) of the net total income (i.e., assessable income after deductions but before allowances, giving the bank a snapshot of the borrower's financial condition).

Different banks in Hong Kong design tax loans in various ways. Some offer tax loans to cover only the actual amount owed to the government, which is the most conservative approach. Others offer loans of up to three times the tax bill if the customer is a professional, and up to two times for other customers. Still others link a personal credit loan to the tax loan, effectively increasing their risk but also their earnings from the loans.

Perhaps because of the perceived relatively low risk, the tax loan market is a crowded one. As a result, banks compete on low interest rates, with existing customers and those whose salaries are deposited directly into the bank charged even lower, and other incentives such as waiver of handling fees are offered. The fierce competition notwithstanding, banks must remain vigilant about extending loans that are of the appropriate amount and must make sure the loans are consistent with their lending policies.

Credit Cards

A credit card is any card, plate, or device that may be used from time to time and over and over again to borrow money or buy goods and services with a promise to pay by a certain date and without an exchange of cash.

A credit card should not be confused with a debit card or prepayment card. A **debit card** looks like a plastic credit card, and may be used to make purchases, but no credit is extended. The funds are electronically withdrawn or transferred from the cardholder's account to pay for the purchases. Debit and credit cards are the preferred method of payment for in-store sales. In the case of prepayment (stored-value) cards, such as Octopus cards, a certain dollar amount is prepaid, and deductions are made for each transaction.

The growth of credit card–related consumer debt is attributable to automation, and the fact that credit cards are mass-marketed like a commodity. Mass mailings of credit card applications are sent to selected segments of the population based on demographic criteria, such as income and housing. The applications are evaluated using credit scoring. Qualified applicants receive cards, and their accounts are monitored by computer programs. The use of automation keeps labour cost at a minimum for the large number of transactions processed.

There are three types of credit card plans for banks. The first type of plan uses a single principal bank to issue the credit card, maintain accounts, bill and collect credit, and assume most of the other functions associated with credit cards. In the second type of plan, one bank acts as a limited agent for the principal bank. The principal bank issues the card, carries the bulk of the credit, and performs the functions described in the first plan. The functions of the agent bank are to establish merchant accounts and accept merchant sales drafts; it receives a commission on the business it generates without incurring costs of a credit card operation. The limited agent bank may have its own name and logo on the card. Cardholders assume that the card is issued and managed by that bank, which is not the case.

In the third plan, a bank affiliates with one of the major travel and entertainment card (T & E) plans such as American Express. A travel and entertainment card is a credit card, but cardholders must pay the entire amount owed when billed. They do not have the option of making small payments over time. However, American Express also issues other cards that are credit cards in the true sense of the word.

Bank-issued credit cards have the following common features:

- The credit card holder has a prearranged line of credit with a bank that issues credit cards. Credit is extended when the credit card holder buys something and signs (or approves) a sales draft at a participating retail outlet. The retail merchant presents the sales draft to its bank for payment in full, less a merchant discount that is based on:
    i. The retail outlet's volume of credit card trade
    ii. The average size of each credit card sale
    iii. The amount of compensating balances kept at the bank
    iv. Some combination of the above factors
- The merchant discounts range from nothing to 6% or more. The merchant's bank will get part of the merchant discount for handling the transaction and routing it to the major credit card company (e.g., Visa, MasterCard) that issued the card. The credit card company determines the amount that the card-issuing bank owes. The card-issuing bank pays the credit card company, and the credit card company pays the merchant bank.
- Most banks allow the credit card holder to pay the bill in full within a *grace period* (say 25 days from the billing date) and not be charged interest on the outstanding balance, or pay a minimum amount each month on an instalment basis. Banks depend on interest income earned on these credit balances as the major source of income from their credit card operations.
- Banks also earn fee income from credit cards. For example, a bank may charge an annual fee (say HK$150) for the privilege of having a credit card, although for competitive reasons, some banks charge no annual fees. Fees are also charged for other account activities such as:
    i. Cash advances;
    ii. Late payments;
    iii. Exceeding credit lines;
    iv. Returned-check fees when payments are not honoured.
- The final feature that all bank credit cards have in common is the plastic credit card itself, which identifies the customer to the merchant. Some credit cards have the customer's picture on the card in order to augment its security for in-person transactions. The card may be encoded with a magnetic strip or computer chip that provides additional information about the cardholder's financial condition.

Consumer Credit Data

Credit scoring is the use of statistical and operational research and data mining models to determine the credit risk of prospective borrowers. In the United States, the credit score is a number that is calculated by a credit bureau or another company, such as the Fair Isaac Corporation's FICO score that is used in making credit decisions and for other purposes.

In Hong Kong, the individual bank assigns credit scores to current and prospective customers based on its own research and credit scoring model, using positive and negative data on individual credits furnished by a credit reference agency such as the Commercial Credit Reference Agency.[5] A number of banks in Hong Kong also tap the services of TransUnion Limited, the former Credit Information Services founded in 1982 and bought by America's TransUnion International in 1999.[6]

The major advantages of using credit scoring models are that they reduce the cost of evaluating credit and increase the speed, consistency, and accuracy of credit decisions. They also help make decisions more impartial. Credit scoring technologies are also used to assess risk-adjusted profitability of account relationships, for delinquency intervention, for fraud detection, and for other purposes. They are typically used in making consumer loans, home mortgage loans, and some commercial loans.

Credit scoring has drawbacks, however. The system has to be based on a large enough sample to make it statistically valid. Wrong, inaccurate, and incomplete information can distort scoring results. Ambitious scoring models for business and income growth as well as an increase in the number of consumers gaming the system could also undermine the reliability of results.

Credit scores are based on the past financial performance of groups of borrowers similar to the one being scored. The models employ variables that are associated with default risk. Past due payments, debt load relative to income, and employment status are examples of factors related to consumer credit and home mortgage loans.

TransUnion uses a proprietary mathematical formula to develop a credit score for an individual or company using information in its centralised database, including account delinquency data, credit enquiry, credit payment history data and public record data.

In Hong Kong, the sharing of consumer credit data through credit reference agencies is governed by the Code of Practice on Consumer Credit Data (Code) issued by the Privacy Commissioner for Personal Data.

When positive consumer credit data sharing (excluding positive mortgage data) was introduced in Hong Kong in 2003, it primarily covered the sharing of positive and negative credit data[7] relating to credit cards and unsecured personal loans, as well as the negative

---

[5] Established in 2004, the CCRA aims to address the need of lending institutions for reliable credit information about small and medium size enterprises, sole proprietorships, and partnerships. It is operated by Dun & Bradstreet (HK), a unit of global provider of commercial information D&B, which has been appointed as a CCRA service provider by the Hong Kong Association of Banks and DTC Association. The role of Dun & Bradstreet (HK) is primarily on commercial credit data.

[6] In addition to Hong Kong, TransUnion operates in 24 other jurisdictions and five continents. By the end of 2009, it claims to have retrieved 66.4 million credit reports in Hong Kong. TransUnion serves some 70 member companies in Hong Kong and says it helps more than 4.3 million consumers understand and use credit better. The role of TransUnion is primiarly on consumer credit data.

[7] Positive credit data refer to information on an individual's credit exposure (e.g., credit limits and outstanding amounts on credit facilities) and payment history. Negative credit data refer to information only on an individual's default record.

credit data relating to mortgage loans. Following the public consultation on the sharing of mortgage data for credit assessment in January 2011, the Privacy Commissioner for Personal Data determined in March 2011 that positive mortgage data sharing ("PMDS") would lead to responsible borrowing and lending. The code was revised on 1 April 2011 as a consequence to allow for the implementation of PMDS. The introduction of positive mortgage data sharing will enhance the credit risk management capability of authorized institutions and thereby promote banking and financial stability in Hong Kong. On 31 March 2011, the HKMA issued a circular to all authorized institutions setting out the steps they need to take to implement PMDS.

Evaluating a Personal Advance Application

The foregoing discussion on general lending principles, types of personal customers, types of lending, consumer credit data, and other issues comprise the elements that banks need to consider in deciding to make advances to personal customers or declining to make them. Unlike corporations, personal customers cannot produce a variety of financial statements and financial ratios, making retail lending more difficult than corporate lending.

Individual banks have their own processes in evaluating a personal credit application. The typical approach is to use a mix of quantitative and qualitative measures on which to base a judgement, based on general principles like CAMPARI and the other elements discussed throughout this chapter. Below are some useful general criteria applicable to the evaluation of personal credit applications in Hong Kong.

Borrower Capacity

In evaluating a personal credit application, the central task is to ascertain the borrower's capacity to pay. At minimum, the bank must verify: 1) his or her occupation; 2) the personal debt service ratio or DSR; and 3) other sources of repayment besides a regular salary. It would also be prudent to check with a credit reference agency for any unfavourable report on the potential borrower.

The Hong Kong Monetary Authority has issued guidelines on the calculation of DSR specifically for residential mortgage loans. The key points include:

- Debt service should be computed to include all monthly repayments relating to the mortgage loan application and all other debt repayments known to the lending institution, such as those arising from personal loans granted by the institution, co-financing loans provided by property developers, and credit facilities from other institutions, if these can be ascertained.

- Institutions should conduct reasonable checks on the extent of the borrower's other financial obligations, for example, by investigating whether the borrower has other existing mortgages or by reviewing the borrower's bank statements and account records.
- If part of the full debt service cost incurred by the borrower is deferred for a period, for example because of an interest holiday, the full eventual servicing cost should be included in the DSR calculation from the start.
- The current income of the borrower should be used in the DSR calculation and no allowance should be made for any expected future income increase.
- The income of other household members should not be taken into account in the DSR test, unless such members have provided a formal guarantee or the property is being acquired jointly with those members.
- The institution must obtain income proof such as a salary statement or tax return from the borrower or guarantor.

In August 2010, the HKMA standardised the limit on DSRs of borrowers to 50% and directed authorized institutions in Hong Kong "to use the prime-based interest rate cap or the prevailing prime-based mortgage rate to calculate DSRs in respect of HIBOR-based mortgage loans" because of the "relatively high volatility of HIBORs and the unusually low HIBOR rates at the moment."

Documentation

The primary basis for determining borrower capacity should be documentary proof of income, such as salary slips, employment letters, and tax demand notes, together with bank statements, in order to check actual earnings, net worth, and existing debt obligations—as well as proof of residence—especially if the borrower does not have an existing relationship with the lending bank or is not a Hong Kong resident or both.

Security

If the loan under application uses a borrower's existing property as collateral, the bank should request to see: 1) the preliminary sale and purchase agreement; 2) a land search and valuation report to ascertain the age, assessed market value, and general conditions of the property (e.g. if there are building orders and other charges); and 3) details of any tenancy agreement, including market rental of the property.

An all-monies legal charge, which is a document that secures all loans the borrower has with the bank, should be taken over the property. If the property is for investment purposes, an assignment of rental should be required. As an added precaution, the bank should require from the borrower a top-up covenant to cover any shortfall should property prices decline during the tenor of the loan.

Summary

This section summarises the issues and topics discussed in this chapter:

- Banks follow general lending principles in making advances to personal customers. One easy-to-remember acronym is CAMPARI, which stands for character, ability, margin, purpose, amount, repayment, and insurance.
- Banks also take into account the type of personal customer, such as a salaried worker or self-employed individual, and the general purpose of personal advances, such as buying a flat or house, in deciding whether or not to lend to an individual.
- There are various types of lending to individuals. Home mortgages are generally more secure with a lower delinquency ratio than other types of lending, which include bridging loans, probate advances, tax loans, and credit cards.
- The Hong Kong Monetary Authority plays a key role in regulating property mortgage lending by recommending LTV, DSR, and other regulatory standards as well as assessing the compliance of authorized institutions with these standards. The Hong Kong Mortgage Corp. helps banks lower risk by buying and insuring their mortgage loans.
- In evaluating a personal credit application, banks must verify borrower capacity through supporting documents such as salary slips, employment letters, and tax demand notes, together with bank statements in order to check actual earnings, net worth, and existing debt obligations.

Key Terms

authorized institutions	interest-only mortgage
balloon mortgage	loan-to-value (LTV) ratio
bridging loans	mortgagee
CAMPARI	mortgagor
consumer credit data	personal loans/overdrafts
credit cards	probate advances
debt service ratio (DSR)	residential mortgage loans
fixed-rate mortgage loan	reverse mortgages
graduated payment mortgage (GPM)	second mortgage/home equity loan
growing equity mortgage	shared appreciation mortgage (SAM)
Home Assistance Loan Scheme (HALS)	tax loans
Home Ownership Scheme (HOS)	Tenants Purchase Scheme (TPS)

Study Guide

1. If Borrower A is a professional with a high income but has issued three bouncing cheques and requested a bank to stop payment on two other issued personal checks, under what circumstances will the bank decide to extend him a loan?

2. How have guidelines and circulars from the Hong Kong Monetary Authority affected home mortgage loans and what were the reasons behind their issuance?

3. Borrower B would like to buy a village house. What would he have to show to convince a bank to extend him a loan? What sort of terms would he have to agree to and why?

4. How were the home ownership schemes that the Hong Kong Housing Authority used to offer different from home mortgage loans offered by banks to their customers on a commercial basis?

5. What are the reasons behind the 70% LTV cap and why has this been adjusted for certain types of home mortgages? Under what circumstances can a borrower gain approval for a loan amount that exceeds the LTV cap?

Further Reading

Gup, Benton E. and James W. Kolari. 2005, *Commercial Banking*. United States: John Wiley & Sons, Third Edition, 2005.

Hong Kong Housing Authority website, http://www.housingauthority.gov.hk/en.

Hong Kong Housing Society website, http://www.hkhs.com/eng/about/index.asp.

Hong Kong Monetary Authority. "Credit Card Business" in *Supervisory Policy Manual*, http://www.info.gov.hk/hkma/eng/bank/spma/attach/CR-S-5.pdf.

———. "New Share Subscription and Share Margin Financing" in *Supervisory Policy Manual*, http://www.info.gov.hk/hkma/eng/bank/spma/attach/CR-S-4.pdf.

———. "Property Lending," updated 28 July 1997, http://www.info.gov.hk/hkma/eng/guide/guide_no/guide_594b.htm.

———. "Proposal on Sharing Positive Consumer Data: Frequently Asked Questions," http://www.info.gov.hk/hkma/eng/pos/faq_index.htm.

———. "Prudential Measures for Property Mortgage Loans," 10 June 2011, http://www.info.gov.hk/hkma/eng/guide/circu_date/20110610e2.pdf.

———. "Prudential Measures for Property Mortgage Loans," 19 November 2010, http://www.info.gov.hk/hkma/eng/guide/circu_date/20101119e1.pdf.

———. "Prudential Measures for Residential Mortgage Loans," 19 August 2010, http://www.info.gov.hk/hkma/eng/guide/circu_date/20100819e1.pdf.

———. "Prudential Measures for Residential Mortgage Loans," 23 October 2009, http://www.info.gov.hk/hkma/eng/guide/index.htm.

———. "Residential Mortgage Loans (RMLs)," 20 March 2008, http://www.info.gov.hk/hkma/eng/guide/index.htm.

———. "The Sharing and Use of Consumer Credit Data Through a Credit Reference Agency" in *Supervisory Policy Manual*, http://www.info.gov.hk/hkma/eng/bank/spma/attach/IC-7.pdf.

Hong Kong Mortgage Corporation website, http://www.hkmc.com.hk/.

CHAPTER 2

Lending Considerations for Corporate Customers

Learning objectives

After studying this chapter, you should be able to:

1 Know the components of the following financial statements: the balance sheet, profit and loss account, cash flow statement, and cash budget

2 Interpret and analyse the information provided by these financial statements, as well as know how they differ and relate to one another

3 Understand which portions of the financial statements are particularly important to a bank lender and why

4 Evaluate the reliability and accuracy of these financial statements

Introduction

In the previous chapter we studied how banks lend to individual customers, what kinds of loans are extended to them, and how lenders assess credit risk using documents like personal bank statements and proofs of income. This chapter[1] will focus on how banks lend to corporate customers.

Assessing the credit risk of corporations is somewhat like examining the physical health of a business executive. Every year, corporate officers are expected to undergo an executive check-up, which includes examining blood flow and analyzing blood chemistry. In the case of a corporation, money is its lifeblood. Measuring how much money goes in and out, how fast money is utilised by the corporation, and for what purpose gives banks an indication of how healthy the company is that is trying to borrow from them.

Corporations are required to issue financial statements such as the balance sheet, profit and loss account, and cash flow statement. In Hong Kong, the manner of disclosures made in the balance sheet and profit and loss account is spelled out by the Hong Kong Companies Ordinance. These documents are important sources of information for financial institutions in deciding whether or not to lend and in what amounts.

The Balance Sheet

Many companies use the last day of the calendar year, December 31, as the indicative date on which to present their financial condition. Others use March 31, the end of the tax year in Hong Kong. Still others use June 30 and other dates because of their history and other reasons.

A balance sheet, known in Hong Kong as the Consolidated Statement of Financial Position,[2] is like an x-ray or a snapshot of a company's financial health on a particular date, say December 31. The balance sheet shows how much the company owns (assets), how much it owes (liabilities), and how much interest or stake its owners have (shareholder's equity) in the company on that particular date.

All balance sheets consist of three major sections: assets, liabilities and owners' equity.

Figure 2.1 shows the consolidated balance sheet of a fictional company called Ajax Corp. and its subsidiaries for two successive years, meaning it provides a summary of the

---

[1] This chapter uses some material from *Commercial Banking* (2005) by Benton E. Gup and James W. Kolari, with permission from publisher John Wiley & Sons.

[2] The Hong Kong Institute of Certified Public Accountants changed the title "balance sheet" to "Consolidated Statement of Financial Position" in 2010, among other changes to HKAS 1, to maintain the convergence of Hong Kong's accounting standards with international standards, arising from the revision of IAS 1 by the International Accounting Standards Board (IASB).

FIGURE 2.1 **Consolidated statement of financial position for Ajax Corp. and subsidiaries, as of December 31, 20YY and 20XX[3]**

	20YY	20XX
Assets		
Non-current assets		
Land	2,593,311	3,223,368
Buildings	173,661,175	151,716,975
Machinery and equipment	546,629,604	504,747,066
Construction in progress	46,727,823	32,118,483
Other assets	35,976,963	36,815,088
Less allowances for depreciation and amortization	(314,475,766)	(268,550,626)
	491,113,110	460,070,354
Current assets		
Bank balances and cash	3,344,075	1,487,676
Temporary investments	10,073,726	11,734,261
Trade and other receivables and prepayments	137,299,371	135,065,650
Inventories	162,086,784	173,168,270
Prepaid lease payments and other current assets	7,896,024	7,269,878
Taxation recoverable	6,406,485	5,725,166
	327,106,465	334,450,901
Total assets	818,219,575	794,521,255
Equity and Liabilities		
Current liabilities		
Notes payable	7,167,285	6,684,796
Accounts payable	23,896,090	38,826,568
Employee compensation	14,355,414	10,523,668
Other	4,456,928	4,921,427
Current tax payable	10,709,170	11,528,267
Current portion of long-term borrowings and capital lease obligations	11,129,575	12,283,430
Total current liabilities	71,714,462	84,768,156
Non-current liabilities		
Long-term borrowings	180,338,551	191,257,695
Deferred tax	48,656,564	49,727,625
Long-term provisions	9,424,669	6,815,997
Total non-current liabilities	238,419,784	247,801,317
Total liabilities	310,134,246	332,569,473
Redeemable Cumulative Preferred Stock		
Par value $0.01 per share authorised 10,000,000 shares; issued and outstanding 558,443 shares in 20YY and 559,943 shares in 20XX	5,584,430	5,599,430
Owners' Equity		
Common stock, par value $0.01 per share; shares outstanding: 40,889,909 in 20YY; 40,919,638 in 20XX	414,200	414,200
Share capital	47,383,897	48,494,262
Retained earnings	465,552,899	422,221,703
Treasury stock	(13,601,818)	(15,811,931)
Currency translation adjustment	2,751,721	1,034,018
Equity attributable to owners of the company	496,916,469	450,752,822
Non-controlling interests	5,584,430	5,599,430
Total equity	502,500,899	456,352,252
Total equity and liabilities	818,219,575	794,521,155

[3] Adapted from Benton E. Gup and James W. Kolari, *Commercial Banking: The Management of Risk* (John Wiley and Sons, 2005) 226–227.

assets, liabilities, and stockholder's equity of the mother firm Ajax and all those companies in which Ajax has a controlling stake (more than 50%).

The Ajax balance sheet represents a statement of the financial condition of the Ajax group on one particular date, December 31. It is also analogous to a snapshot of Ajax's financial condition only on that day, December 31.

As the lender bank, you would do well to inquire whether after December 31 there was a significant change in the balance sheet, such as a sizable asset being disposed of to liquidate a liability.

- Assets represent the resources owned by a company, whereas the liabilities and owners' equity indicate how those resources were financed.
- Liabilities represent what a company like Ajax owes to others. It is the amount that various creditors have invested in the business. Liabilities due to be paid within one year, or within an operating cycle, are called current liabilities.
- The non-current liabilities include long-term debts and leases and deferred liabilities. For example, deferred taxes represent amounts that may be owed in taxes, but due to timing differences in income earned, this is not yet recognised for tax purposes.
- Owners' equity represents the owners' investment in the business. It is a claim against assets. Owners' equity includes the value of the stock purchased by the stockholders, earnings that have been retained, stock that has been repurchased by the company (treasury stock), and an accounting adjustment representing changes in the value of foreign currencies in connection with Ajax's foreign operations.

By definition, total assets must equal total liabilities plus stockholders' equity. In other words, the balance sheet can be expressed using this equation:

$$\text{Assets} = \text{Liabilities} + \text{Stockholder's Equity}$$

In the case of Ajax, its total assets of \$818,219,575 are equal to its combined total liabilities and stockholder's equity, also amounting to \$818,219,575.

To summarise, a balance sheet follows this format:

- **Current assets.** This includes cash and short-term investments, accounts receivable, inventories, and others (such as prepaid expenses).
- **Non-current assets.** Land and buildings, plant and machinery, fixtures and fittings, motor vehicles.
- **Other assets.** Long-term investments, intangible assets (e.g., goodwill), brands, patents, trademarks, licences, amount due from related companies.
- **Current liabilities.** Accounts payable, accruals (e.g., compensation, income taxes payable, dividends).
- **Non-current liabilities.** Bank debts (e.g., mortgages), amount due to associates, loans from shareholders/directors, long-term notes.
- **Owners' equity.** Share capital, retained earnings, reserves (e.g., share premium).

Characteristics and Constraints

A bank lender has to keep in mind that the balance sheet has certain limitations. It is a record of past performance. Therefore, it does not reflect market values, the effects of inflation, or other current information. For instance, assets are recorded on the balance sheet at the price the company paid for them. The figures are therefore presented in terms of historical costs.

Because of this, company balance sheets—and for that matter the profit and loss account and cash flow statement—are better appreciated over time. The bank should examine a company's balance sheets over a span of several years. This could show a trend of how the company is growing or shrinking.

Another thing to keep in mind is that not all liabilities are shown on the balance sheet. For example, post-retirement benefits are described in the notes at the end of the financial statements. Other firms may have commitments or contingent liabilities, or be engaged in hedging (buying and selling futures contracts), all of which are described in the notes.

It is important for the banking professional to read all of the notes. The notes are where companies often try to tuck away embarrassing financial revelations in tiny print. There are even instances where a note referred to in a balance sheet turns out to be missing. You should not dismiss this outright as a misprint error, but would do well to ask about it without embarrassing the potential corporate borrower.

Assets

Ajax's assets total $818,219,575. Assets include *financial assets* (cash, investments, receivables, etc.) and *real assets* (property, plant, and equipment); some firms also have *intangible assets* (patents, trademarks, etc.). Assets that are expected to be converted into cash within one year, or within an operating cycle, are called *current assets*. An *operating cycle* is the period from purchase of inventory until the cash is collected after the goods are sold.

Ajax had total assets of $818,219,575 at the end of 20YY, compared with $794,521,255 at the end of the previous year. The increase in assets indicates that Ajax is growing in size. But bigger may not be better. More analysis is required.

Non-Current Assets

Non-current assets are fixed and other assets held by the company longer than one year. These are intended for the business's own use, rather than to be sold to customers. Tangible fixed assets are those that the business intends to retain for a number of years and puts to use repeatedly in the production and distribution of its products (e.g. land and buildings, plant and machinery, computers, fixtures and fittings, motor vehicles, etc.).

Tangible fixed assets are presented as:

Cost	X
+) Additions	X
−) Disposals	(X)
−) Accumulated depreciation	
= Net book value	

It is essential to ascertain that adequate depreciation is made each year for fixed assets. The problem of obsolescence (e.g. machinery) would cause the assets to run inefficiently and disrupt production. This would result in a reduction in profit margin. A replacement in times of inflation would also create a financial burden to the business.

The closer the amount of accumulated depreciation is to the original cost, the older the assets are and the sooner they would need replacement. Different methods of depreciating fixed assets can affect profitability and financial ratios.

Besides the physical depreciation of fixed assets, the wide use of electronic equipment in business has also introduced a technological type of depreciation. What was state-of-the-art at the time of purchase could now be obsolete or nearly so, with spare parts unavailable or difficult to obtain in case of breakdown.

It is important to check whether the rates used for depreciation are appropriate and consistent. One way to spot this is to see whether the financial statements reflect significant profits or losses on disposals. If so, then the depreciation rates may need to be challenged.

Other Assets: Intangibles

Intangible assets represent the company's capitalised expenses for its long-term benefit (e.g., preliminary expenses, goodwill, research and development, textile quota, patents or trademarks). Due to difficulties in determining the present and salvage value of such assets, they are normally deducted from shareholders' equity to arrive at a company's tangible net worth.

Other Assets: Investments

Under the balance sheet category "other assets," companies may include temporary investments of surplus cash. Money that has been set aside to buy replacements for aged assets can also be considered as investments that fall under the same balance sheet category. These types of investments should be stated at the lower range of cost or market value. If stated at cost, the notes referring to these accounts should indicate the market value.

Investments can either be listed as current or long-term assets. A bank lender should take note of the classification because a company may try to avoid making provisions for investments that have fallen sharply in market value by reclassifying them as long-term assets.

Current Assets

Current assets are those that companies expect to convert to cash within a year. These include accounts receivables less than or equal to one year old (i.e., payments from customers who bought goods on credit). Current assets include stock and works-in-progress, debtors and prepayments, and cash and liquid funds.

- **Inventory and works in progress.** Companies that are in manufacturing, wholesale, or retail list inventories as part of their current assets. For a manufacturer, inventories would include not just finished goods but also raw materials, works-in-progress, and packaging materials. An inventory analysis could detect overstocking or not-so-saleable items.

  Inventories are those items in the balance sheet most susceptible to error and manipulation. An increase or decrease in the value of closing inventory and work-in-progress can result in a corresponding increase or decrease in year-end profits. Inventory and works-in-progress are generally stated at the lower range of cost and net realizable value.

  This is a prudent approach for three reasons. First, materials may have been damaged. Second, finished goods may have turned out defective. And third, the items in stock may be so out of date or out of fashion that these would have to be sold at a discount.

  Company inventory of manufactured goods or goods bought for resale often varies in volume and price per unit throughout the year. Different methods are used to assign value to the inventory remaining at the close of the year and each method would result in a different figure and different profit picture.

  The methods generally used are: the FIFO (First In, First Out), Average, and the LIFO (Last In, First Out). Appendix 2.1 explains the concepts in more detail and gives examples.

  i. **FIFO.** This method assumes that stocks that entered the warehouse first were the goods sold first. Therefore, the goods remaining in the inventory came in to the warehouse last.

  ii. **LIFO.** This method assumes that the stocks that entered the warehouse last were sold first. Therefore, the goods remaining in the inventory came into the warehouse first.

  iii. **Average**. This method merely averages the cost of all the goods that entered the warehouse that entire year.

- **Trade receivables and prepayments.** Customers often buy goods or use services on credit. The items, trade receivables, in the balance sheet, represent the amounts due to a company from customers who have bought goods or obtained services from a company without first paying for these. Often, such amounts emerge directly from the accounting records and could therefore be calculated in precise figures. The only concern is whether any of those customers will not be able to pay.

  Usually, receivables from a trade customer form the largest chunk of trade receivables in the balance sheet. If other receivables (including prepayments) are also important, a breakdown has to be obtained to check the level of trade receivables vs. other receivables. Additional analysis will also be necessary in examining the age and quality of outstanding receivables.

Should companies discount export bills obtained from customers, this would be treated as an off-balance-sheet item and would be revealed in the notes to accounts. If this figure is large, one should add this back to trade receivables, with a corresponding entry to bank debts to reveal more precisely the credit period given.

Prepayments represent any expenses that have been paid for in the financial year but are attributable to succeeding years (e.g. rent, advertising expenditures, or costs in connection with developing a new product.)

- **Cash and cash equivalents.** These include cash in bank such as credit balances in checking or savings accounts and time deposits as well as petty cash for paying small bills.

Cash is one of the easiest items in the balance sheet to window dress. There are ways the company can inflate its cash balances at the balance sheet date and thus appear more liquid than it really is. It can offer discounts to encourage customers to pay early. It can factor or, more usually, delay payments to the company's trade creditors for a brief period.

Liabilities

In the course of business, it is normal for companies to incur liabilities. There are two kinds of liabilities recorded on a balance sheet—current and non-current.

Current liabilities are those owed by a company to third parties that are due for repayment within 12 months from balance sheet date closing. Falling under this category are trade liabilities and accruals. Liabilities falling due longer than 12 months are considered non-current liabilities.

- **Trade liabilities** (also listed under the balance sheet headings—accounts payable and trade accounts) represent amounts owed to suppliers for goods and services rendered, which have not yet been paid for.
- **Accruals** (or accrued expenses) arise from services that have been provided in the financial year—the benefits of which have been used to earn revenues—but which have not been paid for by balance sheet date (e.g., wages, bank interest, electricity, telephone bill, etc.) These are usually paid for in the following year.

Other liabilities a company may incur are debts owed to banks (e.g. mortgages), long-term notes, and amounts due to subsidiaries or associates arising from trade or by loan. Amounts due from or related to companies shall be treated as non-current liabilities, unless it is known that such inter-company balances are genuine trade balances, and that the balances do materially fluctuate.

Owners of a business may also provide additional cash in the form of bank or personal loans rather than as outright capital. Banks should be aware that such loans could be repaid wholly or in part at any time without the bank's knowledge. One way for banks to protect themselves in such a situation is to obtain a letter of undertaking from the company directors promising not to withdraw their loans during the availability of the bank advance.

Equity

Equity represents the claim of the owners of the company. Equity consists of share capital, retained earnings, and other components of equity, such as reserves.

- **Capital** is what shareholders contribute in a business.
- **Retained earnings** are the surplus or deficit transferred from the profit and loss account (income statement).
- **Reserves** are the non-distributable items arising from the issuance of shares at a premium (share premium account) or asset revaluation.

Funding Mismatch

A bank lender would do well to examine the balance sheet of a potential borrower for any mismatch or discrepancy between the source of funds—from either equity or debt—and the purpose for the funds. This could show up as a maturity mismatch between the assets and liabilities in the balance sheet.

- The first type of funding mismatch is the use of long-term funds to buy short-term assets. Long-term funds, whether in the form of equity or debt, provide stability to a business since they are perpetual or have long maturity. This kind of mismatch presents little problem to the business, but if the long-term funds are in the form of long-term debt, that is usually more expensive than short-term debt. From a financial management perspective, this is not a cost-effective way of financing.
- The second type of mismatch is the use of short-term debt to finance long-term assets. In Hong Kong, this type of mismatch is very common because short-term debt is usually cheaper and easier to obtain from banks than long-term loans.

    But this second type of mismatch presents financial risk since the short-term debt will fall due long before the business can generate sufficient cash flow to repay the instalments for the loan taken out to buy long-term assets (i.e. machinery or new building). The company will sooner or later run into liquidity problems, meaning funds for amortising the loan could dry up sooner than the business can generate enough income to pay back the short-term loan.

    This type of mismatch will often lead to business failure even though in the long run the company may have sufficient assets to cover the total liabilities. This danger is greater for smaller firms because of their limited capacity to borrow at short notice.

The Profit and Loss Account

In the previous section you learned about the balance sheet, which records a company's financial health on a particular date. This section will discuss another form of financial

FIGURE 2.2 Consolidated income statements for Ajax Corp. and subsidiaries, as of December 31, 20YY, 20XX and 20WW[4]

	20YY	20XX	20WW
Revenue	804,584,939	713,812,344	687,954,312
Cost of sales and services rendered	(553,159,643)	(461,280,501)	(457,874,872)
Gross profit	251,425,296	252,531,843	230,079,440
Other income (loss)	(310,980)	(2,294,670)	1,983,444
Selling, general and administrative costs	(142,773,638)	(126,269,548)	(109,724,386)
Finance costs	(18,096,696)	(18,884,674)	(15,643,287)
Profit before taxation	90,865,942	109,672,291	102,728,323
Income tax expense	(34,027,000)	(41,725,000)	(37,993,580)
Profit for the year	56,838,942	67,947,291	64,734,743
Preferred stock dividends	559,568	568,943	571,943
Profit for the year attributable to:			
Owners of the company	43,774,807	52,429,944	49,921,157
Non-controlling interests	12,504,567	14,948,404	14,241,643
	56,279,374	67,378,348	64,162,800
Earnings per share	1.38	1.65	1.57
Dividends per share	0.32	0.32	0.28

statement required of companies, the profit and loss account, referred to in Hong Kong as the Income Statement. Figure 2.2 shows the consolidated income statements of our fictional company, Ajax Corp, for three years.

The profit and loss account represents company earnings and expenses during an accounting period such as a year or a quarter. It summarizes results of operations for a particular period. Accountants sometimes refer to this as the "P & L" statement or the income statement.

The resulting net profit or loss, after expenses are deducted from sales, shows the company's bottom line. The net profit or loss is also what is included under the heading "retained earnings" in the owners' equity section of the balance sheet (in order for the balance sheet to balance).

The profit and loss account is reported on an accrual basis rather than on a cash basis. Accrual basis means revenues are recognised when these are earned, regardless of when the cash actually comes into the company.

Expenses are also recorded when these are incurred, not when these are paid. This explains why deferred taxes appear on the balance sheet, which also records on an accrual

---

[4] Adapted from Benton E. Gup and James W. Kolari, *Commercial Banking: The Management of Risk* (John Wiley and Sons, 2005), 227.

basis. In contrast, recording on a *cash basis* means revenues are recognised when these are received and expenses are recognized when these are paid.

In Hong Kong, companies are also required to prepare a Statement of Comprehensive Income, which may form part of the Income Statement (in which case the income statement is styled as the Statement of Comprehensive Income) or be presented as a separate statement from the income statement and styled as Statement of Comprehensive Income (that is, there will be two separate financial statements: Statement of Income, as shown in Figure 2.2, and a Statement of Comprehensive Income).

Figure 2.3 shows a consolidated statement of comprehensive income, separate from the income statement, for our hypothetical company, Ajax Corp.

FIGURE 2.3 Consolidated statement of comprehensive income for Ajax Corp. and subsidiaries, as of December 31, 20YY and 20XX

	20YY	20XX
Profit for the year	56,838,942	67,947,291
Other comprehensive income cash flow hedge:		
Loss on cash flow hedges	(538,833)	(644,140)
Defered tax recognised in relation to cash flow hedges	102,310	122,305
Reclassification adjustment relating to transfer of cash flow hedges	1,365,840	1,632,773
Reclassification adjustment relating to defered tax on transfer of cash flow hedges	(225,423)	(269,479)
Investment revaluation reserve:		
Fair value changes of available-for-sale investments	4,960,334	5,929,760
Reclassification adjustment relating to disposal of available-for-sale investments	(3,617,799)	(4,324,845)
Reclassification adjustment relating to impairment loss on available-for-sale investments	–	1,541,724
Property revaluation reserve:		
Fair value changes on properties transferred to investment properties	88,669	105,998
Translation reserve:		
Exchange differences arising on translation of foreign operations and to presentation currency	2,751,721	1,034,018
Other comprehensive income for the year	10,111,648	12,087,823
Total comprehensive income for the year	71,837,409	83,621,504
Total comprehensive income attributable to:		
Owners of the company	56,699,830	66,000,781
Non-controlling interests	15,137,579	17,620,723
	71,837,409	83,621,504

Note that the items in the statement of comprehensive income are those that are not recognised in profit or loss. The starting point of this statement is the profit for the year in the income statement (which is $56,838,942 in the case of Ajax). The other items of income and expense not recognised in profit or loss are then added to this figure. These include:

- Changes in revaluation surplus.
- Actuarial gains and losses on defined benefit plans recognised in accordance with paragraph 93A of Hong Kong Accounting Standard 19 on *Employee Benefits*.
- Gains and losses arising from translating the financial statements of a foreign operation.
- Gains and losses on re-measuring available-for-sale financial assets.
- The effective portion of gains and losses on hedging instruments in a cash flow hedge.

In effect, the statement of comprehensive income contains earnings or loss that have not yet been realised during the financial reporting period, but may be so realised in the future. This statement is therefore important for the bank to examine because it gives a more comprehensive picture of the borrowing company's financial condition and may indicate future changes in its finances and prospects.

Items in a Profit and Loss Account

As shown in Figure 2.2, the standard items in a profit and loss account are revenue, cost of sales, gross profit, profit before tax, other income (other expenses) and profit for the year (loss). Depending on the company's circumstances, other items may appear in a profit and loss account, including EBITDA (earnings before interest, tax, depreciation, and amortisation), interest, and extraordinary/exceptional items.

Revenue

Represents the total amount of revenue or sales from the normal trading operations of a company, minus the sales discounts and customer returns, during the year or a pre-defined reporting period.

Cost of Sales

In a retail business, this is the purchase cost from suppliers. In a manufacturing operation, cost of sales includes the combined cost of materials, the labour required to make the goods, and the production overhead.

Gross Profit

It is the profit *before* deducting selling, general and administrative costs, distribution costs, finance costs, employee benefits expenses, depreciation and amortisation expenses, impairment of property, plant and equipment, and other expenses.

Profit Before Tax

It is the profit *after* selling, general and administrative costs, distribution costs, finance costs, employee benefits expenses, depreciation and amortisation expenses, impairment of property, plant and equipment, and other expenses, but *before* deducting income tax expenses.

Profit for the Year

It is the profit *after* deducting income tax expenses from profit before tax. This figure is also referred to as net income.

EBITDA

This stands for earnings before interest, tax, depreciation, and amortisation. This figure helps analyse the operating profitability between companies and industries, as it eliminates the effects of financing and accounting decisions. It can also help evaluate different industry trends over time because it removes the impact of capital expenditure or investment, financing, dividend, and depreciation.

Interest

Only the financial interest, not the charges, is recorded under this item.

Other Income

This is income derived from other operations besides the company's principal trading activity (e.g., rent and interest received).

Extraordinary/Exceptional Items

These are costs or revenues that are so unusual in the context of the business that they require separate disclosure. Three conditions normally have to be met for an item to be described as extraordinary. First, the amount is large or material. Second, it arises from an event, transaction, or activity, which the business would not normally be expected to engage in or which is not expected to recur frequently or regularly. And third, if it results from an activity outside the normal routine of business operations (e.g., a company suffers heavy loss from a factory destroyed by fire).

An amount or transaction may be regarded as exceptional but not extraordinary if it is unusually large, or does not happen very often, for example, bad debts.

Standard accounting practice treats exceptional items *above the line*, that is, *before* arriving at the amount disclosed as operating profit for the year. Extraordinary items are added or deducted *below the line* and have their impact lower in the body of the profit and loss account.

The Cash Flow Statement

Cash is important to a business. The survival and success of any business depends on its ability over time to generate cash income beyond outgoing cash.

The method of measuring cash flowing in and out of a business was standardised in 1987 when the U.S. Financial Accounting Services Board (FASB) issued "Statement of Financial Accounting Standards No. 95." This urged U.S. firms to prepare a statement of cash flows instead of a statement of fund flows. All FASB issuance are recognised by the U.S. Securities and Exchange Commission, which requires all U.S.-listed firms to comply with them.

FASB, whose members come from the financial accounting profession and academe, announced a switch to cash flow accounting because the funds flow statement that was then in use had a limitation. It could not measure the cash-generating ability of a company since the figures in a funds flow statement were only derived from the balance sheet and profit and loss account, which are prepared on an accrual basis. This means sales and expenses are recorded at the time they are made, not when the cash actually goes in or out of the company.

FASB felt that cash flow accounting was a better measure of cash going in and out of a company. Even if the figures stated in a cash flow statement, as part of the audited financial report, are historical, they still provide a record of a company's past ability to generate cash. The cash flow statement can therefore indicate the future ability of a company to generate cash and cash equivalents to meet interest, dividend payouts, tax liabilities and bank borrowings.

The cash flow statement has become an international standard in accounting and is among the financial statements required of companies listed at the stock exchange in many jurisdictions, including Hong Kong.

The cash flow statement is of particular interest to bank lenders because:

- It reveals the past financial performance of the borrower, based on historical financial records.
- It is prepared using the balance sheet and the profit and loss account as its basis.
- It explains the changes in the cash level and therefore indicates the liquidity of the borrower.
- It demonstrates the different sources of cash from operating, financing, and investing activities.
- It reconciles the application and use of cash, starting from the operating profit before interest and tax.

A company's cash flow statement should give the following important information:

- Sources of cash for funding expansion;
- Extent of dependence on external financing;

- Feasibility of financing capital expenditures;
- Its dividend policy;
- Ability to meet debt service requirements;
- Financial flexibility for unanticipated needs and opportunities;
- Quality of earnings (earnings = cash flow + discretionary accruals);
- Identification of misleading or erroneous operating results or expectations.

Cash and Cash Equivalents

It is important to note that the cash flow statement is defined as movements in cash and cash equivalents. Financial controllers, when managing the liquidity of their companies, invest in or source from a range of cash and "like cash" equivalents. Without including the cash equivalents, you cannot have a true picture of a company's ability to meet its obligations.

To ensure uniformity and reliability of information, the definition of cash equivalents has been clearly set out by the accounting industry and comprises *only*:

- Cash;
- Short-term liquid investments with remaining maturity shorter than three months.

Presentation Format

Except for some small differences relating to the presentation of interest, tax, and dividends, the format of any cash flow statement is essentially the same. As shown in Figure 2.4, the major headings are cash flows from operating activities, cash flows from investing activities, cash flows from financing activities, and the resulting change in cash and cash equivalents.

Cash Flows From Operating Activities

This is the total cash generated by the main business of a company. It is the primary source of recurrent cash flow, from which a company should be able to meet the normal demands of business such as tax, interest, dividends, and principal repayments.

Cash flow from operations should normally be expected to cover any increases in the working capital requirement of the main business operations. However, growing companies often have a greater requirement for working capital than can be met from cash from operations and so they must raise funds from other sources.

In order to maintain productive capacity at current levels, a company has to have positive free cash flow. Positive free cash flows reflect the amount available for business activities after allowances for financing and investing requirements.

Free cash flow is derived from cash flow from operations minus net capital expenditures required to maintain productive capacity minus dividends on preferred stock and

FIGURE 2.4   Sample cash flow statement

(In Thousands)	HKD	HKD
CASH FLOWS FROM OPERATING ACTIVITIES		
Cash generated from operations		xxx
Returns on Investments and Servicing of Finance		
♦ Interest received / (paid)		(xxx)
Taxation		
♦ Tax paid		(xxx)
Net cash inflow / (outflow) from operating activities		xxx
CASH FLOWS FROM INVESTING ACTIVITIES		
Capital expenditures		(xxx)
(Acquisitions) /disposals		(xxx)
CASH FLOW FROM FINANCING ACTIVITIES		
♦ Issue of shares	xxx	
♦ Repayment of bank loans	(xxx)	
♦ Dividends paid	(xxx)	xxx
Increase / (decrease) in cash and cash equivalents		xxx

Source: HKIB

common stock. Simply put, it is the cash left over after meeting requirements for operations, reinvestment and dividends.

Free cash flow from operations should normally be sufficient to cover dividends paid. For the bank examining the cash flow statement of a potential borrower, dividends that are not covered by operational cash flows will warrant investigation. A persistent shortfall may indicate excessive distribution.

A company that consistently generates cash will either be profitable or is managing its working capital effectively, or both. But in some cases this may indicate a company that is winding down its business and reducing its working capital.

Conversely, when the growth level of the working capital rises more quickly than sales year-on-year, the company may have managed its working capital poorly or may be over trading.

Growth and financial flexibility of a company depends on adequate free cash flow. A positive net cash flow from operating activities is an important consideration for banks to lend, while negative net cash flow from operations is usually a serious indication of financial problems unless accompanied by strong and profitable growth.

If the negative net cash flow from operations persists for two or more consecutive years, a company will eventually run out of cash or willing providers of debt.

In determining cash generated by operating activities, a company can either use the direct method or indirect method.

- The direct method simply reports where the cash came from and what it was used for:

Cash received from buyers − Cash paid to suppliers − Cash paid to employees − Other cash payments = Net cash inflow /(outflow) from operating activities

Under the direct method, all accrual accounts are converted to a cash figure in the cash flow statement. The direct method analyses the various types of operating activities and calculates the total cash flow created by each one.

- The indirect method starts with the company's net income (the figure which is commonly referred to as the "bottom line" in the P & L). The net income is then adjusted in order to deduct or add any items that do not affect cash flows. This includes such items as:

  i. Gains and losses on events reported in other sections of the statement of cash flows;
  ii. Conversion of current operating assets and liabilities from accrual to cash basis (debtors, stocks, and creditors)
  iii. Revenues and expenses that do not involve cash inflow or outflow such as depreciation and amortization

The indirect method uses the following formula:

Operating Profit

± Non cash items (e.g., depreciation)

Adjusted Cash Flow from Operations

± Decline/increase in trade debtors

± Decline/increase in stock

± Decline/increase in trade creditors

Net Cash Flow from Operations

Interest paid

− Tax paid

Net Free Cash Flow from Operations

− Dividends paid

Net Cash Flow before Investing and Financing Activities

A bank lender should be on the lookout for the various ways a company can make its net cash flow from operations look healthier than it really is. For instance, a company can:

- Shorten trade debtor terms
- Extend trade creditor terms
- Sell receivables (giving cash flow a one-time boost, which may ultimately affect earnings)

- Reclassify assets (i.e., assets originally intended for investment purposes are reclassi-fied as core operating assets whose disposal contributes to the operating cash flow)
- Trade credit into cash (i.e., the company lends money to buyers to purchase its prod-ucts in cash to boost operating cash flow. Then the debts are booked as investment, which contributes to a fundamental improvement of core activities.)

Cash Flow From Investing Activities

In the course of business, a company buys or sells property and equipment, hoping this will increase productivity and result in higher profits. This is part of its investing activities.

When operating cash flows are insufficient, a company may be forced to sell assets and investments to generate cash to repay borrowing, interest, and dividends.

A negative cash flow from investing activities may signal that a company is engaged in too broad a range of investments, from fixed deposits, short-term quoted investments, and investments in (and loans to) other companies, to investment in associates and new subsidiaries.

A positive cash flow may indicate that the company is rationalising its business, dis-posing of non-core assets, reinvesting in the core business, or repaying debt.

Cash Flow From Financing Activities

It is particularly important for bank lenders to examine a company's cash flow from financ-ing activities. This will indicate where a company has raised cash to meet shortfalls or where it has used surplus cash to reduce borrowing or equity.

The cash flow from financing activities includes:

- Cash received from shareholders in the issuance of shares;
- Repayments of debt principal;
- Repurchases of previously issued shares of stock;
- Dividends paid.

In summary, the cash flow statement, while historical in nature, tracks the actual cash going in and out of a company, and shows how this is used. Note that the final figure in the cash flow statement—showing an increase or decrease in cash and cash equivalents—should be the same as the figure for "cash and cash equivalents" listed under Current Assets in the balance sheet of the company.

Free Cash Flow (FCF)

As mentioned earlier, it is desirable that a company has positive free cash flow in order to sustain its present productive capacity. Free cash flow, also referred to as FCF, can be examined in various ways depending on the purpose (i.e., to determine share valuation, compute incentive compensation, set loan covenants, and so on).

In general, one can look at free cash flow in relation to the firm or in relation to common equity. Free cash flow to the firm is cash flow provided by operating activities before interest, but after capital expenditures. Free cash flow to common equity is cash flow provided by operating activities after capital expenditures and dividends on preferred stock.

There are three other ways of calculating free cash flow: operating cash flow minus net capital expenditures required to maintain productive capacity and dividends on preferred stock and common stock; EBITDA minus capital expenditures; and net income minus capital expenditures.

In the final analysis, a bank lender examines free cash flow in order to determine a company's ability to repay a potential loan.

Movement of Cash and Equivalents

Cash equivalents, together with cash, signify the cash flow position of a company after taking into account its financing activities, the net cash flows from core operating activities, investment returns, debt servicing, and other capital obligations and investing activities.

A positive number suggests possible higher investment in short-term assets (lasting under three months) or repayment of overdraft with short-term borrowings that mature under three months.

A negative number suggests drawing down new short-term debts (under three months) or increasing the use of overdraft.

For a bank lender, it is important to compare the movement of cash and cash equivalents with the maturity structure of the cash flow statement to identify any term mismatch, i.e. using short-term funding to finance long-term asset acquisition.

EBITDA and Cash Flow

EBITDA is an acronym often used by stock analysts to compare company stocks in and across industries. But for the purpose of bank lending, how useful is EBITDA in measuring cash flow and consequently a company's ability to service borrowings?

EBITDA stands for earnings before interest, tax, depreciation, and amortisation. EBITDA is used to compare the operating profitability between companies and industries, as it removes interest, tax, depreciation and amortization from the calculation of earnings. It can also help evaluate different industry trends over time because it removes the impact of capital expenditure or investment, financing, dividend, and depreciation.

Although EBITDA is calculated before two key non-cash expenses—depreciation and amortisation—it does not adjust for other non-cash items, especially changes in working capital accounts, e.g., bad debt allowances and inventory write downs.

EBITDA also excludes changes in working capital accounts such as trade debtors, stocks, and trade creditors. If all three are growing, they would collectively reduce operating and free cash flows.

EBITDA is a good metric to evaluate operating profitability but not cash flow because it does not consider changes in working capital that also use cash. EBITDA is an earnings-based, modified cash flow metric but is not a true measure of cash flow.

EBITDA does not provide lenders an accurate measure of debt-servicing capacity, as earnings can be kept in debtors and stock but not in cash.

EBITDA is calculated *before* interest expenses and income taxes, which are real cash items, while operating cash flow and free cash flow are computed *after* them.

EBITDA does not consider the amount of required reinvestment, especially for companies with short-lived assets such as production facilities for high tech industries.

EBITDA tells nothing about the quality of earnings.

It also ignores distinctions in the quality of cash flow resulting from different accounting policies, because not all revenues are cash. It leaves out many expenses in measuring profitability.

Cash Flow vs. Profitability

A company may look highly profitable on paper but could actually be losing money to the point of being unable to pay for its normal day-to-day operations.

Profitability is reflected in the bottom figure (the net income) of a Profit and Loss Account. Since figures in this financial statement are recorded on an accrual basis, they do not really give an accurate picture of how much cash a company has on hand. For instance, a company may record profit due to a growth in sales. But extending longer credit terms to buyers might have brought about the sales. Or the profit reported could still be tied up with trade debtors (as reflected in the balance sheet) without actual receipt of cash.

Cash flow, as reflected in the cash flow statement, is therefore different from profitability. Cash flow may be calculated by the indirect method, which uses the net income as the starting figure. This figure is then adjusted upwards or downwards to take into account non-cash profit and loss items such as depreciation and amortisation charges, and movements of the working capital components (e.g. increase/decrease in debtors/stock/creditors).

There are also instances when a company could have positive net cash flow in its cash flow statement, despite showing red ink on the bottom line of its profit and loss account. Such a company may still be able to come up with cash by writing back the non-cash expenses. For instance, it may be charging depreciation against the profit and loss account, or efficiently managing the components of working capital (e.g., stretching creditor terms, speeding up trade debt collections, or unloading stock).

A money-losing company may also increase its positive net cash flow through:

- Early recognition of expenses relative to revenues generated, for example, R&D;
- Entering into valuable long-term sales contracts not yet recognised in income;
- Issuance of debt or equity to finance expansion;
- Sale of assets;
- Delay in cash payments;
- Receipt of cash deposits before completion of sales transactions.

Cash Budget and Cash Flow Forecast

The cash budget is a forward-looking financial management tool for looking at the cash movements of a company. The cash budget provides a cash flow forecast of a company's future cash inflow and outflow based on certain assumptions. It is prepared on a periodic basis, such as monthly or quarterly and is important to lenders as a monitoring mechanism to evaluate future cash surplus and deficit. The projected deficit would in turn determine the funding requirement of a borrower.

As a lender, you have to pay close attention to the cash flow forecast more than the profit forecast because it is cash, not profit, which is crucial for a business to repay its liabilities such as bank loans. Cash flow projections are therefore important as a forecast of a borrower's repayment ability.

On the management side, the cash flow forecast examines the implications of the operating and capital budgets on the cash resources of a business. It is not concerned with profit or loss, or any items not involving inflows or outflows of cash. It is a vital part of the planning and control mechanism of a business.

Cash flow projections provide a company with a means to coordinate the activities of all its managers and make them aware of the liquidity problems facing the business and the part they must play in solving them.

Factors Affecting Future Cash Flow

Several factors can affect the future cash flow of a company. There could be a change in the scope of its business activities, such as its product mix, or in its processes such as more centralisation of operations. The company could change its cost structure by cutting jobs, outsourcing more, or relocating plants to low wage areas.

It could change its product pricing, for instance, by increasing the sales price without affecting volume, or passing on the increased raw material cost to buyers. It could leverage its operations by trying to reduce fixed costs when these are higher than its variable costs, or by generating more sales to cover the high fixed costs.

Cash flow projections can also be affected by a change in the company's financing activities. For example, it can change its capital structure, find access to various financial resources, or even discontinue activities that result in low returns or cash flow or both.

Importance of Borrower's Cash Forecast

The cash flow projections of a potential or existing borrower serve as an early warning signal to both the borrower and lender. The projections allow banks to understand the cash flow drivers of the borrower—how it generates cash and the ways it uses this cash. By understanding the liquidity shortfall indicated in the cash flow projections, banks can then structure the credit facilities in ways appropriate to that particular borrower—or decide not to lend to that corporation.

Reliability of Accounting Information by Source

The potential corporate borrower's cash flow may look great, its P & L may look strong, and its balance sheet may appear robust. The bank lender's work is not yet done, however. Not all financial statements are created equal. Some are more reliable and accurate than others. This section will discuss why this is the case, and how you can fill the gaps of information missing in financial statements, in order to arrive at a fuller picture of the credit risk of a potential or existing borrower.

Types of Reporting

Companies may present bank lenders with various reports, including compilation/management accounts, reviews, and audited reports. In Hong Kong, certain private enterprises and small and medium scale companies are allowed to file S141D accounts, which are less stringent than those prepared by larger corporations under the Companies Ordinance. Each of these reports varies in the degree of reliability and usefulness to the bank lender.

Compilation/Management Accounts

Compilation or management accounts are prepared for internal use. They are usually more detailed, informative and up-to-date than the audited accounts. The American Institute of Certified Public Accountants (AICPA) defines management accounts as "presenting, in the form of financial statements, information that is the representation of management without undertaking to express assurance on the statements."

Management accounts are useful for the following reasons:

- They can be prepared more frequently (i.e., on a half-yearly, quarterly, or monthly basis) than the audited accounts. They can therefore highlight the seasonality as well as the peaks and troughs of the company (e.g., the borrowing requirement throughout the year).
- They can help the company forecast business performance and profitability more reliably.
- They can help banks monitor the performance of the borrower and the usage of bank finances if supplied regularly and on time.
- Since management accounts can be compared with the budgets of the business, they can give a timely review of the state of the business: what has been achieved and

whether the company can reach its targets. Both the company and the bank lender can then take prompt remedial actions if there is any significant variance between the management accounts and the budgets.

- Banks can also use the management accounts to request for satisfactory explanation from the company if the final audited accounts vary significantly from the management accounts.

But management accounts do have their limitations:

- They are not audited. They may not be completely accurate and are less reliable. They can also be inconsistent from one period to the next.
- They may or may not have been compiled by qualified persons.
- They are produced for the company's use and may not contain footnotes or disclosures critical for a sound financial analysis.
- They may also be in a form different from the audited accounts and, being internal documents, need not comply with the Hong Kong Financial Reporting Standards (HKFRS).

Review

The second type of accounting information prepared by companies is the review, which is defined by the US AICP as:

> "Performing inquiry and analytical procedures that provide the accountant with a reasonable basis for expressing limited assurance that there are no material modifications that should be made to the statements in order for them to be in conformity with generally accepted accounting principles, or, if applicable, with another comprehensive basis of accounting."

In short, the review provides "limited assurance" with respect to meeting accounting standards.

Audited Accounts

Among the types of accounting information, audited accounts carry the highest degree of reliability and accuracy. First of all, these are reviewed and examined by someone outside the company. An audit is defined as:

> "The process by which a competent, independent person accumulates and evaluates evidence about quantifiable information related to a specific economic entity for the purpose of determining and reporting on the degree of correspondence between quantifiable information and established criteria."[5]

---

[5] Alvin A. Arens and James K. Loebbecks, *Auditing: An Integrated Approach*, 5th ed. (Englewood Cliffs, NJ: Prentice Hall, 1991).

An auditor gives an assurance that the financial statements follow Hong Kong Financial Reporting Standards. Audited statements provide the most reliable accounting data for recording the economic events that occurred during that accounting period. In other words, if given a choice of accounting information, audited financial statements are better than compilations or reviews.

However, the banking professional should carefully read the independent auditor's report for qualifications. A **qualification** is a statement in the report in which the auditor comments on limitations to the audit examination or process that was conducted, or expresses doubts concerning a reported item. We discuss this issue in the following section, "Audit Report."

Keep in mind that there are also differences in the quality of auditors. Some auditing firms have a better reputation or more resources and expertise than others. These factors must be considered when evaluating audited reports and statements.

S141D Accounts

The reporting requirements of corporations operating in Hong Kong are less strict for certain private enterprises and small and medium scale companies. Section 141D of the Companies Ordinance defines the "power of shareholders of certain private companies to waive compliance with requirements as to accounts." This section permits company shareholders to prepare an abbreviated set of financial statements that exclude the directors' report and cash flow statement and includes only a limited number of notes.

Companies that choose to prepare financial statements under S141D of the Companies Ordinance have to follow the Small and Medium-sized Entity (SME) Financial Reporting Framework & Financial Reporting Standard issued by the Hong Kong Institute of Certified Public Accountants (HKICPA) in August 2005.

The HKICPA defines an SME as one that meets any two of these three conditions:

- Its total annual revenues are less than HK$50 million.
- Its total assets are less than HK$50 million at the balance sheet date.
- It employs fewer than 50 workers.

Under S141D, the balance sheet is the only part of the account that needs to be audited by an independent auditor. The balance sheet is prepared according to Schedule 11 of the Companies Ordinance instead of Schedule 10 of the same ordinance. Schedule 11 has less strict disclosure requirements than Schedule 10.

Companies using S141D cannot assert that its financial statements comply with the Hong Kong Financial Reporting Standards (HKFRS). But they can say their financial statements are in compliance with Hong Kong laws and denote a proper presentation appropriate for small and medium enterprises.

Because of this, an independent auditor examining a company's accounts using S141D can express "…a true and correct view of the state of affairs of the Company as at December 31, 20XX and of its result for the year then ended."

Audit Report

An external auditor or auditing firm conducts the audit and then prepares an audit report. The audit report contains an opinion expressed by the auditor.

Types of Auditor's Opinions

The auditor's opinion can either be "unqualified" or "qualified." If the auditor issues an *unqualified or clean report*, this means the auditor believes the financial statements present fairly in all material respects, the financial position, results of operations, and cash flows of the company, in conformity with generally accepted accounting principles.

The auditor then expresses his written opinion, which should be fairly short and should generally state the following:

> "In our opinion, the financial statements give a true and fair view of the state of affairs of the Company as of December 31, 20XX and of its profit and cash flows for the year then ended and have been properly prepared in accordance with the disclosure requirements of the Hong Kong Companies Ordinance."

But if the auditor states a *qualified opinion*, this means the auditor has certain reservations about portions of the financial statements. Other than those portions, however, the auditor believes the financial statements present fairly in all material respects, the financial position, results of operations, and cash flows of the entity in conformity with generally accepted accounting principles.

Qualifications in the Audit Report

The word "qualification" has a definite meaning for auditors. A qualification is a statement in an audit report that comments on limitations to the audit examination that was conducted or that states the auditor's doubts concerning a reported item.

You should check the entire audit report and the accounting notes for any qualifications made by the auditor. The auditor could express qualifications regarding debtors' or creditors' balances and other items such as deposits not received. Or amounts due from related companies being carried at book value and their recoverability are not ascertained.

The qualifications are often couched in auditor-speak. If the auditor says: "Group accounts were not prepared to consolidate the results of the subsidiaries," it means the auditor is talking of unconsolidated accounts. The bank lender could do the following to address this qualification:

- Obtain the audited accounts of the subsidiaries.

- If the subsidiaries are outside Hong Kong, check the accounting standards of their country of location in order to assess the differences in reporting standards.
- After taking into account the unconsolidated accounts of the group and the separate audited accounts of the subsidiaries, only then can you assess the overall profitability and financial strength of the group.
- To present a true picture of the group's performance and financial status, eliminate any inter-company sales and debts.

If the auditor expresses "doubt on the recoverability of account receivables up to X million," you can do the following:

- Obtain an ageing analysis of the doubted account receivables so you can look at their nature and breakdown.
- Check if the company has taken any action to recover these receivables and estimate the likelihood of recovery.
- And finally, assess the impact on financial performance if the company fails to recover them at all.

If the auditor says, "No physical stocktaking was performed," it means the value of the stock is merely a figure certified by the directors on the balance sheet and profit and loss account. It may not be accurate and cannot be relied upon. The stock figure or inventory may turn out to be higher or lower than what it should be and this could skew the profitability as well as the other accounting ratios of the company.

To address this qualification, you can do the following:

- Appoint an independent surveyor to carry out stock valuation.
- Arrange a site visit to the company warehouse or factory to ascertain the value of the stock.

If the auditor says, ". . . we have not inspected the company's fixed assets which were located outside Hong Kong, and therefore we are unable to satisfy ourselves as to the existence of the fixed assets of net book value of . . ." Find a way to ascertain the existence and value of these fixed assets.

If the auditor says: "Investment properties with a book value of X million have not been revalued," you can do the following:

- Obtain a list of the investment properties booked in the company's accounts.
- Check with the real estate agencies or refer to other available market information on the latest estimated valuation of the properties.
- Compare the investment properties with the net book value of the properties recorded in the accounts.
- Assess the impact of any revaluation on the profit and loss account and company net worth, particularly if the value of the properties will be lower after revaluation.

Summary

This section summarises the issues and topics discussed in this chapter:

- To determine credit risk of corporate borrowers, banks rely on their financial statements—the balance sheet, profit and loss account, cash flow statement, and cash budget. These statements highlight various aspects of the financial health of a borrower company.
- The balance sheet describes the financial position of a company on a particular day, while the profit and loss account summarises the results of its selling or trading over a given period, usually a year.
- The profit and loss account is a statement in which revenues and expenses are compared to arrive at the profit or loss over a period of time. It measures profitability. It records the returns derived from the risks reflected in the balance sheet.
- Every profit and loss account ends with a bottom figure—the net income—which is derived after deducting income tax. The net income can then be used as the starting point to track how cash flows in and out of the company. This cash flow is summarised in a cash flow statement.
- The cash flow statement, along with the cash budget, is very useful for bankers in assessing corporate credit risk. The cash flow statement indicates the liquidity of the company. The cash budget projects future cash surplus or deficit that could require fresh borrowing. The former records the company's past ability to generate cash and the latter predicts its future ability to do the same.
- The bank should look at the company cash flow, not just profitability, which can be window-dressed. It should keep in mind that financial statements are not equal in reliability, completeness, and accuracy. The latter depends on who prepared the statements and for what purpose.
- The most reliable financial statements are those audited by an independent auditor, whose audit report may state qualifications or words of caution that warrant closer examination. Auditors also vary in quality. Some auditing firms may have more resources or expertise than others and this, too, must be considered in evaluating an audit report.

Key Terms

accounts receivable	capital
accrual basis	cash basis
accruals	cash budget
assets	cash flow forecast
audit report	cash flow statement
auditor's qualifications	current assets
balance sheet	current liabilities

depreciation	long term liabilities
EBITDA	management account
equity	net cash from operating, investing, and
FIFO	financing activities
free cash flow (FCF)	profit and loss account
funding mismatch	retained earnings
Hong Kong Financial Reporting Standards	review
(HKFRS)	S141D report
income statement	stockholder's or owner's equity
liabilities	trade liabilities
LIFO	

Study Guide

1. Which of the following statements is/are correct and why? A cash flow forecast:
   (a) is based on the accrual concept
   (b) is improved by the revaluation of property assets
   (c) shows working capital needs
   (d) reveals the profitability of the business
2. Company A has negative net cash flow from operations. Under what circumstances would you still lend money to Company A and why?
3. How do the balance sheet, profit and loss account, and cash flow statement differ from and relate to each other?
4. Company B would like to borrow from your bank and submits its profit and loss account showing a high net profit, higher than the industry average. Should you approve his loan request outright? Why or why not?
5. A manufacturer made 5,000 units of baby dolls in January for $6 each. In April, it finished making 10,000 more units at $3 each. In August, it added 30,000 units of baby dolls to its inventory and it cost $2 each to make; in October another 45,000 units at $1.50 each; and in December 10,000 more units at $1.50 each. On balance sheet date of December 31, its closing inventory of the baby doll was 17,000 units. What was the value of its closing inventory using FIFO, LIFO, and AVR?

Further Reading

Arens, Alvin A. and Loebbecks, James K., *Auditing: An Integrated Approach.* 5th ed. (Englewood Cliffs, N.J.: Prentice Hall, 1991).

Gup, Benton E. and Kolari, James W. *Commercial Banking.* (United States: John Wiley & Sons, Third Edition, 2005).

Hong Kong Government. Companies Ordinance—Sect 141D website. http://www.hklii
.org/hk/legis/ord/32/s141d.html.

Hong Kong Institute of Certified Public Accountants website, http://www.hkicpa.org.hk.

Hong Kong Legal Information Institute website, http://www.hklii.org/.

Appendix 2.1: Comparing FIFO, LIFO, and AVR Inventory Methods

FIFO and LIFO Inventory Methods[6]

	FIFO	LIFO
First inventory purchase (10 items at $5 each)	$ 50	$ 50
Second inventory purchase (10 items at $8 each)	80	80
Total inventory purchases	$130	$130
Cost of goods sold (15 items)		
10 at $5 = $50 10 at $8 = $80	$ 50	$ 80
5 at $8 = $40 5 at $5 = $25	$ 40	$ 25
Total cost of goods sold	$ 90	$105
Inventory balance at end of period		
Beginning inventory (assumed)	$ 0	$ 0
Total inventory purchases	130	130
Less total cost of goods sold	(90)	(105)
Value of ending inventory	$ 40	$ 25
Profit		
Gross sales (15 times at $12 each)	$180	$180
Less total cost of goods sold	(90)	(105)
Gross profit	$ 90	$ 75

Assuming Company A has no other inventory, suppose it bought 10 items at $5 each and
on the second purchase, bought 10 more of the same items at $8 each. The 20 items in all
would have cost Company A $130.

---

[6] Adapted from Benton E. Gup and James W. Kolari, *Commercial Banking: The Management of Risk* (John Wiley
and Sons, 2005), 224.

Suppose the firm then managed to sell 15 items, leaving five items in its inventory at the close of the balance sheet period.

Under the FIFO (first-in, first out) method, Company A would assume that of the 15 items sold, 10 came from the first batch of purchases and the remaining five from the second batch of purchases. The equation would therefore look like this:

15 items sold of which:	
10 items bought @ $5 each =	$50
5 items bought @ $8 each =	$40
Total cost of 15 items =	$90

Since all 20 items in the inventory cost the company $130 and the total cost of the goods sold was $90, using FIFO, the remaining five items in the inventory would therefore be valued at $40.

But if Company A uses the LIFO (last-in, first-out) method, it would assume that it had sold first the goods that it bought last. Under LIFO, therefore, the goods that have been sold are assigned the price of the items last purchased. The items that remain in the inventory are assigned the price of the items first purchased.

Since all 20 items in the inventory were bought by the company at $130 and the total cost of the goods sold was $105, using LIFO, the remaining five items in the inventory would therefore be valued at $25.

The profit picture of a company changes, depending on which method is used. Using the same illustration, assuming that Company A sold the 15 items at $12 each, gross sales would amount to $180.

However, the profit would be calculated differently under FIFO and LIFO:

- Under FIFO, the 15 items sold would be assumed to have cost the company $90 to buy, leaving it with a net profit of $90.
- Under LIFO, the same 15 items sold would be assumed to have cost the company $105 to buy, letting it earn $75.

It is for this reason that during periods of inflation, FIFO can result in the overstatement of profits and, thus, in the overstatement of profitability. Even during periods of price stability—as demonstrated in this example—the two methods yield substantially different profits.

Here is another example. Suppose a computer company bought 1,000 items of a personal computer component each month starting in January. On December 31, the company had 2,000 items of that computer part still left in stock. The purchase price of that component rose three times from the initial price during that year. What was the value of the 2,000 components that remained in the closing inventory?

- 1,000 computer components $\times$ 12 months = 12,000 components
- Jan to Mar (3 months) @$650 per item
- Apr to May (2 months) @$800 per item

- Jun to Nov (6 months) @$900 per item
- Dec (1 month) @$1,000 per item

Valuation of 2,000 items left in stock using FIFO:

1,000 items (Nov price): $900 × 1000   = $ 900,000
1,000 items (Dec price): $1,000 × 1,000 = $1,000,000
Value of closing stock: $1,900,000

Valuation of 2,000 items left in stock using LIFO:

$650 (Jan–Feb prices) × 2,000 items = $1,300,000

Valuation of 2,000 items left in stock using AVR (Average):

[(3months × $650) + (2months × $800) + (6months × $900) + (1month × $1,000)]/
12 months = $829 AVR
Value of closing stock = $829 × 2,000 components left = $1,658,000

3

Financial Ratios and Operating Risks

objectives

After studying this chapter, you should be able to:

1 Derive and use financial ratios as indicators of a company's profitability, liquidity, efficiency, and leverage, as well as other measures of performance to guide lending decisions

2 Analyse the operating risks around a corporate borrower such as business owner risks, management risks, industry risks, and environmental risks

3 Understand frameworks such as CORE analysis, PEST analysis, and SWOT analysis and business growth models such as Porter's Five Competitive Forces model

Introduction

In the previous chapter we studied how to understand the documents issued by corporations, such as the balance sheet, profit and loss account, and cash flow statements, because these are important sources of information for banks in deciding whether or not to lend and in what amounts.

This chapter[1] will show you how the numbers in those financial statements can be further analysed, using mathematical formulas to derive financial ratios that will help evaluate a company's profitability, liquidity, efficiency, leverage, or indebtedness. Ratios help banks decide whether a company is a good credit risk or not.

To complete the examination of the risks surrounding bank lending, we will also look at the borrower in a wider context, using various frameworks and models with reference to the borrower's industry and operating environment, including external threats and opportunities.

Techniques of Financial Analysis

When individual customers apply for loans, bank lenders can interview them personally and obtain proofs of income. Banks take a different approach with corporate customers. They require them to submit various financial documents—balance sheets, profit and loss accounts, a cash flow statement, and forecasts of the current and previous years.

It is through the figures presented in these statements that bank lenders are able to evaluate for themselves the company's profitability, liquidity, efficiency, and leverage. Mathematical formulas to derive financial ratios have been developed for this purpose. Ratio analysis (also known as fundamental analysis) is the main technique of financial analysis that we focus on in this chapter.

There are other techniques that bankers can use, including percentage analysis. This involves transforming figures in the financial statements into percentages of a base amount. For example, each line in the balance sheet can be translated into percentages of total assets. This can be done on the same set of figures over a period of time and the results compared, an approach known as horizontal or time-series analysis.

The financial statements of different sizes of companies can also be reduced to a "common size" by expressing the figures as a percentage of a base value, such as revenue (for the income statement). Such common-size financial statements allow the banker to compare the corporate borrower's financial results with those of other companies in its industry, regardless of their different sizes, known as cross-sectional analysis or vertical

---

[1] This chapter uses some material from *Commercial Banking* (2005) by Benton E. Gup and James W. Kolari, with permission from publisher John Wiley & Sons.

analysis. This method can be combined with time-series analysis by translating financial information across time periods into common-size financial statements.

The various financial ratios can also be related to each other in a more comprehensive analysis. One such method is known as the DuPont Analysis (also known as DuPont Decomposition, DuPont Model, or DuPont Identity). Developed by America's DuPont Corporation in the 1920s, it allows bankers to measure the combined impact of operating efficiency, asset efficiency, and financial leverage on return on investment and return on equity, and thus on the company's ability to repay its loans.

Understanding Ratio Analysis

Ratio analysis helps bank lenders compare the performance of a corporate borrower over a number of years. By using ratios we can eliminate the distortions that can arise when absolute figures fluctuate significantly. Financial ratio analysis uses the various numbers in the balance sheet and profit and loss account to assess, for instance, a company's ability to pay financial obligations.

This chapter will introduce these financial indicators, which are grouped into four categories that concern most bank lenders: profitability, liquidity, efficiency, and leverage. The borrower's financial ratios are compared over time (horizontal analysis) and also with the "industry average," which is the average financial ratios of other companies in the same industry (vertical or cross-sectional analysis). In the following examples, the industry average is the average ratios of three firms similar to Ajax, the hypothetical company we introduced in Chapter 2.

Profitability

Profitability is the ultimate test of management's effectiveness. It can be measured using the following ratios: 1) return on assets, 2) return on equity, 3) gross profit margin, 4) operating profit margin, 5) net profit margin, 6) earnings per share, and 7) dividend payout ratio.

1. Return on Assets (ROA)

The ROA ratio is the most comprehensive measure of profitability. It measures productivity for creditors, bondholders, and shareholders. ROA is calculated by dividing the profit for the year[2] (the bottom line in the income statement) by the total assets (stated in the balance sheet).

---

[2] The terms used in the formula for ROA and other financial ratios in this chapter follow the terminology used by the Hong Kong Institute of Certified Public Accountants in its revision of HKAS 1 in January 2010. The terms "revenue" and "profit for the year," for example, are drawn from the illustrative presentation of financial statements in the annexes to HKAS 1 (Revised), specifically "XYZ Group—Statement of comprehensive income for the year ended 31 December 20X7." In older literature, terms such as "net income" ("profit for the year" in the revised HKAS 1) and "common stockholders' equity" ("total equity" in HKAS 1) are used in these formulas.

The ROA formula below draws the numbers from a fictional company called Ajax Corporation, whose balance sheet and income statement were shown in Chapter 2. The ROA ratios, using year-end figures of two successive years, reveal that the overall profitability of Ajax declined and was below the industry average.

$$ROA = \frac{\text{Profit for the Year}}{\text{Total Assets}}$$

$$\frac{\text{Profit for the year 20YY}}{\text{Total assets 20YY}} = \frac{\$56,838,942}{\$818,219,575} = 6.95\%$$

$$\frac{\text{Profit for the year 20XX}}{\text{Total assets 20XX}} = \frac{\$67,947,291}{\$794,521,255} = 8.55\%$$

$$\text{20YY industry average} = 7.83\%$$

The 20YY industry average of 7.83% is based on the results of three similar firms. This simply means Ajax management made nearly seven cents out of every dollar of invested assets, compared to the industry average of nearly eight cents. In short, Ajax did not manage company assets as well as its three rivals.

2. Return on Equity (ROE)

The ROE ratio measures the rate of return on the stockholders' investment in a corporation, which includes their paid-in capital and retained earnings. ROE is calculated by dividing profit for the year by total equity.

In calculating for ROE, only the figures for common stockholders' equity (both owners of the company and non-controlling interests) are used. If a firm has large amounts of preferred stock outstanding, a similar ratio may be computed by dividing income available to common stockholders by common equity.

According to Ajax's balance sheet, the company has redeemable cumulative preferred stock outstanding. A preferred stock is redeemable at the stockholder's option, and all dividends due to preferred stockholders must be paid out before any dividends can be paid on common stock.

Technically, preferred stockholders are owners of the corporation but they have limited voting rights and they receive fixed cash payments (dividends), similar to the fixed interest payments on debt. Thus, this hybrid preferred stock has some features of both debt and equity investments. Therefore, it is listed in the liability section of the balance sheet, and it is not considered part of stockholders' equity.

$$ROE = \frac{\text{Profit for the Year}}{\text{Total Equity}}$$

$$ROE\ 20YY = \frac{\$56,838,942}{\$502,500,899} = 11.31\%$$

$$ROE\ 20XX = \frac{\$67,947,291}{\$456,352,252} = 14.89\%$$

$$\text{20YY industry average} = 12.54\%$$

This means Ajax made nearly 12 cents for every dollar invested by its stockholders in 20YY, while rival firms made nearly 13 cents per dollar of equity.

Later in this chapter, when we discuss the leverage ratio, we will examine the relationship between ROA and ROE. At this point, let us look at ROE and ROA in further detail. The ROE is equal to the ROA times LR, which is a leverage ratio. The LR (assets/equity) is one indicator of financial leverage. It indicates the dollar amount of assets that are financed by each dollar of equity.

Assume that:
　PY = profit for the year
　　E = total equity
　　A = total assets
　LR = leverage ratio (A/E)

$$ROE = ROA \times LR$$

$$PY/E = PY/A \times A/E$$

Using 20YY data for Ajax companies, we see that the leverage ratio is 1.63. In other words, about $0.61 in every dollar of asset is funded by equity. The remainder of the assets is financed by debt (including current liabilities). The relationship between debt and equity is called financial leverage.

$$ROE = ROA \times LR$$

$$PY/E = PY/A \times A/E$$

$$11.31\% = 6.95\% \times 1.63 \text{ times}$$

Suppose the leverage ratio was 1.00, which means that every dollar of equity finances only $1 in assets. If net income remains the same, ROE will decline to 6.95%.

$$ROE = ROA \times LR$$

$$6.95\% = 6.95\% \times 1.00 \text{ times}$$

This means that ROE is a function of both financial leverage and net income. Observe that ROA is not affected directly by financial leverage. Both measures—ROE and ROA—are affected indirectly because interest expense affects profit for the year.

3. Gross Profit Margin

Gross profit margin is the profit *before* deducting distribution, selling, and administrative costs. It measures the profitability of the company's core business and is expressed as a percentage of revenue in the formula below:

$$\frac{\text{Gross profit}}{\text{Revenue}} \times 100\%$$

Among other things, a declining ratio could signify that:

- Cost of raw materials and/or cost of direct labour has increased, and this has not been passed on to the customer;
- Cost of imported raw materials has risen due to weakening of the local currency;
- Competition within the market has increased, forcing the company to accept lower margins on its sales;
- The company is increasing its market share by undercutting the prices of its competitors
- The product-mix of a company is changing because different margins on different product lines could alter the gross profit margin; and
- The stock valuation method has been changed.

A rising ratio can signify the opposite of the above, as well as increased production efficiency.

4. Operating Profit Margin

Operating profit is the profit *after* deducting distribution, selling, and administrative costs but *before* taxation—i.e., profit before taxation. By measuring the operating profit against the revenue from the core business, this ratio measures company efficiency in generating profits from the core business. It is derived using the following formula:

$$\frac{\text{Profit before taxation}}{\text{Revenue}} \times 100\%$$

If this ratio is changing in line with the gross profit margin, the change is being caused by changes in the gross profit margin and may not need a separate investigation. But if the ratio changes out of line with the gross profit margin, this may be due to an increase or decrease in indirect overhead. Watch out, too, for expenditures in housing, travel, and entertainment, where an increase may include payments to directors. Beware of changes in accounting policies on depreciation charges as well.

5. Net Profit Margin

Previously, we measured profitability in terms of the rate of return on assets, equity, and sales. The net profit margin ratio measures how much profit (profit for the year) a company earns on every dollar of revenue.

The formula below uses the profit for the year and revenue figures in the income statement of Ajax (Figure 2.2 in Chapter 2).

$$\text{Net profit margin} = \frac{\text{Profit for the year}}{\text{Revenue}} \times 100\%$$

$$\text{Net profit margin 20YY} = \frac{\$56,838,942}{\$804,584,939} = 7.06\%$$

$$\text{Net profit margin 20XX} = \frac{\$67,947,291}{\$713,812,344} = 9.52\%$$

$$\text{20YY industry average} = 9.48\%$$

The sharp decline from 9.52% to 7.06% in net profit margin is a red flag telling us that further analysis of the profit and loss account statement is required.

6. Earnings Per Share (EPS)

The earnings per share (EPS) is one financial ratio often quoted by stock analysts when discussing corporate profitability. The reason for its popularity is that it is relatively easy to understand and easy to relate to stock prices. EPS is derived by dividing profit for the year attributable to owners of the company and non-controlling interests by the number of common stocks outstanding.

Profit attributable to common stockholders is profit for the year minus preferred stock dividend. Some companies have sinking fund payments that must be deducted too. Sinking fund payments are periodic payments made to retire debts.

The EPS can either be reported as "basic EPS" or "diluted EPS." Basic EPS represents income from continuing operations and net income. Diluted EPS takes into account the potential effects of conversion of convertible securities, warrants, and stock options.

Because the number of shares outstanding can change from year to year, a firm with no change in income could have higher EPS if the number of shares decline. Many firms buy back their own stock to be cancelled or held for reissue (known as treasury shares), for employee stock option plans (ESOP), and for other purposes. One effect of such purchases is to increase the EPS.

If a firm has an extraordinary income or charge, such as a one-time adjustment due to changes in accounting methods, earnings before and after the charge should be examined to gain a better understanding of the trend.

Suppose the number of shares outstanding for Ajax was 40,889,909 in 20YY and 40,919,638 in 20XX. Its EPS was therefore $1.38 in 20YY compared with $1.65 the year before.

$$\text{Earnings per share} = \frac{\text{Profit attributable to common stockholders}}{\text{Number of shares outstanding}}$$

$$\text{EPS 20YY} = \frac{\$56,279,374}{40,889,909} = \$1.38 \text{ per share}$$

$$\text{EPS 20XX} = \frac{\$67,378,348}{40,919,638} = \$1.65 \text{ per share}$$

7. Dividend Payout Ratio

Firms may retain earnings to help finance growth, or distribute earnings to shareholders in the form of cash dividends. The extent to which earnings are paid to common stockholders in the form of cash dividends is called the dividend payout ratio. Strictly speaking, it is not a measure of profitability.

The payout ratio is computed by dividing cash dividends per share on common stock by earnings per share (EPS). Suppose Ajax paid a cash dividend of $0.32 per share in both 20YY and 20XX.

$$\text{Payout ratio} = \frac{\text{Cash dividends per share}}{\text{Earnings per share}}$$

$$\text{Payout ratio 20YY} = \frac{\$0.32}{\$1.38} = 23\%$$

$$\text{Payout ratio 20XX} = \frac{\$0.32}{\$1.65} = 19\%$$

$$\text{20YY industry average} = 20\%$$

Because the dividend per share remained unchanged while earnings per share declined in 20YY, the payout ratio increased from 19% to 23%, slightly above the industry average of 20%. Ajax's relatively low payout ratio indicates that management believes it has growth opportunities that they want to fund, in part, with retained earnings.

In summary, looking at the various ratios that measure profitability, all of them point to a decline in the profitability of Ajax. But while profitability ratios tell us *what* happened, they do not tell us the precise reasons. More qualitative analysis is required with help from more supporting data and management information.

Liquidity and Working Capital

A company must survive the short run in order to prosper in the long run. A firm has to have enough liquidity for it to survive the short run. This is why keeping tabs on a firm's liquidity is so important. The following financial ratios and indicators help assess a firm's liquidity or ability to meet short-run or current liabilities, which fall due within one year: 1) net working capital, also known as working capital, 2) restrictive net working capital, 3) net sales over working capital, 4) current ratio, 5) acid test ratio, 6) average collection period, and 7) days payable outstanding.

These ratios indicate the short-term stability of the company, since poor liquidity and bad working capital management can severely affect the financial health of a company in a very short time.

1. Net Working Capital

Working capital, also known as net working capital, is the firm's current assets minus its current liabilities. As a general rule, companies use current assets to pay their current liabilities. For example, cash is used to pay accounts payable. It also represents a company's investment in net current assets that can be converted into cash within a year or less.

The management of net working capital, also known as short-term financial management, is the lifeblood of a business. Net working capital provides a firm with a cushion to meet creditors' short-term loans. In other words, having more working capital is better than having less working capital, especially from the viewpoint of creditors.

However, too much working capital may also be detrimental to the company, because it may indicate that funds are not being used effectively. Holding excess non-earning assets, such as cash and accounts receivable, can hold down profits. Cash, for example, might be better used in stocking up inventory or acquiring more fixed assets.

An examination of Ajax's balance sheet reveals that net working capital increased from about $250 million in 20XX to $255 million in 20YY:

$$\text{Net working capital} = \text{Current assets} - \text{Current liabilities}$$

$$\text{NWC 20YY} = \$327,106,465 - \$71,714,462$$

$$= \$255,392,003$$

$$\text{NWC 20XX} = \$334,450,901 - \$84,768,256$$

$$= \$249,682,645$$

2. Restrictive Net Working Capital

Some banks may use a more restrictive definition of net working capital because the other items in current assets and current liabilities, for example, other debtors, other creditors, cash, overdraft, etc., do not vary in direct proportion to a company's turnover. The following equation shows a stricter definition of net working capital:

$$\text{Working Capital} = \text{Stock} + \text{Trade Debtors} - \text{Trade Creditors}$$

Tight control of working capital is essential for profitability and survival. It should be the aim of every business to minimise the amount of working capital needed to support a given level of activity.

3. Net Sales/Working Capital

This financial ratio measures a company's efficiency in using working capital to generate sales:

$$\frac{\text{Net sales (Revenue)}}{\text{Working capital}}$$

It is also the money invested in net current assets used in the core business as a percentage of sales. A rising ratio may imply more efficient working capital management but can also be the result of rapid growth in sales, requiring a company to stretch accounts payable, push accounts receivable for repayment, and/or maintain low inventory levels.

Cash based businesses (e.g. retail, restaurants) will have a relatively high ratio because the working capital requirement is small. Suppliers typically provide credit, sales are predominantly in cash, and inventories turn over quickly.

4. Current Ratio

The current ratio is a broad measure of liquidity because it divides all current assets by all current liabilities. It assesses how much current assets, for example, receivables, cash, and prepayments, can cover current liabilities, and therefore indicates the ability of a business to meet its short-term obligations, that is, all current assets can be converted into cash within 12 months.

The current ratio for Ajax increased sharply in 20YY and was well above the industry average. This means Ajax could pay its current liabilities 4.56 times. Another way of putting it is that Ajax has $4.56 worth of current assets for every $1 worth of current debt. This is more than enough and is therefore a red flag that requires further analysis. The high current ratio, particularly with a lot of cash, suggests that Ajax may be too liquid and not optimal in profitability.

$$\text{Current ratio} = \frac{\text{Current assets}}{\text{Current liabilities}}$$

$$\text{Current ratio 20YY} = \frac{\$327,106,465}{\$71,714,462} = 4.65 \text{ times}$$

$$\text{Current ratio 20XX} = \frac{\$334,450,901}{\$84,768,256} = 3.95 \text{ times}$$

$$20\text{YY industry average} = 2.97 \text{ times}$$

The ideal ratio cited by accountants is 1.5 times. If the ratio falls below 1, the company is technically illiquid. But the trading practice within some industries may make a ratio below 1 acceptable, if not ideal, for example, in cash businesses such as retail outlets and supermarkets.

A declining ratio can be caused by a number of factors, acting together or independently, such as:

- Diversion of funds out of working capital assets (i.e. short-term) into non-core long-term projects;
- Increasing dependence on creditors and banks as a source of short-term finance for long-term assets; or
- Rapid growth in sales without a corresponding increase in the capital structure of a company, which causes greater reliance on short-term creditors and lenders.

Each business must determine what its most effective current ratio is, such that it neither creates short-term liquidity problems (as seen in too low a ratio) nor sacrifices profitability for safety (seen in too high a ratio). If the ratio is too high, a company has too much money tied up in working capital that is not earning a profit.

5. Acid Test Ratio

Compared to the current ratio, which is a broad measure of liquidity, the acid test ratio is a narrow measure of liquidity derived by dividing cash, marketable securities, and accounts receivable by current liabilities. Also known as the quick ratio, it is considered a measure of current liquidity because it excludes the least liquid current assets (i.e., inventory, prepaid expenses, and future tax benefits) from the comparison of current assets and liabilities.

The acid test ratio for Ajax increased in 20YY, which may explain its high current ratio and lower profits. Notice that Ajax's acid test ratio is high compared with the industry average. Sometimes a high acid test ratio is due to conservative financial policies. Alternatively, the firm may be building its cash and investments in anticipation of capital expenditures or an acquisition. Finally, the firm may not be succeeding in collecting its receivables, thus making the numerator (comprising cash, securities, and accounts receivable) larger and the acid test ratio correspondingly higher. Further analysis is required to determine which explanation is the correct one.

$$\text{Acid test ratio} = \frac{\text{Cash} + \text{Securities} + \text{Accounts receivable}}{\text{Current liabilities}}$$

$$\text{Current ratio 20YY} = \frac{\$150,717,172}{\$71,714,462} = 2.10\text{ times}$$

$$\text{Current ratio 20XX} = \frac{\$148,287,587}{\$84,768,256} = 1.75\text{ times}$$

20YY industry average = 1.48 times

Compare the liquidity ratios of these two Hong Kong companies:

	A	B
Current assets (excl. inventory)	150,000	170,000
Current liabilities	200,000	200,000
(Within which bank borrowing of)	10,000	190,000
Acid test ratio	0.75	0.85
Total bank facilities available	200,000	200,000

Looking at their acid test ratio, it appears that Company A has poorer liquidity. But A still has $190,000 of unused bank facilities available, while Company B has used all but the last $10,000 of its facilities. It seems that A is then in a better situation. Let us see what happens if both companies draw down their facilities in full and put the resultant funds into current assets, say cash:

	A	B
Current assets (excl. stock)	340,000	180,000
Current liabilities	390,000	210,000
(Within which bank borrowing of)	200,000	200,000
Acid test ratio	0.87	0.86

The acid test ratio now reflects the true picture: A has a slightly better liquidity than B.

6. Average Collection Period

Average collection period indicates the average number of days that a firm waits before receiving cash from sales made on credit. All of Ajax's sales are made on credit, so it is important for the firm to minimise the collection period in order to get paid as soon as possible.

Two steps are required to calculate average collection period:

- Step 1: Determine the dollar amount of credit sales per day. We do this by dividing revenue by 360 days. Either 360 or 365 days may be used as long as the number is used consistently.
- Step 2: Divide the accounts receivable by credit sales per day.

For Ajax, the average collection period declined from 68 to 61 days, indicating that it was doing a better job of collecting its funds compared to the previous year and compared to its competitors. Therefore, the high level of the acid test ratio noted earlier is either a result of conservative management policies or an intentional increase in liquid assets for future expansion.

$$\text{Credit sales per day} = \frac{\text{Net sales}}{360 \text{ days}}$$

$$\text{Credit sales per day 20YY} = \frac{\$804,584,939}{360 \text{ days}} = \$2,234,598$$

$$\text{Credit sales per day 20XX} = \frac{\$713,812,344}{360 \text{ days}} = \$1,982,812$$

$$\text{Average collection period} = \frac{\text{Accounts receivable}}{\text{Credit sales/day}}$$

$$\text{Average collection period 20YY} = \frac{\$137,299,371}{\$2,234,958} = 61.43 \text{ days}$$

$$\text{Average collection period 20XX} = \frac{\$135,065,650}{\$1,982.812} = 68 \text{ days}$$

$$20YY \text{ industry average} = 63 \text{ days}$$

An alternative formula that is more recognised in Hong Kong is shown below:

$$\text{Average collection period} = \frac{\text{Accounts receivable}}{\text{Revenue}} \times 360 \text{ days}$$

An increase in the average collection period is generally a worrying sign that can indicate any of the following:

- The company is giving longer credit terms to protect market share and/or sales level and growth.
- It is relaxing credit controls.
- There is a general decline in the industry (i.e. textiles and garments in recent years).

A decrease in the average collection period, as is the case with Ajax, is generally a good sign, but be alert. If the period decreases severely, the company may be discounting its accounts receivable.

If the discounting is with recourse, this is a form of off-balance sheet finance that should be shown in the financial statements by means of a note on contingent liabilities. If the amounts involved are material, consider adding back the discounted accounts receivable to the balance sheet, increasing the short-term external finance (e.g., overdraft) by the same amount, and seeing what effect this will have on the gearing or external debt to tangible net worth ratio of the company.

7. Days Payable Outstanding

Days payable outstanding indicates how a firm is managing its current liabilities. A company usually tries to obtain as much credit from suppliers as possible, since this is a cheap form of finance. The following steps are used to compute days payable outstanding:

- Step 1: Determine the dollar amount of credit purchases per day. For Ajax, credit purchases comprise 80% of the cost of sales and services rendered.
- Step 2: Divide accounts payable by the credit purchases per day.

$$\text{Days payable outstanding} = \frac{\text{Accounts payable}}{\text{Credit purchases/day}}$$

$$\text{Credit purchase/day 20YY} = \frac{0.80 \times \$553,159,643}{360 \text{ days}} = \$1,229,244$$

$$\text{Days payable outstanding 20YY} = \frac{\$23,896,090}{\$1,229,244} = 19 \text{ days}$$

$$\text{Credit purchase/day 20XX} = \frac{0.80 \times \$461,280,501}{360 \text{ days}} = \$1,025,068$$

$$\text{Days payable outstanding 20XX} = \frac{\$38,826,568}{\$1,025,068} = 38 \text{ days}$$

$$\text{20YY industry average} = 35 \text{ days}$$

There was a sharp decline in the dollar amount of accounts payable in Ajax from 20XX to 20YY and in days payable outstanding. At just 19 days, days payable outstanding in 20YY is also far below the industry average of 35 days.

We don't have the information here to explain the sharp reduction in time. Nevertheless, we can guess that if Ajax had sufficient liquidity, the reduction in the payment period may have been due to the company's early payment of bills in order to take advantage of trade discounts.

An alternative formula that is more recognised in Hong Kong is shown below:

$$\text{Days payable outstanding} = \frac{\text{Accounts payable}}{\text{Cost of sales}} \times 360 \text{ days}$$

An increase in days payable outstanding is a positive sign, as long as stretching payments to trade creditors is not harming the reputation of the company. However, it may also be a warning sign that the company is illiquid and is stretching creditor payment.

A decrease in days payable outstanding, as is the case with Ajax, may indicate that the company is becoming more liquid and less reliant on trade credit. It may also indicate poor working capital management or a shift from creditor to bank finance.

In summary, the profitability and liquidity ratios for Ajax indicate a decline in profitability, but a rise in liquidity. At this point, the high liquidity could be due to conservative management policies or an increase in liquid assets for future expansion. More investigation is required to determine either.

Efficiency Measurements

Efficiency indicators measure how effectively certain assets and liabilities are being used in producing goods and services. The average collection period can be considered a measure of both liquidity and efficiency. Efficiency can be measured using the following financial ratios: 1) stock turnover period, 2) fixed assets turnover, and 3) asset turnover.

1. Stock Turnover Period

Also known as days inventory held, this formula measures the number of days required to turn over the company's inventories and gives an insight into the operating efficiency of a company:

$$\text{Stock turnover period} = \frac{\text{Closing inventories}}{\text{Cost of sales}} \times 360 \text{ days}$$

$$\text{Stock turnover period 20YY} = \frac{\$162,086,784}{\$553,159,643} \times 360 \text{ days} = 105 \text{ days}$$

$$\text{Stock turnover period 20XX} = \frac{\$173,168,270}{\$461,280,501} \times 360 \text{ days} = 135 \text{ days}$$

$$\text{20YY industry average} = 120 \text{ days}$$

A bank lender should not make quick judgments on absolute stock turnover periods without first looking at industry norms. Service industries normally have low stock turnover periods, while companies with large distribution networks will have considerably higher stock turnover periods.

A decrease in the stock turnover period, as is the case with Ajax, is generally a good sign because the company is using up its inventory quicker and not stockpiling. But it may also imply the company is illiquid and cannot afford to keep an adequate buffer of stocks to cater to sudden demand increases. This may cause the company to lose potential sales and the goodwill of its customers.

An increase in the stock turnover period is generally a poor sign since the company could be tying up capital in inventories and using more capital than is necessary. A high stock turnover period may imply slow-moving stocks, over-buying, or possible obsolescence. An extremely low stock turnover period may indicate that the production floor is overstretched, continually flat out, and unable to meet demand.

In the previous example, we used the closing inventories for 20XX and 20YY to compute the stock turnover period for each of those years. In calculating stock turnover in 20YY, it may be more prudent to use "average" inventories (instead of closing inventories) by adding closing inventories in 20XX and in 20YY and dividing by two. Thus:

$$\text{Average inventories} = \frac{\text{Inventories 20XX} + \text{Inventories 20YY}}{2}$$

$$\text{Average inventories} = \frac{\$173,168,270 + \$162,086,784}{2}$$

$$\text{Average inventories} = \$167,627,527$$

$$\text{Stock turnover period 20YY} = \frac{\$167,627,527}{\$553,159,643} \times 360 \text{ days} = 109 \text{ days}$$

2. Fixed Assets Turnover

This ratio indicates how effective a company has used its fixed assets during the financial year. It may be calculated with the following formula:

$$\text{Fixed assets turnover} = \frac{\text{Fixed assets}}{\text{Sales}}$$

However, this ratio has the following limitations:

- It may not be meaningful due to old fixed assets or if applied to labour-intensive operations, which would cause the ratio to be substantially lower.
- It is calculated using the historic cost of the fixed assets. A ratio based on current costs of fixed assets may reveal a much less satisfactory return.
- Construction in progress may be excluded since this does not contribute to current sales.
- Depreciation policies and the extent to which fixed assets are leased rather than owned would also affect the percentage.

3. Asset Turnover

The asset turnover ratio is a broad measure of efficiency because it encompasses all assets. It is computed by dividing net sales by total assets. The ratio for 20YY indicates that Ajax is using its assets more efficiently compared with the industry average and compared with 20XX. This is consistent with the improvements noted in the management of accounts receivable and inventory.

$$\text{Asset turnover} = \frac{\text{Revenue}}{\text{Total assets}}$$

$$\text{Asset turnover 20YY} = \frac{\$804{,}584{,}939}{\$818{,}219{,}575} = 98.33\%$$

$$\text{Asset turnover 20XX} = \frac{\$713{,}812{,}344}{\$794{,}521{,}255} = 89.84\%$$

20YY industry average $= 93.15\%$

Leverage and Capital Structure

Financial leverage indicates the amount of money the company owes to third parties, compared with the amount of money due to its owners. It also has to do with the capital structure of a company, whether it raised money by selling common stocks or bonds or through loan borrowings. Companies with a high proportion of borrowed funds are said to be highly leveraged. Financial leverage increases the volatility of earnings per share and the risk of bankruptcy.

The ratios and indicators to measure a company's capital structure and leverage are the following: 1) debt to assets, 2) debt to tangible net worth, 3) gearing, 4) long-term debt to total capital, 5) interest cover, 6) dividend cash cover, 7) short-term debt cash cover, and 8) external debt repayment period.

Earlier in this chapter, we looked at liquidity ratios as a measure of short-term viability of a firm. Over the longer term it is the capital structure that can have a great bearing on the ultimate stability or health of a company. One way to monitor this is through leverage ratios.

1. Debt to Assets

The debt to assets ratio indicates how much of the firm's total assets is financed with borrowed funds. It is calculated by dividing total liabilities by total assets.

The easy way to compute total liabilities is to subtract common stockholders' equity from total assets. Some analysts consider preferred stock to be in the same category as debt because of the obligation to pay preferred dividends. We will follow that practice because the balance sheet for Ajax does not include the preferred stock in the stockholders' equity.

Using the formula, the debt to assets ratio for Ajax declined in 20YY. The reason can be found in the balance sheet, which reveals both an increase in equity and a decrease in liabilities. The principal changes in liabilities were lower long-term debts and accounts payable.

$$\text{Debt to assets ratio} = \frac{\text{Total liabilities}}{\text{Total assets}} \times 100\%$$

$$\text{Debt to assets ratio 20YY} = \frac{\$315{,}718{,}676}{\$818{,}219{,}575} = 38.59\%$$

$$\text{Debt to assets ratio 20XX} = \frac{\$338{,}169{,}003}{\$794{,}521{,}255} = 42.56\%$$

20YY industry average $= 40.18\%$

2. Debt to Tangible Worth

The formula below measures the company's total debts as a ratio of total equity and preferred stock minus intangible assets.

$$\text{Debt to tangible worth} = \frac{\text{Total liabilities}}{\text{Total equity} + \text{Preferred stock} - \text{Intangible assets}}$$

$$\text{Debt to tangible worth 20YY} = \frac{\$315{,}718{,}676}{\$502{,}500{,}899 + \$5{,}584{,}430 - \$35{,}976{,}963}$$

$$\text{Debt to tangible worth 20YY} = 0.66 \text{ times}$$

The debt to tangible worth ratio serves as an indicator of the company's long-term debt repayment ability and how well creditors are protected in case the company goes bankrupt. In the case of Ajax in 20YY, debt to tangible worth is 0.66 times, which means creditors, in theory, are 1.5 times covered for every dollar they have loaned. If the ratio reaches 1:1, it means the creditors may have as much claim to the company as the owners and non-controlling interests.

Note that intangible assets such as goodwill, trademarks, patents, and copyrights are not included in the debt to tangible worth ratio. Such intangible assets, which are usually categorised under "other assets" in the balance sheet, are deducted from total equity and preferred stock. This makes the ratio a more useful indicator of creditor protection because intangible assets do not provide resources to pay creditors in case of bankruptcy.

3. Gearing

Gearing is usually expressed as the ratio of debt to equity, as measured by the amount of long-term borrowings and stockholders' funds plus preferred stock. Bank overdrafts and other bank debts are often included in the calculation for the purpose of measuring gearing on a more conservative basis.

$$\text{Gearing} = \frac{\text{Total external borrowing}}{\text{Tangible net worth}} \times 100\%$$

$$\text{Gearing 20YY} = \frac{\$180{,}338{,}551}{\$472{,}108{,}366} = 38.19\%$$

Ajax is not particularly highly geared, which is usually defined as gearing of 50% or higher. Its total external borrowing in 20YY is just 38% of its tangible net worth, meaning that it can repay all of its external debts and still have 62% of tangible assets left.

Highly geared companies are more vulnerable to business downturns than low-geared ones because the interest burden of highly geared firms becomes disproportionately heavier as profits decline. They are also highly vulnerable in a rising interest rate environment.

An increase in gearing could be caused by the following:

- The company is making losses, which reduces the tangible net worth.
- The company is expanding sales faster than it is able to increase tangible net worth.

- The assets of the company are growing fast enough to accommodate rapid growth, but further funding is required. In such instances, the company could be overtrading.

4. Long-Term Debt to Total Capital

Total capital includes long-term debt and equity. In 20YY, for example, the total capital of Ajax was:

Long-term borrowings	$180,338,551
Preferred stock	5,584,430
Total equity	502,500,899
Total capital	$688,423,880

The calculations below show that Ajax was able to reduce its long-term debt and bring it below the industry average.

$$\text{Long-term debt to total capital} = \frac{\text{Long-term debt}}{\text{Total capital}} \times 100\%$$

$$\text{Long-term debt to total capital 20YY} = \frac{\$180,338,551}{\$688,423,880} = 26.20\%$$

$$\text{Long-term debt to total capital 20XX} = \frac{\$191,257,695}{\$652,939,377} = 29.29\%$$

$$\text{20YY industry average} = 32.13\%$$

5. Interest Cover

By reducing the amount of debt outstanding, a company is better able to cover or pay outstanding debts, thereby cutting its financial risk. Interest cover is computed by dividing earnings before interest and taxes (EBIT) by interest expense (finance costs). In 20YY, the EBIT of Ajax was $108,962,638.

Profit before taxation	$ 90,865,942
Interest expense	18,096,696
EBIT	$108,962,638

There was a slight decline in interest cover in Ajax in 20YY compared to 20XX due to a lower EBIT. But Ajax still has ample interest cover, which is well above the industry average as shown below:

$$\text{Interest cover} = \frac{\text{EBIT}}{\text{Interest expense}}$$

$$\text{Interest cover 20YY} = \frac{\$108,962,638}{\$18,096,696} = 6.02 \text{ times}$$

$$\text{Interest cover 20XX} = \frac{\$128,556,965}{\$18,096,696} = 6.81 \text{ times}$$

$$\text{20YY industry average} = 5.38 \text{ times}$$

A decrease in the interest cover can indicate a decline in sales volume or margins on sales, bank financed expansion, or rising interest rates. If the ratio reaches 1:1, this means that virtually the entire earnings before interest and tax goes to paying interest expenses—a phenomenon that is sometimes called "working for the bank." When the ratio drops further to less than 1:1, this means the situation is critical.

In a rising interest rate environment, a low interest cover combined with a high level of floating rate debt will expose the company to a high risk of losses.

6. Dividend Cash Cover

This measures a company's ability to generate enough cash to meet ordinary dividend commitments during the year. A company is generally expected to meet dividend payments using internally generated cash, especially for listed companies.

$$\text{Dividend cash cover} = \frac{\text{Net free cash flow from operations}}{\text{Dividend paid and proposed}}$$

The dividend cash cover compares the number of times a company's net free cash flow from operations can meet the dividends paid and proposed. As discussed in Chapter 2, net free cash flow is net cash flow from operations[3] minus interest paid and tax paid. Because interest payments and taxes can be substantial, net free cash flow can be a considerably smaller amount than net cash flow. Net free cash flow therefore gives a more accurate measure of the company's ability to fund dividends.

If the dividend cash cover ratio is less than 1:1, the directors are paying the shareholders more than what the company has earned. This can indicate that the company is not producing sufficient profits to give the owners a nominal rate of return on their investments. It can also mean that the owners are milking funds out of the company.

Sometimes a ratio of less than 1:1 is acceptable. If a company has had a bad year, it may not want to upset its shareholders, particularly if it is listed on the stock exchange. However, if this practice is continued over the next few years, the tangible net worth will necessarily decline and the stability of the company will be weakened. A ratio of less than 1:1 is acceptable only in an isolated bad year.

An even lower ratio may still be reasonable for a mature company that has no pressing need for funds, but for a company that is expanding and requesting an increase of facilities from its banks, this may be unacceptable.

---

[3] As discussed in Chapter 2, net cash flow from operations is derived from adjusted cash flow from operations (operating profit plus or minus non cash items) plus or minus decline/increase in trade debtors, decline/increase in stock, and decline/increase in trade creditors.

7. Short-Term Debt Cash Cover

This measures a company's ability to repay short-term debts such as short-term loans, the current portion of any long-term debt, overdraft, and trade finance. The formula is as follows:

$$\text{Short-term debt cash cover} = \frac{\text{Net free cash flow from operations}}{\text{Short-term debts}}$$

The short-term debt cash cover ratio should at least be 1:1 or ideally should be higher (approaching 2:1) because of the short-term nature of the debt obligations. A lower ratio means the company is not making enough money in the current year to cover repayment of its short-term debts as they come due.

8. External Debt Repayment Period

This shows how many months it would take a company to repay all of its interest-bearing debt based on the current year's net free cash flow from operations. The shorter the repayment period, the more comfortable creditors will be with the company's financial condition.

$$\text{External debt repayment period} = \frac{\text{Total interest-bearing debt}}{\text{Net free cash flow from operations}} \times 12$$

We cannot derive the last three leverage and capital structure ratios for Ajax from the balance sheet and income statement presented in Chapter 2, but there is enough information about its finances now to make a tentative assessment of its creditworthiness.

The ratios show that Ajax's profitability declined from 20XX to 20YY. The ratios that measure liquidity indicate that Ajax is very liquid, but this high degree of liquidity does not account for the decline in profitability. The efficiency ratios show that Ajax has become more efficient in the most recent period. Finally, the leverage ratios show the firm has reduced its financial debt.

It would seem that, in the final analysis, Ajax is a good credit risk for the bank. However, following the usual credit monitoring procedures, the bank should track the company's financial performance, particularly in the areas shown to be relatively weak, after it has granted the loan.

DuPont Analysis

Earlier in this chapter, we alluded to a technique of financial analysis known as the DuPont Analysis, which looks at return on investment (ROI) and return on equity (ROE) from the interplay of the various financial ratios discussed above.

To measure ROI, the DuPont formula is:

$$\text{ROI} = \frac{\text{Net income}}{\text{Sales}} \times \frac{\text{Sales}}{\text{Assets}}$$

Using the nomenclature of the balance sheet and income statement of Ajax, "net income" is "profit for the year" ($56,838,942 in 20YY), "sales" is "revenue" ($804,584,939), and "assets" is "total assets" ($818,219,575). Note that the DuPont formula for ROI is, in effect, a combination of the net profit margin ratio and the asset turnover ratio.

Using DuPont analysis, the 20YY ROI for Ajax is 6.94%, meaning that for every dollar of investment, the company returns around seven cents. When compared in a cross-sectional analysis with the ROI of similar companies and the industry average (which bankers may retrieve from commercial financial information providers such as the Dun & Bradstreet Index of Key Financial Ratios or calculate themselves), this ROI may be shown to be efficient or inefficient in the use of investments—and therefore an indication of the likelihood that the company will be able or unable to service its loans.

As discussed previously, a simple way to measure ROE is by dividing profit for the year with total equity. The DuPont formula for ROE is more complicated, as it combines five financial ratios:

$$ROE = \frac{Net\ profit}{Pretax\ profit} \times \frac{Pretax\ profit}{EBIT} \times \frac{EBIT}{Sales} \times \frac{Sales}{Assets} \times \frac{Assets}{Equity}$$

Using the terms in the balance sheet and income statement of Ajax, "net profit" is "profit for the year" ($56,838,942 in 20YY), "pretax profit" is "profit before taxation" ($90,865,942), EBIT is $108,962,638 (from the interest cover ratio above), "sales" is "revenue" ($804,584,939), "assets" is "total assets" ($818,219,575), and "equity" is "total equity" ($502,500,575).

The 20YY ROE of Ajax using the DuPont formula, comes to 11.31%, which is exactly the same as the financial ratio derived by simply dividing profit for the year with total equity. But the simple and comprehensive calculations of ROE may sometimes diverge, since DuPont analysis also takes assets, profit before taxation, and EBIT into account.

Because DuPoint analysis is more finely tuned, bankers may consider using DuPont analysis to calculate ROE in cases involving large amounts of loans or in analysing complicated businesses.

Limitations of Financial Ratios

Nowadays, many banks use financial analysis software and electronic spreadsheets to perform ratio analysis and make comparisons with collected industry data. Computerised systems are useful because they reduce the time required to compute ratios and generate variance and trend analysis. We have explained how to do it manually in order to give the reader hands-on experience.

Calculating ratios is easy, requiring only basic mathematical knowledge and a calculator. The difficult part is in determining whether the figures used in the equation are appropriate and trustworthy (which we discussed in Chapter 2) and in interpreting the ratios in context.

Interpretation has to take into account key events and changes inside and outside the company. Even comparisons between companies in the same industry or across industries have to be done with care to see whether their results are meaningful.

The banker has to keep in mind the following limitations of financial ratios and comprehensive financial analysis techniques such as DuPont Analysis:

- Creative accounting techniques can make ratios look better.
- Comparison with industry averages is difficult if the company operates in many different business lines and divisions.
- Seasonal factors can distort ratios.
- Different accounting practices or policies distort comparisons.
- Ratio analysis would not give the true picture if it uses only the financial figures provided in the accounts without considering contingent liabilities or capital commitments, post-balance sheet events, personnel changes, quality of management, skill sets of the labour force, and so on.
- A ratio is meaningless by itself. It becomes meaningful only when it is tracked over a period of time or when it is compared to the industry standard or those of competitors.
- Variations in trends may only serve as an alarm bell. It is dangerous to draw definite conclusions from ratio trends and variations without determining the underlying cause.
- If a change in a ratio is expected, it is wrong to assume there is no need to inquire if it has not changed significantly.
- A number of ratios are based on figures in the balance sheets. While balance sheets are snapshots in time, there is a need to question whether the year-end figures are typical for the business. Window-dressing year-end numbers is not an unknown practice.
- There is no such thing as an "ideal" ratio. What is unacceptable or optimal depends on the type of company, industry, time frame, and the external environment.

The banker has to ensure that every question raised by these financial indicators are asked and adequately answered. Wrong assumptions can lead to wrong conclusions. Ratio analysis should then be followed by an overall analysis set in a wider context, as discussed in the following section.

Operating Risks of the Borrower

Nick Rouse of Barclays Bank observed in his book, *Applied Banking Techniques,* that users of applied banking techniques "fairly readily interpret accounting ratios and financial information such as gearing, interest cover, etc., to see that a corporate has a capital structure, which contains high financial risk. Where they then fall down is that they are not able to put this high financial risk into a wider context and so are often unable to decide whether high financial risk can be tolerated in the overall circumstances of the company."

FIGURE 3.1   The wider context of borrower risk

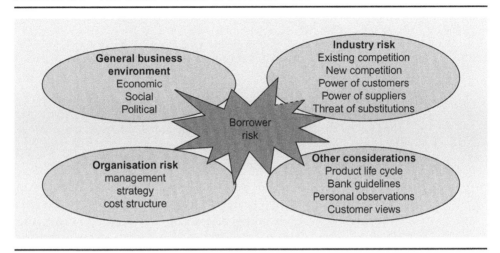

Source: HKIB

That "wider context" is represented by other risks aside from financial risk that surround the corporate borrower. In bank lending, it is important to take into account all the risks that can affect a business's ability to repay its bank loans, as Figure 3.1 graphically shows.

Taken together, all these risks do not automatically mean that the bank will not lend, but they could alert the bank to the need to adjust upwards the interest rate charged, for example, or to closely monitor the company's operations and financial condition.

What are these operating risks? Table 3.1 categorises them into six groups: owners' risks, management risks, company risks, industry risks, market risks, and external environment risks.

TABLE 3.1   Categories of borrower risks

Owners	Management	Company	Industry	Markets	Environment
Names	Names	Premises	Size	Position	Domestic/
Background	Responsibilities	Business	Domestic	Size	International
Experience	Background	strategy	International	Share	Political
Net worth	Experience	Production	Structure	Profitability	Economic
Other interests	Capability	process	Competitors	compared to	Social
Related	Depth	Products	Barriers to	competitors	Technology
companies	Balance	Raw materials	entry		Legal
	Age/Succession	Labor/staff	Development		Regulatory
	Insurance	Energy	Growing		
	Expertise	Distribution	Mature		
	Controls	Buyers	Declining		
		Investment			

Source: HKIB

Owners' Risks

Let us start the evaluation by assessing the potential operating risks related to company ownership. Every assessment of a corporation should begin by looking at:

- Names of the real owners.
- Their backgrounds and experience.
- Their net worth, particularly assets unrelated to their business, which may serve as key alternative sources of repayment.
- Their other interests, which can have both positive and adverse impacts on the business (i.e., if the other interests will contribute to or drain company resources).
- Their related companies. A lender has to be alert about the impact of related companies on the business, primarily in the form of inter-company transactions that can pose difficulties in evaluating the actual performance and financial strength of a corporate borrower.

Management Risks

The next area to consider in assessing the wider context of operating risks is the company's top management:

- Find out the names of key managers and their responsibilities, backgrounds, experience, and capabilities.
- Assess the effectiveness of the division of labour and expertise according to functions or responsibilities in such areas as sales, production, and finance.
- Examine the quality and range of management control, in particular whether management exhibits close financial control on management accounts, forecasting, and budgets.
- Gauge the style of management to determine its suitability to the particular business.
- Look at the net worth of the managers, who could be different from the owners, since they can be a key alternative source of repayment if the management guarantees the liabilities of the business to the bank.
- Assess the depth, balance, age of management, and succession issues and insurance. For instance, is there an effective succession plan for the business to continue without the original owner(s) at the helm? Is there adequate insurance to cover operational and financial risks in the form of contingency measures and key-man cover?
- Finally, a bank should avoid the practice of name-lending, which refers to the practice of extending credit based solely on the identity of the owner, who may be a high profile businessman known in the local business community, or the reputation of the company.

Company Risks

The company's operating risks should also be assessed in terms of the following areas:

- Its premises: location, obligations, adequacy, suitability, valuation, and insurance.
- Business strategy: costs, differentiation, focus.
- Production process: condition of equipment, technology, production costs, efficiency, controls.
- Products: range, quality, price, life cycle, research, and development.
- Raw materials: source, terms, form of currency.
- Labour: supply, skills, wages, unions.
- Energy or power: source, cost, backup.
- Distribution: process, channels, after-sale service.
- Buyers: number, spread, standing, payment terms, form of currency.
- Investment: expansion, rationalisation.

Many companies in Hong Kong have relocated their production facilities out of the SAR to take advantage of lower costs and other competitive advantages available elsewhere, particularly in southern China. Find out if these production facilities bring actual benefits to a business:

- Look at the location. An understanding and analysis of the various political, social, and economic risks of the country where the facilities are located will be crucial in assessing the operating strengths of the business.
- Identify the legal structure of the overseas establishment. For instance, a wholly owned foreign enterprise and a joint venture entity in China will create different levels of risk, which a lender has to take into account.
- Ascertain the investment costs and future capital commitments.
- Find out whether the assets located overseas can be charged and if not, whether a charge on the shareholding of the overseas companies or factories can be imposed, or at least whether a negative pledge can be executed to protect the lender's interests.

Industry Risks

Operating risks can arise as well from trends and developments in the industry sector that the business is in:

- Look at the size of the industry as a whole, domestically and even internationally, if the business is competing overseas.
- Ascertain the level of competition and the barriers to entry.
- Evaluate the nature and prospects of the industry, whether it is growing, mature, or declining.
- Investigate environmental protection issues applicable to the company's operations.

Market Risks

The company's market share, size and profitability in relation to its competitors are also part of the operating risks that should be reviewed. A company whose financial and operational performance is much worse than its rivals in the same market should raise concerns with the bank. The borrower's financial ratios and actual results may look adequate standing on their own, but the bank should be concerned as well by the company's ability to compete and therefore survive in the future.

External Environment

The external economic, social, political, legal, and regulatory environment—both domestic and overseas—could also have an impact on the company's operating risks and therefore, from the bank's point of view, its creditworthiness. A company that sells most of its goods to a country that is undergoing political upheaval, for example, can be expected to suffer financially if the disruptions go on for some time.

Other external risks include new environmental standards that may increase the company's costs (e.g., higher fuel emissions standards for cars), higher taxes on the company's goods (e.g., "sin" taxes on cigarettes), and the rise of new technologies that can make the company's products obsolete.

Analysis Tools and Approaches

How does a bank analyse the operating risks borrowers face and how do borrowers manage those risks? Market researchers and business planning strategists have developed a number of tools and models for this purpose. They include PEST analysis, SWOT analysis, the five competitive forces model, and the stages model of business growth.

PEST Analysis

PEST stands for the political, economic, social, and technological forces that exert an influence on the company from the outside. Figure 3.2 shows a graphic illustration of PEST analysis.

Political Forces

In analysing the "P" in PEST analysis, the factors to be considered include the following:

- **Political instability.** Businesses with manufacturing bases in politically unstable places may encounter production disruptions because of the breakdown in law and order. It typically takes years for a country to return to political stability. The bank will have to

FIGURE 3.2   PEST analysis

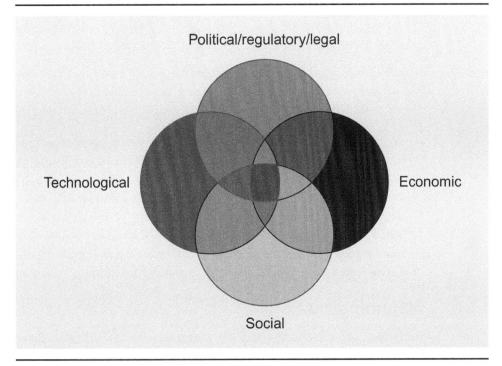

Source: HKIB

gauge the extent of the current and future disorder and the impact on the corporate borrower's business and ability to repay its loans.

- **Trade protectionism.** The World Trade Organisation now counts most of the world's economies as members, including China and Vietnam. Still, trade disputes continue to erupt, in part because of protectionist trade policies in places where citizens blame other countries for supposedly taking away local jobs, manipulating their currency to boost exports, as well as other accusations. The bank needs to assess how higher tariffs and the erection of non-tariff barriers could impact the borrower's financial condition.

Economic Forces

The bank should examine the impact of economic storms on the corporate borrower and how it copes with them. The factors to be considered include:

- Currency devaluations, such as those that happened during the 1997 Asian financial crisis, which destabilised industry equilibrium, stoked inflation, forced interest rates up, and so on.
- Economic downturn and recessions, which typically weaken consumer confidence. For instance, car manufacturers facing static, declining national markets need to increase promotional campaigns and offer a number of free services to secure market share.

- Overcapacity, which may happen when the economy is growing and new businesses join the borrower's industry and market.

Social Forces

Societies do not stand still; those in Asia are particularly changing fast. A company that is in tune with these changes is better equipped to survive and thrive as consumer consumption and taste patterns evolve. The social factors to be considered include:

- **Ageing population.** Corporate borrowers that target younger consumers may struggle to remain in business. Those that embrace the ageing trend and develop goods and services aimed at this growing segment of the market may improve their creditworthiness.
- **Environmentalism.** Borrowers in highly polluting industries may be punished by environmentally conscious consumers. Conversely, borrowers that are perceived to have good "green" credentials may benefit, and thus improve their credit standing with the banks.
- **Lifestyle changes.** In some markets, certain sectors like breweries and cigarette manufacturers have fallen out of favour with consumers, who have embraced healthy living.

Technological Forces

Technology can profoundly affect the way companies do business. The advent of the iPhone, for example, has shaken up the mobile phone industry. The following are amongst the factors to examine in analysing how technological forces can affect a company's business, and therefore its creditworthiness.

- **Product cycle.** Technological advances can reduce product development time and make existing products outdated and obsolete more quickly than before. Is the borrower subject to this trend? How is it responding to product cycle changes?
- **E-commerce.** The rapid growth of the Internet and broadband infrastructure worldwide is blurring physical borders in the sale and distribution of products. A borrower may find itself under pressure if its e-commerce initiative fails or if it is unable to compete with online businesses.

SWOT analysis

SWOT stands for strengths, weaknesses, opportunities, and threats. Developed by Albert Humphrey, a prominent American business and management consultant, this analysis tool looks at both internal and external factors that could have a favourable or unfavourable impact on a corporate borrower.

Strengths and Weaknesses

The analysis of the strengths and weaknesses of a company takes an internal view of its performance from the following angles:

- **Management:** The level of management skills, expertise, and experience and their impact on the competitiveness of a business.
- **Capital:** Liquidity, profitability, and asset structure and their impact on the business.
- **Accounting records:** Whether the business has an effective Management Information System to help track performance and whether management is well-informed about the financial position of the company.
- **Marketing:** The market position and market share of a business compared to its main competitors.
- **Product:** Its life cycle—durables or fashionable items; its nature—mass market, niche, or branded; its quality—cost or differentiation.
- **Premises:** Location, condition, and suitability for present and future needs.
- **Plant, machinery, and other physical assets:** Their current state and the company's policy on assets replacement.
- **Labour:** Cost, quality, supply, and labour relations. Is the trade union influential?
- **Stock:** Proportion of raw materials, work-in-progress, and finished goods. Is there any obsolete stock?

Opportunities and Threats

The analysis focuses on the range of factors external to the business, which can influence performance but are essentially beyond the company's control:

- **Political:** Changes in government legislation.
- **Economic:** Business cycles, exchange rates, interest rates, inflation, and changes in labour markets.
- **Social:** Demographic and lifestyle changes such as birth rate, number of children per family, and average age of the population (e.g., food producers reacting to trend, towards health-consciousness).
- **Technological:** New technological innovations and process developments may cause obsolescence of major company assets.
- **Competitiveness:** Level of competition.
- **Ecological:** Environmental "friendliness" of the business (e.g., high levels of effluent discharge could result in greater fines in view of increased environmental awareness).

Five Competitive Forces Model

Noted American economist Michael Porter developed a framework widely used today by academics and business strategists to examine what he calls "the five forces that shape industry competition." Porter theorised that it is "industry structure [that] drives competition and profitability, not whether an industry produces a product or service, is emerging or mature, high tech or low tech, regulated or unregulated." He explained that "while a myriad of factors can affect industry profitability in the short run—including the weather and the business cycle—industry structure, [as] manifested in the competitive forces, sets industry profitability in the medium and long run."

The five competitive forces that Porter believes shape competition are the following: 1) threat of new entrants, 2) threat of substitute products or services, 3) bargaining power of buyers, 4) bargaining power of suppliers, and 5) rivalry among existing competitors.

The banker can use Porter's Five Forces Model to help assess what operating risks a borrower faces and how well (or how badly) it is responding to these forces.

1. Threat of New Entrants

The factors to consider include the following:

- Economies of scale deter entry of newcomers by forcing them either to come in on a large scale themselves or to accept a cost disadvantage. A company that enjoys economies of scale may be well-positioned to meet the threat of new entrants.
- Brand identification creates a barrier by forcing new entrants to spend heavily to overcome customer loyalty to existing players. Advertising, customer service, and product differences are amongst the factors that foster brand identification. Large switching costs from one brand to another may also deter customers from switching to a new brand.
- The need to invest large sums in order to compete creates a barrier to entry, particularly if capital is required for unrecoverable expenditures in upfront advertising or research and development (R&D).
- Entrenched companies may have cost advantages not available to potential rivals, irrespective of their size and attainable economies of scale. Examples include patents, proprietary technology, experience, access to the best raw materials sources, assets purchased at pre-inflation prices, government subsidies, and favourable locations.
- Availability of self-owned space, retail outlets, and warehouses can deter new entrants. The more limited the wholesale or retail channels are and the more that existing competitors have tied these up, the more difficult it is for new entrants.
- The government can limit or even close entry to industries with such controls as license requirements, limits on access to raw materials, quotas, subsidies, and tax incentives. The government can also play an indirect but major role by affecting entry barriers through controls such as air and water pollution standards and health and safety rules.
- The potential rival's expectations about the reaction of existing competitors will influence its decision on whether or not to enter the market.
    i. Existing players possess substantial resources to fight back, including excess cash and unused borrowing power, productive capacity, or clout with distribution channels and customers.
    ii. Existing players seem likely to cut prices because of a desire to keep market share or because of industry-wide excess capacity.
    iii. Industry growth is slow, affecting its ability to absorb new entrants and may result in less earnings for all parties involved.

2. Threat of a Substitute Product

This refers to existing or potential products/services that perform the same function as rival goods, or new products/services created from technological innovation, which can reduce costs and/or provide better quality performance. The key considerations include:

- Whether the product is easily replaceable or is indispensable
- Comparative price and performance
- Impact from technological innovation (e.g., the impact of product life cycle on stock obsolescence). One way to cope with this is to set up an inventory ageing list to monitor the stock movement

3. Bargaining Power of Suppliers

The bargaining power of suppliers is strong if:

- The market is dominated by a few companies and is more concentrated than the industry it sells to. For example, oil producing countries formed OPEC and in its early stages it was able to dictate price increases at the expense of customers.
- Products are unique or differentiated or switching costs are high. (Switching costs are the fixed costs that buyers absorb when changing suppliers.) This is the case, for example, when buyers have invested heavily in specialised ancillary equipment or in learning how to operate a supplier's equipment. This may also happen if production lines are connected to the supplier's manufacturing facilities. Another example is when customers rely on the suppliers for assuring product quality and nurturing brand image.
- Suppliers pose a credible threat of integrating forward and thus directly competing with the companies they used to supply. This may happen, for instance, when a bauxite mining firm expands to aluminium smelting, then to extrusion or manufacturing aluminium into complex shapes.
- The industry is not an important customer of the supplier group. This may be the case with one-off or small customers, which do not command a significant share of the supplier group's business.
- The supplier's input is crucial to the success of the customer's product. For example, a computer manufacturer may rely on improvements and enhancements by its supplier for a key component like the microprocessor.

4. Bargaining Power of Buyers

The bargaining power of buyers is strong if:

- The industry is concentrated. For example, one or some buyers have a dominant position and are able to force down prices, reducing industry margins. The dominant buyers are inclined to exert pressure on the suppliers if:
    i. Their purchases from the industry represent a significant portion of their total costs. A price reduction can generate substantial cost savings and improve profitability for the buyers.

ii. They cannot pass on cost increases to their customers easily, so they try to squeeze suppliers instead.

iii. They are bulk buyers. High fixed-cost companies purchasing in large volumes can force down supplier prices or increase supplier costs by demanding higher quality products.

- Products are standard or undifferentiated, allowing buyers to easily find alternative sources of supply.
- Buyers pose a credible threat of integrating backward (e.g., a wholesale trader acquiring the manufacturing source).
- Industry input is not crucial to the success of the buyer's product.
- There are risks in buyer concentration. Suppliers will therefore want to diversify, increasing the power of the buyers they want to keep in their customer mix to avoid over dependence on too few buyers.
- Order cancellations can cause serious disruption to operations.
- Corporate failure or winding-up of buyers can result in payment default or liquidity squeeze for the supplier.

The bank can assess whether a borrower company has addressed the risks posed by strong buyer concentration by looking for the following mitigating actions:

- Does the company have contracts on hand to assure a minimum guaranteed business level?
- Does the company avoid unfavourable terms and conditions in its contracts with buyers such as product buy-backs?
- Does the company monitor debtors with a debtors ageing list? Has the company conducted a credit check on the financial status of drawees by contacting the latter's banks or the credit agencies?
- Has the company arranged insurance cover with credit insurance agencies including the Export Credit Insurance Corporation and factoring companies in case of non-payment?
- Does the company impose a ceiling limit for each buyer to avoid concentration?
- Does the company have a list of approved buyers, accompanied by satisfactory background and credit status checks?
- Has the company diversified its market?

5. Rivalry Amongst Existing Competitors

The intensity of the rivalry amongst existing players in the same industry poses a challenge to those companies, and should be considered by the bank in lending decisions. The rivalry among competitors may intensify if:

- Industry-wide growth is slowing, precipitating a fight for market share amongst companies that are roughly equal in size and capabilities. In an ageing market with fewer children, for example, demand for toys may be static or may decline, causing toymakers to compete more aggressively for the attention of a shrinking pool of customers.

- The product or service lacks differentiation, making it easy for buyers to change suppliers without incurring heavy costs and thus intensifying competition among companies to retain customer loyalty.
- A competitor adds to its existing capacity (usually to gain economies of scale), disrupting the demand/supply dynamics.
- Low profitability or losses do not deter competitors from closing down because they are motivated by non-commercial factors (e.g., specialised assets, closure costs, loyalty to employees, job security for management, government pressure).

Stage Models of Business Growth

Every corporation goes through various stages of development, according to Prof. Richard Nolan, who first formulated the stages-of-growth model to explain the growth of information technology in a corporation in the 1970s. Nolan's theoretical model has since been widely adopted to try to explain the growth of any company and to assess the risks encountered in every stage of development.

The following are the five stages of growth: existence, survival, growth, consolidation, and maturity.

Stage 1: Existence

At this infant stage, a business usually needs to find customers and deliver products or services. The company structure is simple, usually a one-man operation and under the owner's direct supervision. The owner is involved in every decision. Planning is non-existent or minimal. Banks are usually wary of lending.

Stage 2: Survival

At the survival stage, a business usually establishes enough products and customers to become a viable business. Company structure is evolving and growing, but owner dominance and direct supervision are still strong. There is some short-term planning involving cash flow forecasting. Banks may be more open to lending, but will perhaps require more documentation than normal.

Stage 3: Growth

At the growth stage, a business has established a market niche to pave the way for further growth. A functional company structure with delineated marketing, finance, and administrative operations has emerged. The business owner has formed a clear strategy based on his vision and has obtained resources for growth. Banks are usually happy to lend to growth companies.

Stage 4: Consolidation

This is often the dangerous and critical stage before a business can become very successful and large. The business owner needs to ensure enough financial resources, internal controls, and good management practices are in place. Banks are one source of financing, but the company may tap other sources such as the stock market, bonds and private equity.

Stage 5: Maturity

At this stage, a corporation has developed the characteristics of a stable and large enterprise with professional management, formal information systems, and a strategic planning process in running the business. It has usually established good relationships with banks, which may extend credit lines and long-term credit for new capital expenses and investment.

Summary

This section summarises the issues and topics discussed in this chapter:

- To evaluate a corporate borrower's profitability, liquidity, efficiency, leverage, or indebtedness, banks derive financial ratios from the financial statements of the corporate borrower. Banks pay particularly close attention to liquidity and leverage ratios, which indicate the ability to pay short-term liabilities and how deep into debt the borrower is.
- Ratios do not mean much by themselves. They become meaningful only when tracked using figures across several years and when compared to industry rivals. It is also best to ask the borrower to provide more information and explain the changes in the ratios before drawing final conclusions.
- Ratio analysis is only part of a full evaluation of a borrower's operating risks. A business also has to be examined in the context of its internal and external operating environment. The bank lender can make use of various models and frameworks for this purpose, including the PEST Analysis model, which looks at the external factors affecting risk, and the SWOT framework, which looks at both external and internal factors.
- Both PEST and SWOT can be used in conjunction with other models. The Five Competitive Forces Model assumes it is the industry that drives competition and profitability. The stages-of-growth model identifies the risks that a company faces in the different stages of company development.

Key Terms

acid test ratio	current ratio
age of inventory	debt ratio
asset turnover	debt to tangible net worth

dividend cash cover

dividend payout ratio

earnings per share (EPS)

efficiency measurement

external debt repayment period

Five Competitive Forces Model

fixed assets turnover

gearing

gross profit margin

interest cash cover

interest coverage

long-term debt to total capital

net profit margin

net sales over working capital

net working capital

operating profit margin

PEST analysis

return on assets (ROA)

return on equity (ROE)

short-term debt cash cover

stage models of business growth model

stock turnover period

SWOT analysis

trade creditor days

trade debtor days

working capital

Study Guide

1. What ratios should be used to determine if a firm can meet its current and long-term financial obligations?
2. When comparing a firm's ratios to an industry, is it bad to be below average? Explain your answer.
3. What would be the expected turnover ratios for *Time* magazine and for a high priced jewellery store, and why?
4. Why does a bank lender need to go beyond the examination of a corporate borrower's financial statements, using financial ratios, in order to assess the overall operating risk?
5. Using Michael Porter's Five Competitive Forces model, why do you think many newspapers are now in danger of folding up?

Further Reading

Basu, Sam N. and Rolfes, Harold L. Jr. 1995, *Strategic Credit Management*. United States: John Wiley & Sons.

Gup, Benton E. and Kolari, James W. 2005, *Commercial Banking*. United States: John Wiley & Sons, Third Edition.

Porter, Michael E. "The Five Competitive Forces That Shape Strategy" in *Harvard Business Review* 86, no. 1 (January 2008).

2

CORPORATE CREDIT

4

Credit Assessment

After studying this chapter, you should be able to:

1. Understand the use of the decision tree for credit assessment

2. Explain the basic elements of opportunity assessment, preliminary analysis, repayment source analysis and facility arrangement and loan management

3. Describe how credit scoring works

4. Summarise the credit process from analysis to decision

Introduction

In the previous chapters, we looked outwards at how banks assess borrowers and the tools they can use to decide whether to lend to them or not. In this chapter,[1] we look inward at the bank's internal credit assessment process. The assessment of the borrower's credit-worthiness is part of this process, but there are other steps that need to be taken before and after the decision to lend is made.

Because the amounts involved are generally larger compared to lending to individuals, lending to a corporation follows a rigorous process. Understanding how that process works will go a long way to helping the bank lender mitigate risk while at the same time getting on with the business of lending, which is what banking is all about. After all, a bank that turns down most credit applications is as bad as one that approves almost all of them.

Lending Principles

In Chapter 1, we discussed general lending principles such as CAMPARI, which are applicable to advances to personal customers. There are also lending principles specifically for lending to corporations.

The process of lending begins before a loan is made. The bank's board of directors establishes a loan policy and considers the risk reduction techniques previously described in Chapters 2 and 3. The process ends when the loan is repaid or when it is determined to be uncollectable. At that point, if it no longer has value, it is removed as an asset from the bank balance sheet. Even then, the bank still may be able to collect some of the proceeds. Both lender and borrower perform certain tasks over the term of the lending process.

In evaluating loan requests from corporations, banks have to keep in mind the long-established 6 Cs of credit, which are character, capacity, capital, collateral, conditions, and compliance.

Character

Banks must "know their customer" before they make loans, and character is the place to start. Character refers to a combination of qualities that distinguishes one person or a group from another. To some extent, the words *character* and *reputation* overlap in meaning. We use the term character here to refer to a borrower's honesty, responsibility, integrity, and consistency, from which we can determine their willingness to repay loans. Evidence of character traits can be found in reports from credit bureaus and credit reporting agencies.

---

[1] This chapter uses some material from *Commercial Banking* (2005) by Benton E. Gup and James W. Kolari and *Strategic Credit Management* (1995) by Sam N. Basu and Harold L. Rolfes, Jr., with permission from publisher John Wiley & Sons.

Capacity

This refers to the success of the borrower's business as reflected in its financial condition and ability to meet financial obligations via cash flow and earnings. Banks generally require prospective borrowers to submit their financial statements and income tax statements in order to determine their credit worthiness.

Capital

Capital represents the amount of equity capital that a firm has that can be liquidated for payment if all other means of collecting the debt fail. Equity capital is equal to total assets less total liabilities. However, there can be a substantial difference between the *book value* and the *market value* of assets and liabilities. For example, land purchased 20 years ago can be carried on the books at its historical cost. However, the market value of the land could be substantially higher or lower than the book value.

Collateral

Collateral refers to assets that are pledged for security in a credit transaction. The fact that borrowers may lose their collateral if they default on their loans serves as an incentive for them to abide by the loan contract. Notwithstanding the availability of collateral, the primary consideration for deciding whether to extend credit facilities to a borrower remains that borrower's ability to repay.

Conditions

Conditions refer to external factors beyond the control of a firm that may affect their ability to repay debts. Excess capacity in the commercial real estate sector is one example. The lender should take that into account before granting a loan that would add to the capacity. It is changes in conditions, such as recessions, interest rate shocks, and asset price deflation that adversely affect borrowers and contribute to loan defaults.

Compliance

While the previous Cs refer to the borrower, compliance applies to the lender. Compliance with court decisions, laws, and regulations is an important part of the lending process. In Hong Kong, the most important legislative source are the Banking Ordinance (Cap. 155), and the Banking (Capital) Rules (Cap. 155L). Other relevant laws include the Hong Kong Association of Banks Ordinance (Cap. 364), Exchange Fund Ordinance (Cap. 66),

Companies Ordinance (Cap. 32), Partnership Ordinance (Cap. 38), Bankruptcy Ordinance (Cap. 6), Conveyancing and Property Ordinance (Cap. 219), and Bills of Exchange Ordinance (Cap. 19).

Banks must also follow the Hong Kong Monetary Authority's Supervisory Policy Manual, which contains the latest banking supervisory policies and practices, the minimum standards that authorised institutions are expected to meet to satisfy the requirements of the Banking Ordinance, and recommendations on best practices that banks in Hong Kong should aim to achieve.

The specific guidelines for bank lending include General Principles of Credit Risk Management, Credit Approval, Review and Records, Connected Lending, Large Exposure and Risk Concentration, Credit Administration, Measurement, and Monitoring. Banks must also comply with circular letters and guidelines issued by the HKMA from time to time.

Banks are also expected to comply with the Code of Banking Practice, which was issued jointly by the Hong Kong Association of Banks and the DTC Association (the industry group for restricted licence banks and deposit-taking companies) and endorsed by the HKMA.

Credit Decision Tree

The use of decision trees has become popular as an evaluation tool because they are graphic and easy to understand. Figure 4.1 shows a decision tree that illustrates the typical steps a bank lender takes in doing what a bank is supposed to do—lend money in order to earn interest on that lending.

In this decision tree, the credit process starts with opportunity assessment by loan officers or, in some instances, with a potential borrower approaching the bank to request credit. A preliminary analysis is done on the application or an identified opportunity.

If the credit application or identified opportunity passes the preliminary screening, which includes the identification of a clear borrowing cause, the loan officer moves on to analyses of industry, business, and financial statements, which we discussed in the previous chapters. If this stage is successfully negotiated, the bank goes on to repayment source analysis and completes the process with the grant of facility arrangement and disbursement of the funds. But the process does not end there. It is also important for the bank to practice loan management, which includes monitoring the performance of the corporate borrower to detect red flags early enough so the bank can protect itself from defaults.

Opportunity Assessment

There are many ways for banks to start the lending process to corporate borrowers. They include soliciting loans, refinancing, overdraft, buying loans, and use of loan brokers.

FIGURE 4.1 Credit decision tree

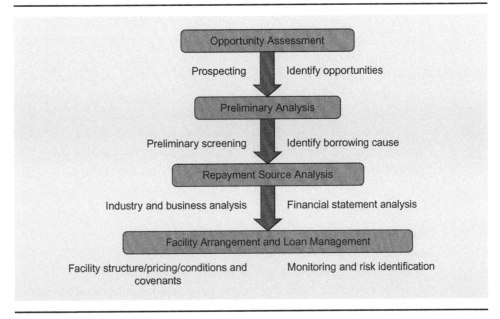

Source: HKIB

Soliciting Loans

Banks actively solicit loans in person, by mail, and via the Internet. These sales efforts are typical for seeking new customers or trying to cross-sell bank services. For example, a branch manager or loan officer may explain to a prospective borrower how the bank's cash management services can improve the company's cash flow.

Many potential commercial loan requests are unfortunately rejected by banks or turn out to be unsuitable for the client because the client does not know what information the bank needs to grant the loan. Some borrowers, for example, do not know what type of loan (i.e., line of credit, term loan) will meet their financial needs best, or what type of collateral (i.e., accounts receivable, bill of lading, or second mortgage) is suitable for their loans.

With prospective borrowers who do not know the procedures, good loan officers take the time to explain what information they must provide to the bank and even suggest the type of loan most suited to their needs.

Refinancing

Borrowers can request banks to refinance existing loans. Suppose that interest rates on loans decline from 10% to 6%. Borrowers with high fixed rate loans would naturally want to avail of the lower rate. They can make out a new loan at the lower rate and pay off the high-rate loan. The refinancing is at the borrower's option, and occurs only when it is to their advantage.

Buying Loans

Suppose a large bank is making a $100 million loan to an airline, but the originating bank does not want to keep such a large loan in its loan portfolio. It may sell parts (called participations) of that loan to other banks. The sale of participations "downstream" to smaller banks allows smaller banks to participate in loans that they could not originate. In addition, it is one way for a bank with slack demand for loans to increase its loan portfolio. It also allows all the banks involved to diversify their loan portfolios.

Participations can originate from small banks too. Suppose a small bank wants to make a loan that exceeds its lending limits. It can make the loan and sell participations "upstream" to larger banks. Banks also buy and sell securitised loans.

Overdraft

An overdraft occurs when a customer writes a check on uncollected funds, or when funds are insufficient in an account to cover a withdrawal. If a bank pays on a check written against insufficient balances, it is in effect extending an unsecured loan.

Some overdrafts are written with prior permission from the bank, but most are not. In the latter case, the overdraft represents a loan that the bank may not want to make. The borrower did not ask the bank for the funds in advance.

Loan Broker

Loan brokers sell loan propositions to banks and other lenders. Loan brokers are individuals or firms acting as agents or brokers between the borrower and the lender. For example, a loan broker may come to an arrangement with a real estate developer on a deal for the broker to find financing for a particular project. The broker will seek out lenders and arrange the loan. Once the loan is made and the borrower has paid the broker's fees, the broker is out of the picture.

Preliminary Analysis

Regardless of how the opportunity to lend was identified, a well-designed and implemented credit assessment system will have a provision to conduct a preliminary assessment of the opportunity. This step asks the questions: What is the borrowing cause? How valid is that borrowing cause?

Identifying the Borrowing Cause

The borrowing cause can either be for a general corporate purpose or a special purpose. If for a general purpose, the loan is typically going to be used to:

- Provide working capital to replenish inventory, pay for accounts payable, and so on;
- Finance general growth, such as entering a new line of business or market;
- Purchase assets.

If the borrowing cause is for a special purpose, the loan will typically be used for:

- Project financing;
- Acquisition financing;
- Construction financing;
- Trade financing;
- Other purposes.

Evaluating the Borrowing Cause

The borrowing cause must not only be identified; it should also be evaluated. To come to a conclusion about the credibility of the borrowing purpose, it is helpful for the bank lender to ask the following questions:

- *Does the purpose make good business sense?* Although American businessman T. Boone Pickens, head of the relatively small Mesa Petroleum, made a successful greenmail attempt on Gulf Oil, a company many times larger, by buying enough Gulf Oil stock so as to threaten a takeover, it is unlikely that financing for such a business purpose would make sense for most commercial banks.
- *Is the purpose legal?* Bankers should take into account legal and reputation risk. It is possible for a bank to end up ultimately financing a helicopter used by a well-known drug lord. Honesty and integrity are the pillars upon which the banking industry rests. The slightest hint of scandal or irregular and/or illegal activities could bring the bank under intense regulatory scrutiny, control, or—in an extreme case—closure.
- *Is the purpose consistent with the bank's commercial lending policy?* The commercial lending policy of a bank is driven by its strategy, its market, and the ensuing environment. Each of these factors may change over time. With a change in strategic focus, a bank may decide to de-emphasise or exit one area of lending and enter or grow another.

  The evolution of the market may create yet another change in lending policy. In Japan in the 1960s and 1970s, most large corporations tended to be more leveraged than their U.S. counterparts. In the 1980s, however, large successful companies like Toyota Motors carried so much liquidity that their bank borrowings were way down and it was informally referred to as "Toyota Bank." Consequently, Japanese banks had to adjust their commercial lending policy to respond to this change in market conditions, such as targeting smaller companies.

  In addition, certain banks may have their own ethical guidelines with respect to lending decisions. In the 1980s, for example, lending to South African companies or gaming operations were not acceptable practices among major U.S. banks. Nowadays, lending to "green" companies may be encouraged in today's environmentally conscious society.
- *Does the loan require special expertise or handling?* Certain loan purposes typically would require specific loan structures and perhaps special expertise on the part of the lender. Project loans would be one such area where specialised skills such as engineering

feasibility analysis and merchant banking expertise would be critical. Even ordinary inventory financing would require expertise in secured lending, including management of an efficient collateral control system. A commercial bank may not have such expertise or may not want to grow this segment of loans for a variety of reasons at a given time.

- *Does the borrower signal that he values the project enough to do his homework?* Aside from informing a bank lender about the loan purpose, a well-thought-through request that makes business sense indicates disciplined analysis and strategic preparation on the part of the potential borrower. Any banker would rather have thoughtful borrowers who do relevant homework by performing defensible financial programs and plans, than those who fly by the seat of their pants.

Repayment Source Analysis

As any experienced lender would say, cash, and only cash repays loans; accounting income does not. A suitable stream of cash flow must be identified as the primary source of repayment. It is also important to designate a backup or secondary source of repayment in case the main one comes up short. A number of major banks have a standard policy of not making a loan unless two independent sources of repayment are identified. It is worthwhile to be able to systematically identify these sources and to assess their repayment potential.

Sources of Repayment

The usual sources of repayment can be categorised into two groups: primary sources and secondary sources. Primary sources include the following:

- *Operating cash flow.* This is the main source of most loan repayments. Not only is this the most common source, there is no incremental transaction cost involved. Furthermore, the generation of operating cash flow is an ongoing process and it does not depend on successful completion of a deal, unlike in the case of refinancing, asset sale, acquisition or liquidation, or a public securities offering.
- *Refinancing.* This is perhaps the second most common source of repayment. It comes in two variations:
  - i. takeout financing by another institution, where the original bank loan is paid off by a new loan from the incoming institution, and
  - ii. public or private placement of the borrower's security, where proceeds from an equity or debt issue are used to pay off the loan.
- *Acquisition of the borrower by another company.* This often (but not always) results in repayment of existing bank loans out of the cash flows generated by the deal. There are also cases where the buyout triggers a takeout financing by the acquiring company's bank, which may end up taking over the primary banking relationship. In this case, takeout financing is defined as the incoming bank essentially taking over the outgoing

bank's loan to the acquired company. In practice, though, it is difficult to count on an uncertain event like an acquisition as a planned repayment source.

- *Liquidation of the borrowing entity.* This is typical in the case of some specific-purpose business borrowers such as real estate limited partnerships, which are often liquidated upon reaching their investment objectives. Bank loans are paid off from the proceeds of liquidation.

Secondary sources are functionally the same ones discussed above. The key thing to remember is that the two sources—primary and secondary—must be independent of each other. In short, the same source cannot be double-counted under both primary and secondary categories. Thus, if the primary source of repayment is identified as operating cash flow, the secondary one should be any of the other types of repayment.

Financial Statement Analysis

A bank does not depend on the mere say so of a corporate borrower that it can repay the loan, but must make an independent assessment of the matter. This can be accomplished by examining the potential borrower's financial statements, as discussed in Chapter 2.

Ratio and Operating Risks Analysis

As discussed in Chapter 3, the bank can evaluate the financial health of the business and compare it with its rivals by performing a ratio analysis and other financial analysis techniques. The bank should also assess the internal and external strengths and weaknesses of the business and the external environment through tools and approaches such as PEST and SWOT analyses, the Five Competitive Market Forces Model, and stages model of business growth.

Table 4.1 shows a matrix of general observations about the level of risk a bank may be running when lending to a corporate borrower. The levels of risk are rated on a sliding scale (very low, low, moderate, high, and very high) according to three categories: the borrower's business, its financial condition, and its level of liquidity.

Loan Management

This last step in the credit decision tree refers to credit administration. The bank's job is not done just because a solid credit assessment process had been followed and it genuinely believes it had done all it could to vet the borrower. Indeed, we can argue that the hard work is just beginning. The bank lender must now monitor the borrower's performance and make sure it remains as creditworthy as it was when the loan was extended. This process will be discussed in greater detail in Chapter 7 of this book.

Figure 4.2 shows a more detailed decision tree that sums up what has been discussed in this section and in the previous chapters.

TABLE 4.1 Levels of credit risk according to borrower characteristics on three categories

	Very Low	Low	Moderate	High	Very High
Business	◆ Uncontested market leader ◆ Diversified & stable cash flow sources ◆ Recognized growth record	◆ Leader in more competitive sector ◆ Regulated protection ◆ Diversified cash flow sources ◆ Competitive operations	◆ Large established competitors ◆ Leaders of less stable sectors ◆ Successful niche players with little indebtedness	◆ Sector-tier players ◆ Worse-than-average operating profile ◆ Potential industry leaders with very high debt levels	◆ Struggling competitors ◆ Weak operating profile, e.g., wrong business model
Financial	◆ Low debt coverage ◆ Consistent dividends	◆ Superior operating profitability ◆ Low debt coverage but moderate for growth	◆ More aggressive financial strategy ◆ Stable debt servicing capacity ◆ Modest dividends	◆ Tight debt-servicing ratios ◆ Cash flow volatility ◆ Leveraged capital structure	◆ Very tight debt-servicing ratios ◆ Negative cash flow ◆ No dividends ◆ Highly leveraged
Liquidity	◆ Consistent free cash flow ◆ Strong access to debt & equity markets ◆ Huge undrawn bank & capital market lines	◆ Consistent free cash flow ◆ Strong access to debt & equity markets ◆ Available medium-term committed bank lines	◆ Weak access to debt capital markets ◆ Available medium-term committed bank lines with financial covenants	◆ Marginal cash flow ◆ Bank debts with financial covenants or secured ◆ Uncertain access to debt capital markets	◆ Insecure debt servicing capability ◆ Secure bank debt and tight financial covenants

Source: HKIB

FIGURE 4.2　Process of credit analysis from loan request to loan decision

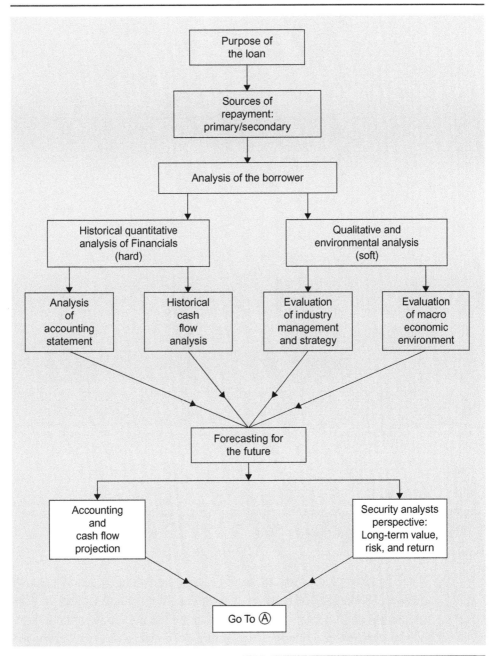

Source: Sam N. Basu and Harold L. Rolfes, Jr., *Strategic Credit Management* (John Wiley & Sons, 1995), 75–76.

(Continued)

FIGURE 4.2 *(Continued)*

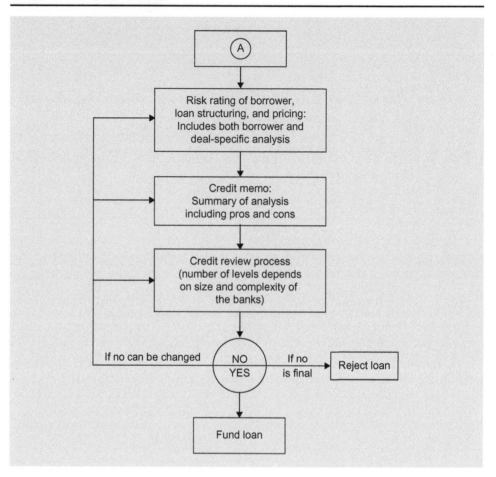

Credit Risk Rating

Banks are integrating credit scoring by external credit rating agencies into their corporate lending decisions. Note, however, that the credibility of such ratings has been questioned in the wake of the global financial crisis in the late 2000s, when the international credit rating agencies were criticised for assigning investment grades to collateralised debt obligations (CDOs) that had some U.S. sub-prime mortgages as underlying assets, along with triple-A credits. Questions about conflict of interest have also been raised regarding the practice of the companies being rated paying the credit rating agency for the rating.

Even so, an internal credit risk rating system, whether or not external ratings are integrated into it, is considered best practice for banks. A system of rating credits based on predetermined and accepted definitions has proven to be effective. It is critical for all officers participating in the evaluation and monitoring process to have a common understanding of these ratings and possess the ability and experience to use this system of ratings fairly and objectively.

Effective credit risk management rating systems have a number of common characteristics:

- One common credit risk rating system is used throughout the organisation.
- Officers responsible for using and implementing the rating system receive common and regular training in its use.
- Senior management supports and reinforces discipline in system implementation.
- The system adequately differentiates risk.
- Portfolio risk is managed centrally.
- The system provides for continuous review and update of the ratings.
- The ratings reflect the risk inherent in each individual credit.
- The system provides for scheduled and regular internal audits.

An internal credit risk rating system may consist of numerical, alphabetical, or descriptive ratings. Banks can devise their own system of credit risk rating according to their particular circumstances and the characteristics of their credit portfolios.

The number of risk levels of a rating system is not necessarily important, provided portfolio credit risk is adequately differentiated. However, the Hong Kong Monetary Authority recommends in its Supervisory Policy Manual module on General Principles of Credit Risk Management (CR-G-1) that authorised institutions "seek to improve the sophistication of their loan classification system beyond the 5-grade system currently employed for regulatory reporting." The HKMA advises institutions "to adopt multiple grades for loans that are not yet irregular and to develop the ability to track the migration of individual loans through the various internal credit ratings."

A nine-level rating system, for example, may use the first four levels to differentiate levels of acceptable risk. The next two levels may refer to marginally acceptable risks requiring special attention and watchfulness. The remaining three may be designated problem or classified levels requiring intensive management attention and follow-up. Figure 4.3 shows an example of an internal credit risk rating system.

An effective internal credit risk rating system is an important and necessary tool for good portfolio management and is key to determining adequate loan loss reserve levels. However, it should be remembered that the ratings are interpreted and applied by bank officers and managers, whose judgements may be coloured by their experience, personal beliefs, and varying capabilities. In this regard, officer training is essential to ensure consistent and accurate application of the ratings.

HKMA Loan Classification Framework

The HKMA has issued guidelines on how authorised institutions in Hong Kong should classify loans and advances, balances due from banks, investment debt securities,

Figure 4.3 Risk evaluation and ratings (illustrative only)[2]

ACCEPTABLE RATINGS

Credit risk rating: Best

Highest quality credit risk. Past performance and future outlook for the client meet the highest financial and business standards. Prospects for performance consistency and stability are very strong and the client possesses substantial capacity to deal with unexpected adversity. Holds a "AAA" (Standard & Poor's) securities rating. The credit product, country, and economic risk do not pose any incremental risk.

Credit risk rating: Very Good

A very strong customer who has displayed most of the characteristics of a "Best" risk rated credit. However, prospects for consistency and stability of performance may not be as strong as a "Best" rated credit. Holds a "AAA" (S&P) securities rating. The credit product, country, and economic elements do not pose any material risk.

Credit risk rating: Good

A strong customer with good performance and financial results and future prospects. Prospects for performance consistency are good but may be adversely affected by industry, economic, or market events. Holds a "AA" (S&P) securities rating. Credit product and country risk may pose some incremental exposure.

Credit risk rating: Average

An acceptable customer who has demonstrated good business performance with average financial resourcefulness. Future prospects are good but adverse economic, industry, and market factors will directly affect performance and results. Holds an "A" (S&P) securities rating. Credit product and country risk may present incremental exposure.

Credit risk rating: Below Average

An acceptable customer who has demonstrated acceptable but at times inconsistent levels of performance. The financial health and resources of these clients are below average. Economic, industry, and market factors directly affect performance and results. Credit products and country risk present incremental risk. Credits rated at this level may demonstrate weaknesses requiring special attention and monitoring. Holds a "A/BBB" (S&P) securities rating. Country risk may present incremental exposure.

Credit risk rating: OAEM (Other Assets Especially Mentioned)

The lowest level of acceptable risk. A clear below average risk due to inconsistent results and levels of performance, and marginal financial resources to accommodate weak economic cycles or markets. These credit assets are potentially weak and have demonstrated trends which require correction. The client's ability to correct potential deficiencies is considered acceptable. However, special attention and monitoring of the credit is required. Holds a "BBB" (S&P) securities rating. Country risk may present incremental exposure.

[2] Sam N. Basu and Harold L. Rolfes, Jr., *Strategic Credit Management* (John Wiley & Sons, 1995), 58–59.

Figure 4.3 *(Continued)*

PROBLEM RATINGS

Credit risk rating: Substandard

An unacceptable credit risk which places collection of the asset in jeopardy. Adverse financial performance or collateral trends are evident, and if not corrected will endanger credit collection. Credit products and country risk affect the rating determination. Credit risks rated substandard are normally managed by the loan workout team. Company holds a securities rating (if available) below investment grade.

Credit risk rating: Doubtful

An unacceptable credit risk wherein collection of the credit in full is in doubt. Financial condition, performance, and collateral potential are such that full repayment of the obligation is unlikely. That portion of the credit which is determined to be non-collectible should be risk rated "Loss." Credit risks rated doubtful are normally managed by the loan workout team.

Credit risk rating: Loss

Credit assets rated loss are considered to be uncollectible and should be written off. These credits are managed by the loan workout team.

acceptances and bills of exchange held, and credit commitments and contingent liabilities. There are five categories: 1) Pass, 2) Special mention, 3) Substandard, 4) Doubtful, and 5) Loss.

- **Pass.** These are loans where borrowers are meeting their commitments and the bank does not doubt that full repayment of interest and principal will be made.
- **Special mention.** The bank may classify loans as "special mention" when it judges the borrowers to be experiencing difficulties which could be a threat to its financial position. The bank does not expect ultimate loss at this stage, but it is aware that loss could occur if adverse conditions persist. Special mention loans exhibit one or more of the following characteristics:
    i. early signs of liquidity problems such as delay in servicing loans;
    ii. inadequate loan information such as annual audited financial statements not obtained or available;
    iii. the condition of and control over collateral is questionable
    iv. failure to obtain proper documentation or non-cooperation by the borrower or difficulty in keeping contact with him;
    v. slowdown in business or an adverse trend in the borrower's operations that signals a potential weakness in the financial strength of the borrower, but which has not reached a point where servicing of the loan is jeopardised;

    vi.   volatility in economic or market conditions which may in the future affect the borrower negatively;

   vii.   poor performance in the industry in which the borrower operates

  viii.   the borrower or in the case of corporate borrowers, a key executive, is in ill health

    ix.   borrower is the subject of litigation which may have a significant impact on his financial position; and/or

     x.   even if the loan in question is current, the borrower is having difficulty in servicing other loans (either from the institution concerned or from other institutions)

- **Substandard.** Loans referred to as substandard are those made to borrowers who are displaying a definable weakness that is likely to jeopardise repayment. Substandard loans include loans where some loss of principal or interest is possible after taking account of the "net realisable value" of the security put up by the borrower, and rescheduled loans where concessions have been made to a customer on interest or principal, such as to render the loan "non-commercial" to the bank. Substandard loans exhibit one or more of the following characteristics:

     i.   repayment of principal and/or interest has been overdue for more than three months and the net realisable value of security is insufficient to cover the payment of principal and accrued interest;

    ii.   even where principal and accrued interest are fully secured, a "substandard" classification will usually be justified where repayment of principal and/or interest is overdue for more than 12 months;

   iii.   in the case of unsecured or partially secured loans, a "substandard" classification may also be justified, even if the overdue period is less than three months, where other significant deficiencies are present which threaten the borrower's business, cash flow, and payment capability. These include:
    - credit history or performance record is not satisfactory;
    - labour disputes or unresolved management problems which may affect the business, production, or profitability of the borrower;
    - increased borrowings not in proportion with the borrower's business
    - the borrower experiencing difficulties in repaying obligations to other creditors
    - construction delays or other unplanned adverse events resulting in cost overruns that may require loan restructuring; and/ or
    - unemployment of an individual borrower.

- **Doubtful.** Collection in full of doubtful loans is judged by the bank to be improbable, causing the bank to expect a loss of principal and/or interest even after taking into account the net realisable value of security. Doubtful loans exhibit one or more of the following characteristics:

     i.   repayment of principal and/or interest has been overdue for more than six months and the net realisable value of security is insufficient to cover the payment of principal and accrued interest; and/or

    ii.   in the case of unsecured or partially secured loans, a shorter overdue period may also justify a "doubtful" classification if other serious deficiencies, such as default, death, bankruptcy, or liquidation of the borrower are detected or if the borrower's whereabouts are unknown

- **Loss.** Loans are considered uncollectible after the bank has exhausted all collection efforts such as realisation of collateral, institution of legal proceedings, and so on.

The HKMA expects every authorized institution in Hong Kong to have a formal loan classification system in place so it can conduct internal monitoring of the asset quality of its loans. However, this classification system should be consistent with the framework discussed here.

International Credit Rating Agencies

Credit rating agencies such as Standard & Poor's (S&P), Moody's Investor Service, Fitch, and Duff and Phelps provide credit ratings that reflect their opinions about the general creditworthiness of debt and equity issuers in the capital markets. Their ratings also take into account the type of security, collateral, and other factors. The ratings indicate the credit agency's view of the obligors' ability to meet its financial obligations. The ratings for bonds, for example, range from AAA (S&P) or Aaa (Moody's) indicating the highest investment grade and least default risk, to C, the lowest grade and highest default risk.

An S&P rating of D means there is a default on a payment. The ratings have finer gradations, AAA, AA, A, and + and –, to show their relative standings. Investment grade bonds meet the minimum standards as legal investments for trusts and fiduciaries. The ratings of AAA, AA, A, and BBB are considered investment grade. Junk bonds are those with a BB/Ba rating or lower, and they are speculative in quality. Investors in the riskier bonds/companies require higher rates of return.

Ratings by international credit rating agencies are useful guides for banks to classify their debt securities. These ratings, however, should not replace the institution's own judgement of the credit soundness of the issuers.

Local Credit Rating Agencies

In Hong Kong, the Commercial Credit Reference Agency (CCRA) was set up in 2004 for the benefit of authorised institutions providing credit to small and medium-sized enterprises. SMEs with an annual turnover of HK$50 million or lower are eligible to join the scheme, provided they give consent to the bank to transfer all their credit data to the agency.

Banks are to encourage their SME customers to agree to be rated by the CCRA. They must also provide both positive and negative credit data to the CCRA. In turn, SME customers benefit through easier access to bank financing at a relatively cheaper cost due to the transparency of their credit track records.

Some private-sector organisations have set up local commercial credit rating agencies. One such body is CTRISKS (Credit Rating and Risk Consulting), which has been providing banking institutions with obligor ratings since 2008. The agency says it now covers more than 4,000 corporations in Greater China, including mainland China, Hong Kong, and Taiwan.

The Rating Wheel

The elements of credit risk ratings are put together in "The Rating Wheel," which is shown in Figure 4.4. This chart is a handy reference that hopefully will help the reader gain a better understanding of the concepts and practices discussed in this chapter. Note that external

FIGURE 4.4   The Rating Wheel

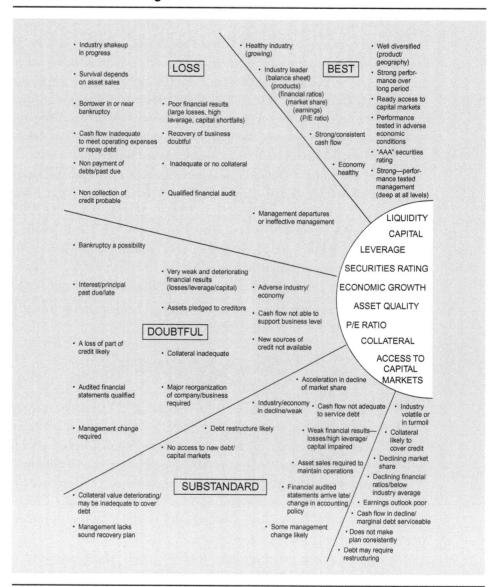

Source: Sam N. Basu and Harold L. Rolfes, Jr., *Strategic Credit Management* (John Wiley & Sons, 1995), 72–73.

FIGURE 4.4 *(Continued)*

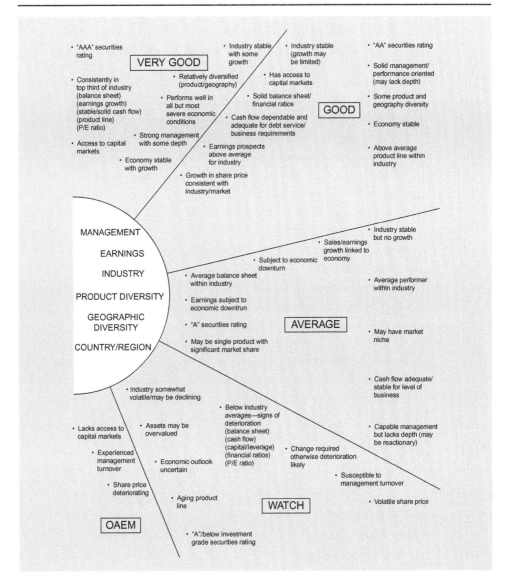

factors such as the state of the economy and the performance of the borrower's share price (if listed) are included in the Rating Wheel, which was devised by Sam N. Basu and Harold L. Rolfes, Jr. in their book *Strategic Credit Management*. Some banks consider these factors to be irrelevant to internal credit ratings because a company may fail in a strong economy and succeed in a weak one. But the authors believe that banks should treat economic and market conditions as potential elements, although possibly as minor ones.

Summary

This section summarises the issues and topics discussed in this chapter:

- One approach to lending to corporations is the 6Cs, which looks at six lending principles: character, capacity, capital, collateral, conditions, and compliance. The process of lending to corporations typically starts with opportunity assessment by loan officers or, in some instances, with a potential borrower approaching the bank to request credit. The other steps are preliminary analysis, repayment source analysis, disbursement of the funds or grant of facility arrangement, and loan management.
- Many banks now integrate credit ratings by external credit rating agencies into their corporate lending decisions. Credit rating agencies such as Standard & Poor's (S&P), Moody's Investor Service, Fitch, and Duff and Phelps provide credit ratings that reflect their opinions about the general creditworthiness of debt and equity issuers in the capital markets.
- In Hong Kong, the Commercial Credit Reference Agency (CCRA) tracks the credit data of small and medium-scale enterprises. Some private-sector organisations have set up local commercial credit rating agencies.
- An internal credit risk rating system, whether or not external ratings are integrated, is considered best practice for banks. It is critical for all officers participating in the evaluation and monitoring process to have a common understanding of these ratings and possess the ability and experience to use this system of ratings fairly and objectively.

Key Terms

6 Cs of credit
Commercial Credit Reference Agency
credit risk rating system
external credit rating agencies
facility arrangement

loan management
opportunity assessment
preliminary analysis
repayment source analysis

Study Guide

1. How does the use of financial ratios and the five stages of business growth model fit into the corporate credit assessment process?
2. What are the characteristics of an effective credit risk rating system?
3. The credibility of external credit rating agencies like S&P and Moody's has been questioned because of their business model, which involves the company to be rated paying the rating agency for a rating. How do you think this conflict of interest can be eliminated?

4. Suppose you are a loan officer who is considering a loan request from a packaging business. Under what circumstances will you classify this borrower as a "moderate" risk? When will you consider it a "very high" risk?

5. Under what circumstances could the credit risk rating system of a bank prove ineffective? Give two circumstances and explain your answer.

Further Reading

Basu, Sam N. and Rolfes, Harold L. Jr. *Strategic Credit Management.* United States: John Wiley & Sons, 1995.

Commercial Credit Reference Agency website, http://www.dnbasia.com/hk/english/ccra/default.asp.

CTRISKS website, https://www.ctrisks.com/#/en_US/page/main.html.

Fitch Ratings website, http://www.fitchratings.com/index_fitchratings.cfm.

Gup, Benton E. and Kolari, James W. *Commercial Banking.* United States: John Wiley & Sons, Third Edition, 2005.

Hong Kong Monetary Authority. "Collateral and Guarantees," in *Supervisory Policy Manual,* http://www.info.gov.hk/hkma/eng/bank/spma/attach/CR-G-7.pdf.

―――. "Connected Lending," in *Supervisory Policy Manual,* http://www.info.gov.hk/hkma/eng/bank/spma/attach/CR-G-9.pdf.

―――. "Credit Administration, Measurement and Monitoring," in *Supervisory Policy Manual,* http://www.info.gov.hk/hkma/eng/bank/spma/attach/CR-G-3.pdf.

―――. "Credit Approval, Review and Records," in *Supervisory Policy Manual,* http://www.info.gov.hk/hkma/eng/bank/spma/attach/CR-G-2.pdf.

―――. "General Principles of Credit Risk Management," in *Supervisory Policy Manual,* http://www.info.gov.hk/hkma/eng/bank/spma/attach/CR-G-1.pdf.

―――. "Large Exposures and Risk Concentration," in *Supervisory Policy Manual,* http://www.info.gov.hk/hkma/eng/bank/spma/attach/CR-G-8.pdf.

―――. "The Sharing and Use of Consumer Credit Data Through a Credit Reference Agency," in *Supervisory Policy Manual,* http://www.info.gov.hk/hkma/eng/bank/spma/attach/IC-7.pdf.

Moody's Investor Service website, http://www.moodys.com/cust/default.asp.

Standard and Poor's website, http://www.standardandpoors.com/home/en/us.

CHAPTER 5

Structuring a Loan Facility

Learning objectives

After studying this chapter, you should be able to:

1 Explain the importance of security in the structuring of loan facilities and differentiate the various types of security

2 Evaluate the conditions and covenants as well as risk factors of facility structures

3 Be familiar with the various funding schemes for SMEs offered by the Hong Kong government

4 Understand how loan facilities are priced, the reasons behind such pricing, and the issues of overpricing and underpricing

Introduction

In this chapter,[1] we focus on the terms for a loan facility to a corporate borrower, including the types of security banks may require to make sure they have something to hold on to in case of default, and the conditions and covenants they may impose. We will also examine how banks price their loans at the most optimum level to attract the highest quality corporate borrowers while still making a profit from the transaction.

Security in Bank Lending

Banks should always expect loans to be paid back in cash, British author John Holden wrote in his book *The Law and Banking Practice*. "Any security should be regarded as a last line of defence to fall back upon in exceptional circumstances. To lend money against security knowing full well that one is likely to have to realise that security is bad banking practice."

That said, the collateral a borrower puts up against the money borrowed from the bank provides some comfort that the lender can get something back should the borrower renege on promises to repay the loan. "Security should be taken wherever and whenever available, especially with loans to smaller companies where the level of financial information may be limited," Holden wrote. "In these situations, the existence of a larger amount of security relative to the proposed amount of the loan can provide a stronger justification for making the advance."

Reasons for Security

Banks require security for the following reasons:

- *As a demonstration of borrower commitment.* It shows the borrower's commitment to the venture's success, in particular, where the security is in the form of director/shareholder guarantees. It will also show the parties are committed to the success of the venture.
- *As an alternative source of repayment.* Regardless of how good the credit analysis by the bank was conducted at the outset, businesses do occasionally fail. The projects financed may not be able to produce the anticipated cash flow necessary to repay the loan. The key reason for taking security is that as a last resort, if that venture fails, banks can realise the principal assets of a company in order to get repaid.
- *As a way of deterring other lenders or creditors.* If the bank has security over the assets of a company, the bank will be paid out of the proceeds before any of the other unsecured

---

[1] This chapter uses some material from *Commercial Banking* (2005) by Benton E. Gup and James W. Kolari and *Strategic Credit Management* (1995) by Sam N. Basu and Harold L. Rolfes, Jr., with permission from publisher John Wiley & Sons.

creditors when the company is liquidated. In such cases, the assets of the company are invariably smaller than the liabilities, and therefore the unsecured parties are far less likely to get repaid. Where a bank has security, this is likely to deter other lenders from claiming payment ahead of the rest.

- *As a way of obtaining access to assets or cash flow outside those of the borrower.* If the borrower company fails and the security is in the form of a guarantee from the borrower's parent company, then the bank can have recourse to the parent company's other cash flows.

Features of Good Security

Almost anything that is lawful may be used as collateral, but some assets are better than others. A security, to be considered an adequate guarantee, should have the following key features:

- **Stability.** The price of a loan security should remain stable since it is supposed to back the full value of the loan. For this reason, a cash deposit is perhaps the best and the most stable form of security, as long as the deposit is in the same currency as the loan.
- **Certainty.** Certainty in value of the security is crucial, especially when this is in the form of shares. Shares in a company listed and widely traded on reputable stock exchanges have a more certain value than those of a non-listed private company, for which the price and marketability of the shares are often unknown.
- **Marketability.** A lender will need to consider marketability of the assets, particularly the less liquid ones such as old and less popular properties when taking them in as security (e.g., residential flats over 30 years old and village houses).
- **Durability.** The assets have to be able to withstand wear and tear up to the end of its useful life. Durable goods make better collateral than nondurables. For instance, crushed rocks make better collateral than fresh flowers.
- **Identification.** Certain types of assets are readily identifiable because they have definite characteristics or serial numbers that cannot be removed. Two examples are a large office building and an automobile that can be identified by make, model, and serial number.

Types of Security

The legal instruments that banks accept as security to back a loan include the following: lien, pledge, hypothecation, assignment, mortgage, debenture, guarantee and comfort letter.

Lien

A bank can take a "lien" or physical possession over a specific asset. However, the asset remains the property of the customer and the lender does not have any title to it.

The lien is most commonly used for cash deposits, but is occasionally applied to other assets that are easily held such as gold, shares, bonds, and certificates of deposit. Placing a lien over cash deposit has its pros and cons. It is advantageous as a security because cash deposit is immediately realisable, totally liquid, and its precise value is easily known.

But placing a lien over cash deposit has a disadvantage. Since the lender does not have undisputed title in a lien over cash deposit, the lender may have to go to court to prove it is more entitled to that cash for repayment than the defaulting customer's other creditors.

To avoid that complication, a lien over a cash deposit is normally supported by a letter of set-off that gives the lender the immediate right to use that cash to repay advances in the event of default. Once legally watertight, a cash deposit is perhaps the most liquid and easily realisable form of security, and is classified as a tangible security.

Pledge

A pledge arises when assets (e.g., goods and shares) are delivered by one person (the "pledgor") to another person (the "pledgee") as security held for a debt or obligation. The arrangement has an express or implied understanding that the assets under pledge will be restored to the pledgor once the debt or obligation is discharged.

A pledge gives the bank the title over the assets until the facility in question has been repaid. Despite the fact that ownership of the assets remains with the borrower, the pledgee usually has a power of sale when there is default in repayment of the debt at a stipulated time or, if no time has been fixed, after an unsuccessful demand for repayment.

The pledge is most commonly used over two types of assets: goods and stocks and shares.

Goods

- The goods are conveyed to the lender and remain in the lender's control by means of a title or documents to the goods such as the bills of lading. While the goods remain in the lender's control, such a pledge over goods is considered as tangible security.
- Title of the goods is restored to the customer once the debt is discharged. But in case of default, the lender has the right to sell the goods in question.
- It would be prudent for the lender to monitor the security over the goods regularly as their value may fluctuate. Some goods may perish easily and their value will fall over time, e.g., a box of six-week-old tomatoes will probably have little resale value.
- It often happens that a customer would need to use the goods that have been pledged even before the debt is fully paid. In such cases, the bank lender would have to give the pledgor physical possession of the goods and therefore the title documents. One way that banks protect themselves is to require the pledgor to sign a trust receipt whereby the goods and documents are released to them "on trust." In this way, the lender maintains a "constructive title" to the goods (i.e., the lender still has a pledge over the goods but the customer is allowed to process and ultimately sell them).

- Goods released "on trust" are considered as intangible security because the lender loses control over the goods. In many practical instances it is hard to trace or recover the goods in question once released.

Stocks and shares

When a pledge is taken over stocks and shares, ownership of these shares is transferred to the lender. If the shares are quoted on a reputable stock exchange, they are readily realisable. In contrast, unlisted shares are not normally considered a good form of security as their value depends mainly on whether there are interested buyers.

Lenders should not accept as security the shares of a company (or group) to which they are lending. If the company runs into difficulties, its shares would become worthless. The security would therefore not provide an alternative source of repayment if the company fails.

Hypothecation

Another way of securing a loan is through hypothecation. This is a legal transaction where assets may be made available as security for a debt without transferring either the title of the property or the possession to the lender. The lender's interest in the assets is merely noted and the owner of the assets may undertake to transfer possession when called upon to do so. Hypothecation is rarely seen in Hong Kong since a stronger form of pledge or lien is preferred.

Assignment

Through an assignment, a corporate borrower passes on to the bank lender the right to receive future proceeds until its debt is repaid.

- **Assignment of debts.** For instance, third parties are asked to repay debts owed to the borrower direct to the bank lender. The third party needs to acknowledge such an arrangement, after which they will be obliged to do so. As a precaution, the bank lender should first ascertain from the third parties whether there are any prior assignments over the proceeds in question.

  The assignment of debts should, whenever possible, be registered at the Companies Registry in order to alert and establish priority over other creditors to the company.

  Under a legal arrangement called a debenture, a bank lender can establish the first right to future proceeds above all other creditors even if the latter are located in many other countries. A debenture, however, is mainly backed by the borrower's integrity and is basically unsecured by collateral. We will discuss the debenture in greater detail later in this chapter.
- **Assignment over insurance.** Particularly with smaller companies, one or two individuals may be crucial to the success or failure of a business. If the future success of the business depends largely on the continuing personal efforts of these key people, the bank's exposure would be at risk if the business loses these key people suddenly.

By asking the business to take out key man insurance on its key personnel and assigning the key man insurance to the bank as a condition for the loan, the bank can protect itself and the business from the risks arising from the loss of the key personnel. Key man insurance can be defined as an insurance policy covering the life of the key or most important personnel of a company. The payee of the policy will be compensated with cash if the company loses the services of the insured (key personnel) due to serious injury, illness, or death.

This key man insurance has to designate the bank lender as the first "loss payee" so it can collect on the insurance should the person in question be unable to carry out the job, fall ill, or die.

This insurance must be from a reputable insurance company, which will acknowledge the lender as the sole beneficiary. It is essential to detail the key man's true age and state of health on the insurance application. Otherwise the insurance may be void and the insurance company will not pay.

In addition, where particular assets are important to a company, these should also be insured generally, and if material, the insurance proceeds should be assigned to the lender. This is particularly important where the loss of that asset, say through fire, would leave the company unable to pay the loan.

The insurance company should confirm that no prior claims on the proceeds exist. The bank lender should constantly monitor that the insurance premiums are paid on time.

Mortgage

Security over land and buildings is taken by way of a mortgage, which is the most common form of security. A mortgage is the conveyance of a legal or equitable interest in property as security for the payment of a debt or for the discharge of some other obligation. The borrower is called the "mortgagor" and the lender is the 'mortgagee.'

The lender should be able to obtain a safe, perfect title without undue trouble or expense, as it may need to realise it quickly.

When taking mortgages, the bank has to consider the nature or type of the property and determine whether the property has a stable or fluctuating value. Different types of properties command different values in different market situations. Property value should be readily ascertainable and reasonably stable over the years and provide a sufficient margin for depreciation. A market for the property must also be readily available in case there is a need to realise it for debt repayment. The security should be readily realisable in all conditions. The more complicated and difficult an asset is to realise, the greater will be the loss on its realisation if hurriedly done.

To ensure maximum realisable value, the bank has to get a regular update of the property's valuation from a professional valuer, make sure the insurance premiums (i.e., for fire and key man insurance) are current, and countercheck the title of the security.

The bank should also consider the quality and marketability of the property (i.e. , type, location, age, condition, and permitted land use). For leasehold property where the lease has an expiry date, its value falls as the date approaches. Where a property has long-term tenants who cannot be evicted, this may seriously reduce the resale and hence security value of the property. Property is a very common and good form of tangible security, but the bank still needs to be careful in accepting it because:

- Property prices can fall as well as rise.
- The forced sale value of a mortgaged property is usually lower than the selling price that can be obtained between a willing buyer and a willing seller.
- The bank would incur extra costs in selling the mortgaged property such as estate agent fees and other disbursements.
- The carrying cost (including incidental disbursements) incurred by a bank in a falling market may be high in case there is no demand in the market. The bank will not be earning any income from that asset as well.

There are basically four types of mortgages: all monies mortgage, legal mortgage, equitable mortgage, and second mortgage.

All Monies Mortgage

Mortgages, whether legal or equitable, can either be used to back a specified amount or for "all monies." An all monies mortgage is one that secures all outstanding debts of the borrower to the limit of the value of the property used as collateral.

Legal Mortgage

This conveys title to the lender until the debt is repaid. In case of default, the bank has the right to take possession of the property, sell the property, or appoint a receiver over the property without court proceedings. For a legal mortgage to be valid in Hong Kong, the bank's charge over the property must be registered at Companies Registry (if the mortgagor is a limited company) and at the Land Registry.

Equitable Mortgage

This is a form of mortgage where only the title deeds of the property are deposited with the bank, with a certificate of deposit showing the property is being used to secure a loan. The title is not transferred and the security is not necessarily registered. Due to this, the bank is not assured of its claim being given first priority. The bank may have to go to court to contest its claims against other company creditors.

Second Mortgage

There are cases when a bank obtains a "second mortgage" over a property. In case of default, the bank would be paid after the first mortgagee. As a precaution, the bank should always take a legal second mortgage, register its interests at the Companies Registry and the Land Registry, and immediately inform the first mortgagee. This way, the bank ensures its ranking among creditors, and signals to the first mortgagee not to lend any more money, which would reduce the value of the second mortgagee's (i.e., the bank's) security.

Debenture

A debenture is an umbrella document under which security is taken over all or most company assets. This type of security is issued only by limited companies. Debentures can be for a specified amount or for all "monies." Under a debenture, the lender has the right to appoint a receiver to take whatever steps necessary to ensure repayment.

There are two types of debentures: fixed charges and floating charges.

Fixed Charges

These are given over the fixed assets of a company by way of a mortgage. Under a fixed charge, as with a mortgage, the bank has the right to immediately take possession and sell the asset and will rank ahead of all creditors, including preferential creditors, in its rights to the proceeds.

Floating Charges

These are given over the floating assets of a company (i.e., assets that keep changing, principally stock, cash, and debts). Specific assets are not named, and the company can continue to trade these assets in the normal course of business.

With floating charges, the lender has the right to appoint a receiver to take control of the borrower's unencumbered assets. The receiver will arrange to realise the value of these current assets and have the bank's loans repaid.

Floating charges have at least three disadvantages compared to fixed charges:

- In case of default, the charge "crystallises" against those specific assets present at that time. In terms of repayment, floating charges rank behind fixed charges and preferential creditors, but ahead of all unsecured creditors and preferred unsecured creditors.
- Precisely because the assets in question "float," it is possible that during times of trouble these assets might be removed from the business and this would diminish the value of the floating charges. In addition, partly finished stock may be hard to sell. For these reasons floating charges are classified as intangible security.
- Finally, because of the concept of "unfair preference," the validity of floating charges is subject to challenge by other unsecured creditors if the borrower is put into liquidation within 12 months from the date the charge is executed. This right of unfair preference is only set aside if new advances to the borrower are granted or the borrower's financial position can be proven to be solvent.

Guarantees

Banks accept as a form of security guarantees from parties other than the borrower. This is particularly important where the strength of the borrower needs further assurance. It is also particularly common where a parent company guarantees the obligations of a small or undercapitalised subsidiary. A guarantee is classified as intangible security unless backed by tangible assets.

There are four basic types of guarantees deemed acceptable by banks: bank guarantee, standby letter of credit (L/C), company guarantee, and individual guarantee.

Bank Guarantee

This is the strongest and most reliable guarantee as long as the banks in question are well rated and have no exchange control problems in paying the funds if called upon.

A bank guarantee is a written promise made by a bank to repay the debt of its customer to the beneficiary in case of default or non-performance. Such a promise is made to a third party to whom the customer is, or will become, liable. To draw on this guarantee, the beneficiary would have to submit a declaration that a default or non-performance has taken place and show proof of this event.

Bank guarantees are usually subject to the jurisdiction of a country that will be agreed on beforehand by the parties concerned. The liability of the issuing bank can be direct or indirect, depending on whether there is an indemnifying clause in the guarantee. Without an indemnifying clause, the beneficiary might have to prove the default before it can serve the demand for payment under the guarantee. Even with an indemnifying clause, the beneficiary would have to demand payment. This is normally more cumbersome than just drawing against a standby letter of credit.

Standby Letter of Credit (L/C)

A standby letter of credit is a guarantee issued by the bank in the form of a Documentary Credit but it possesses all the elements of a commercial Documentary Credit. It is similar to bank guarantees and is used to cover the default or non-performance of the bank's customer. A standby letter of credit is issued in favour of the beneficiary stipulating that a sum will be paid to the beneficiary upon demand, in the event that the beneficiary simply submits a signed statement saying there has been default or non-performance.

Issuance of standby letters of credit is subject to the Uniform Customs Practice 600 (UCP 600), which is issued by the International Chambers of Commerce (ICC). The beneficiary can easily obtain repayment by simply drawing against the standby letter of credit, provided he can comply with all the terms and conditions which are normally simple and agreed on between the beneficiary, the applicant, and the issuing bank before the standby L/C is opened.

An L/C is simple and straightforward. It does not require the beneficiary to prove that the default has happened. Given the choice, standby letters of credit are more favoured by lenders because they are governed by UCP600, which is an internationally accepted regulation issued by the ICC. This is useful because when a dispute arises, they can be settled by simply going to the ICC for arbitration instead of through a lengthy legal procedure.

When determining the acceptability of a bank guarantee or standby letter of credit as security, lenders should take into account the following factors:

- Ensure that there are no unfamiliar terms that are considered to be ambiguous, which could affect the enforceability of that guarantee or standby letter of credit.
- Agree on a date to remind the parties concerned of the impending expiry of the bank guarantee or standby letter of credit, to ensure there is sufficient time to call on them if required.
- Ensure that any trigger clause is simple and unconditional. Difficulty may arise if the guarantee/standby letter of credit is conditional upon the happening of a trigger event.

Company Guarantee

This kind of guarantee is commonly issued by parent companies in support of their subsidiaries or between sister companies or companies related through a common shareholder.

The legal issues that banks have to consider when taking a corporate guarantee are:

- **Power and authority.** The bank has to check the Memorandum and Articles of Association (M&A) of the guaranteeing company to ensure a company has the power to give the guarantee and the individuals giving the guarantee are empowered to do so. Check particularly for any clauses in the M&A barring the company from providing such guarantees.
- **Commercial consideration.** "Commercial benefit" is a key consideration in this kind of guarantee. It must be clear that it is in the interest of a business to give such a guarantee, otherwise the courts may not recognise the validity of the guarantee and disallow it. This law is common in many countries to protect creditors of the guaranteeing company. The guarantee will be void if there is no such consideration between the contractual parties.
- **Past consideration.** If the loan is booked before the documentation, the guarantee is a past consideration. A past consideration is not a good consideration from a legal angle, and renders the guarantee voidable.
- **Interested directors.** If there are interested directors on both sides (i.e., the lender and the guarantor), a special board resolution or shareholders' resolution is required to support the guarantee. The interested directors should not vote on matters in which they have a personal financial interest in conflict with the interests of the company. For example, in a vote to repay a loan that would lead to the release of a director from a guarantee, the interested director should not vote.
- **Misrepresentation.** The guarantee will be void if the guarantor can prove it has been misrepresented when entering into the contract.
- **Unfair preference.** A bank lender should proceed with caution if the borrower repays the bank in order to be released from the guarantee. The bank runs the risk of being

charged with having an "unfair preference" should the borrower subsequently default on other obligations. Citing unfair preference, other creditors may seek legal recourse against the bank to reimburse the repayment, which will then be shared equally among creditors of the same class.

To counter such a charge, the bank could try to prove that the borrower was solvent and showed no financial difficulty at the time of repayment, or that the bank had already demanded loan repayment in accordance with the terms of the loan agreement. To be on the safe side, the bank should retain the guarantee for an extended period, typically six months after repayment is made in order to have recourse to both the borrower and the guarantor.

Individual Guarantee

When a personal guarantee is required for bank finance, a statement of net worth should be obtained from the individual guarantor and his or her financial standing should be analysed. The apparent existence of personal wealth of the guarantor should not be sufficient in itself. The lender must also be satisfied with the integrity of the guarantor as the guarantor can easily transfer or sell his or her assets without the bank's knowledge.

The Code of Banking Practice requires lenders to request individuals giving such guarantees to seek independent legal advice from their own solicitors before signing the guarantee document. As we discussed in Chapter 1, this is also the same advice given to those third-party individuals who issue personal guarantees in support of individual loan customers.

If a borrower's spouse extends the guarantee, the bank must proceed with caution. Under extreme circumstances, the spouse may say the security was tainted by undue influence and claim it was obtained under duress. The security may be rendered void if "duress" can be proven.

To ensure that the security offered by a spouse will stand up to question or challenge, the bank lender should take reasonable steps, such as asking the spouse-guarantor to seek independent legal advice. It is very important for the lender to ensure that the guarantor is well aware of what he or she is doing by offering the security. The spouse-guarantor must be given the chance to obtain independent legal advice.

Comfort Letter

A comfort letter is a letter from a parent company to the bank, expressing awareness of the latter's proposed banking facility to the subsidiary and stating that it is a normal business practice of the parent company to ensure the subsidiary remains in good financial standing.

This is also known as a letter of awareness or a letter of moral intent. Comfort letters are not legally enforceable, and thus the document has no security value except a moral obligation from the parent company. But there is still a strong reason for requesting such a letter, along with other forms of security, to prove that the parent company is sanctioning the subsidiary's actions.

Conditions and Covenants

To reduce the risk of default and ensure payment in case of default, the bank and the corporate borrower negotiate a comprehensive agreement that the borrower should follow during the life of the loan facility. The terms and conditions are spelled out in loan covenants. Appendix 5.1 shows an illustrative example of a loan agreement. Section 5 of the agreement covers the covenants of this sample contract.

The following are some special conditions and covenants designed to enhance protection for the bank and tighten the operating targets of the borrower:

- **Subordinated loan agreement.** The covenant has to be clear under what terms the bank lender would be repaid in case of default. By securing a Subordinated Loan Agreement from the borrower and any of its unsecured creditors, the ranking of the bank lender in receiving the liquidation payout, if any, will be higher than the other unsecured creditors.

  If there is evidence the borrower has repaid an unsecured creditor ahead of a bank holding a Subordinated Loan Agreement, the bank has the right to go after the unsecured creditor for any amount it received from the borrower up to the amount the bank is owed.

- **Minimum net worth.** The bank has to ensure that the company has sufficient capital to support business growth and so requires the company to maintain a minimum level of capitalisation as part of the loan covenants. The bank can track this measure by examining the financial statements (see Chapter 2) and deriving financial ratios (see Chapter 3).

- **Total liabilities to net worth.** The bank has to ensure that the borrower maintains tight control over the leverage of the company, which it can do by requiring the company to maintain a stipulated ratio of total liabilities to net worth.

- **Interest bearing debts to net worth.** The bank must monitor the borrowings of the company to make sure its total debts do not endanger the financial health of the company. The bank and the company expressly agree on the level of interest bearing debts to net worth that the company must maintain.

- **Maximum dividend payout ratio.** The company has to agree to limit the distribution of retained profits as dividends so that more earnings are available to support business operations.

- **Negative pledge.** A negative pledge is a common form of undertaking obtained by lenders from borrowers, in which borrowers undertake to restrict the encumbrance of assets. It can also restrict borrowers from further borrowings or lending to third parties and bars the borrower from pledging its assets to other creditors. A negative pledge helps prevent a reduction in the net worth of the borrower and an increase in its gearing. It ensures that the bank maintains a *pari passu* position (meaning, on equal footing) with other unsecured creditors.

  But a negative pledge gives little practical comfort to a bank because the negative pledge is only enforceable against the party providing the undertaking, but not against a third party lender or general creditor who may benefit in its breach by receiving a security interest in violation of the covenant.

When a negative pledge is breached, the borrower's assets are no longer available to repay the loan because the borrower has broken its promise and granted a security interest in the restricted assets to a second lender and dissipated the proceeds of the second loan.

Any breach provides the bank recourse only for breach of contract or the trigger for an event of default. This will be of little value if the borrower is in liquidation. It is difficult and cumbersome for commercial bankers to monitor such a covenant against the financial statements of the company. It is also hard to determine whether an asset is unencumbered since land records may not be up to date.

- **Top-up covenant**. A major risk associated with security is the possibility that the value of security will fall below its original value when repayment becomes necessary. This often happens in a forced sale when a borrower gets into trouble. In a winding up situation, assets on a balance sheet are generally not realised up to their book value.

  For this reason a lender should, whenever possible, ask for a top-up arrangement when taking collateral so as to provide an adequate security margin. The margin should not only allow for a future fall in asset value but should also cover the costs of sale, costs in keeping the saleable assets, and a reasonable amount of interest. When the top-up covenant is exercised by the bank, the borrower will have to provide additional security or reduce the loan outstanding in order to satisfy the prescribed security margin.

Further Considerations

In lending to a customer group, it is preferable to extend the structured facility to the operating entity rather than to its holding company for the following reasons:

- The operating entity holds the assets and generates profit and cash flow. In case of default, banks can go after these items for repayment. Holding companies usually hold the equity of subsidiaries as an asset and do not generate profits or cash flow from operations. They rely on dividends paid out by subsidiaries.
- Under a liquidation scenario, a lender that lends directly to the operating entity can be ranked as either a secured or unsecured creditor of the operating entity. But if the lender lends to the holding company, the holding company will rank last in the payout list during a liquidation scenario since it is just an ordinary shareholder of the operating entity.
- By lending to the operating entity, the lender can have a higher level of control over the use of the credit facility or loan. The facility could also be more appropriately structured to suit the actual requirements of the operating entity and the lender will be closer to the actual sources of repayment.

Authorised institutions in Hong Kong also have to make sure credit facilities to small and medium-sized enterprises (SMEs) are properly registered with the Commercial Credit Reference Agency. As discussed in Chapter 4, the CCRA was set up in 2004 under the guidance of the Hong Kong Monetary Authority for the benefit of authorised institutions which provide credit facilities to SMEs in Hong Kong.

Authorised institutions are obliged to provide both positive and negative credit data to the agency, provided the borrower concerned agrees to have its credit data reported to the CCRA. The HKMA encourages authorised institutions to make use of the services of CCRA to assist them in their credit decisions.

Appendix 5.2 details the funding schemes that the government of Hong Kong has devised to nurture the growth of SMEs in the short and longer term. Around 46 banks in Hong Kong participate in some of the SME funding schemes.

Pricing a Loan Facility

One key element in the process of commercial lending is loan pricing—determining what interest rate to charge the borrower and how to calculate that rate. The interest rate may be determined by using a loan pricing model. The purpose of loan pricing models is to determine the minimum price that a bank should charge on a commercial loan. Before we examine loan pricing, let's consider the effective yield.

Calculating Effective Yield

There is a difference between the nominal interest rate—the interest rate that is stated in the loan agreement—and the effective yield, which takes the payment accrual basis and the payment frequency into account. The method for calculating effective yields will be explained after some terms have been defined.

The payment accrual basis refers to the number of days used in the interest rate calculation. One part of the calculation involves the number of days in a year. Interest may be calculated on the basis of a 365-day year or a 360-day year.

To illustrate the difference, consider a $1 million loan at a 10% nominal rate of interest. The daily interest payment (interest income to the bank and interest expense of the borrower) of the loan is determined by multiplying the amount of the loan by the nominal interest rate and then dividing by the appropriate number of days (365 or 360), and multiplying that figure by the amount of the loan.

Accordingly, the daily cost of a $1 million loan at 10% interest is $273.97 on a 365-day basis and $277.78 on a 360-day basis.

Another part of the calculation involves the number of days that the loan is outstanding. One can use the actual number of days the loan is outstanding, or one can use a 30-day per month base.

The final variable is the frequency of interest payments. Typically, term loans are structured with monthly, quarterly, or annual payments. Because of the time value of money (money is worth more today than the same amount received in the future), frequent payments are favoured by bankers but harder to sell to borrowers. The effect of payment frequency on interest earned and yields will be explained shortly.

To illustrate the effective yield, let's consider a 345-day term loan beginning on January 1 and ending on December 11. The principal amount is $1 million and the interest rate is 10%. The calculations for a 360-day year and 30-day month are as follows:

1.	$1,000,000	Principal amount
2.	× 0.10	Annual interest rate
3.	$100,000	Annual interest amount
4.	360	Divide by number of days in year (360 or 365)
5.	$277.78	Daily interest payment
6.	× (30 days × 11 months + 11 days)	Times 11 months of 30 days plus 11 days (341 days) or the actual number of days
7.	$94,722.22	Total interest paid

$$\text{Effective yield} = \frac{\text{Total interest paid}}{\text{Principal amount}} \times \frac{365}{\text{Term of loan in days}}$$

$$= \frac{\$94,722.22}{\$1,000,000.00} \times \frac{365}{345} = 10.02\%$$

The same process (with the appropriate number of days in lines 4 and 6) may be used to calculate the effective yields for 360-day years with actual number of days and 365-day years with actual number of days. The effective yields for the three methods are as follows:

	Effective Yield
360-day year/30-day month	10.02%
360-day year/actual number of days	10.14%
360-day year/actual number of days	10.00%

Effect of Payment Frequency

The frequency of loan payments has a major impact on interest earnings and the yield received on loans. Suppose that a bank is considering making a one-year, $100,000 loan at 12% interest. The $100,000 loan will be repaid at the end of the year. The bank earns $12,000 if interest is paid annually, and $12,747.46 if it is paid daily. The bank earns more when interest is collected frequently.

Payment Periods	Interest Earned on $100,000 Loan	Yield
Continuous	$12,748.28	12.748%
Daily	12,747.46	12.747%
Monthly	12,682.50	12.683%
Quarterly	12,550.88	12.551%
Annually	12,000.00	12.000%

The amount that the bank receives at the end of the period may be determined by the equation for the future value of $1:

$$FV_n = PV_0(1 + i/m)^{nm}$$

where

FV_n = future value at end of n periods

PV_0 = present value ($100,000 in this example)

i = interest rate

n = number of periods

m = number of interyear periods (days, months, quarters)

Thus, the amount earned if interest is collected monthly is:

$$FV_{12} = \$100,000(1 + 0.12/12)^{1 \times 12}$$

$$= \$112,682.50$$

Interest earned is the difference between FV_{12} and PV_0, which is:

$$\$112,682.50 - \$100,000 = \$12,682.50$$

It follows that the annual yield is:[17]

$$FV_n = PV_0 (1 + 0.12/12)^{n \times 12}$$

$$= 12.683\%$$

Many loans are amortised, which means the principal is reduced with periodic payments.

Loan Pricing

When profit margins on commercial loans are razor thin, precise estimates of cost are necessary to price the loans correctly. Overpricing of loans results in some borrowers going elsewhere to obtain loans. Underpricing of loans results in banks earning less than they should for a given level of risk. Consistent underpricing could adversely affect both the profits and the market value of the banks making such errors.

Mark-Ups

Many banks price commercial loans by using an index rate (e.g., prime rate) plus a mark-up of one or more percentage points. Other banks use the cost of borrowed funds (e.g., 90-day Certificate of Deposit rate) plus a mark-up. The advantage of using mark-ups above prime for the cost of funds is that they are simple and easy to understand.

Mark-ups are supposed to compensate the bank for the risk it takes in making a loan, as well as provide a return on its investment. The disadvantage of using mark-ups is that they may not properly account for risk, the cost of funds, and operating expenses. The result may be that some loans are mispriced.

The alternative is to use loan pricing models that properly account for risk, costs, and returns. There are many types of loan pricing models. We examine some of these models in the following sections.

Return on Net Funds Employed

This loan pricing model establishes the required rate of return that the bank wants to earn on the loan, and then determines the net income that the loan must generate to provide that return. If the loan cannot generate sufficient net income to earn the required rate of return, the bank should consider rejecting it. The formula below illustrates this pricing model:

Marginal cost of funds + Profit goal
$$= (\text{Loan income} - \text{Loan expense})/\text{Net bank funds employed}$$

In this model, the required rate of return is equal to the marginal cost of funds plus a profit goal. The marginal cost of capital (funds) is the rate of return required by debt and equity investors on newly issued funds they provide to the bank. That rate may differ from the rate of return required by the bank's management.

Loan expense includes all direct and indirect costs associated with making, servicing, and collecting the loan. This does not include the bank's cost of funds. Making effective cost estimates to be used in the model is difficult to do. To illustrate the difficulty, suppose that a loan officer spent 35 hours of work time trying to attract a new loan customer.

Let's consider only the officer's time, which is worth $100 per hour. The cost is $3,500. If the customer borrows $10,000 for 90 days, the equation suggests that the bank would have to charge more than $3,500 (35%) to cover that cost alone. Obviously, the bank would not attempt to charge that amount. Nevertheless, someone has to pay for the loan officer's time. This is done using cost accounting data and trying to make reasonable estimates about the cost of making, servicing, and collecting loans.

The net bank funds employed is the average amount of the loan over its life, minus funds provided by the borrower, net of regulatory reserve requirements.

Borrowers provide banks with funds in the form of compensating balances or other balances held at the bank. The bank cannot use the entire amount on deposit because it is required by regulators to maintain a specified amount of reserves against those balances.

To illustrate the use of the equation for return on net funds employed, let us make the following assumptions:

- Marginal cost of funds is 6%
- Profit goal is 2%
- Loan expense is $2,000
- Net bank funds employed is $100,000

Marginal cost of funds + Profit goal =

(Loan income − Loan expense)/Net bank funds employed

(6% + 2%)	= (Loan income − $2,000)/$100,000
((6% + 2%) × $100,000) + $2,000	= Loan income
(8% × $100,000) + $2,000	= Loan income
$8,000 + $2,000	= Loan income
$10,000	= Loan income

The $10,000 is the amount of income this loan must generate in order for the bank to earn its required rate of return. This figure understates the correct amount because it does not take the time value of money into account. Nevertheless, it is a good ballpark estimate of the income that is needed.

This loan pricing model is best suited for banks that have effective cost accounting data and that can estimate the order data that are required. If this model is used to price variable rate loans, the rate of return to the bank will change whenever the loan rate changes.

This problem is resolved in relationship pricing, the next loan pricing model we consider.

Relationship Pricing

The loan pricing model we just examined did not take into account other business relationships the borrower may have with the bank. For example, the borrower may be using its cash management services or have a pension fund managed by the bank. Each of these activities generates positive income for the bank. When, and under what circumstances should a borrower's relationships be considered?

To answer that question, we must think about making a loan as a new investment opportunity. All the relevant cash flows must be evaluated. If the loan is the only business the borrower has with the bank, then only the cash flows associated with the loan are relevant. However, if the loan is one of many services provided by the bank, then all the cash flows associated with that borrower's relationship with the bank must be evaluated.

The projected cash flow from each service, including the loan, should be adjusted to take risks into account. In *relationship pricing*, the rate charged on a loan may differ from the rate indicated by the loan pricing model presented previously.

Minimum Spread

Some banks price loans by determining the minimum spread they will accept between their lending rate and their costs plus a profit margin. For example, assume that a bank's costs are 12% and the profit margin is 2%. If the bank wants to encourage lending, it will accept a smaller profit margin and charge borrowers 13%. If the bank wants to retard lending, it will increase the spread and charge borrowers 15% percent.

Encouraging and discouraging lending is a common practice and reflects banks' changing financial needs. Banks know that many large commercial loans are repriced every day or every 30, 60, or 90 days. Large borrowers regularly shop for the lowest rates. A bank that increases its lending rate in one period to discourage a borrower may decide to make the loan the next time it is repriced.

Average Cost vs. Marginal Cost

The costs used in this type of model include the cost of funds and operating costs. Here, too, are problems in determining the relevant costs. Let us focus the discussion on the cost of funds. Should the bank use the average cost of funds or the marginal cost of funds? In the explanation on the cost of capital, the marginal and average costs were the same (see the discussion under "required rate of return" in this chapter). But that is not always the case.

To illustrate this problem, suppose a firm wants to borrow $1 million for 90 days. The bank's lending rate is the cost of funds plus 1 percentage point per annum. The hypothetical bank raised $0.5 million by selling a 90-day CD at 12%. In addition, the bank has $0.5 million in other interest-rate sensitive liabilities that cost 8%. For simplicity, we ignore equity.

The average cost of borrowed funds, which is determined by dividing total interest cost by total funds employed, is 10%. The marginal cost of funds, or the 90-day CD rate, is 12%. Should the bank use the average cost of funds or the marginal cost of funds to price the loan?

When market rates of interest are rising, the bank is better off using the marginal cost of funds because it is higher than the average cost of funds. However, when market rates of interest are falling, it is better off using the average cost of funds, which is higher than the marginal cost.

Another consideration is how the loan is funded. If the $1 million, 90-day loan was match funded by selling a $1 million 90-day CD, the CD rate could be used to represent the borrowed funds. Although not mentioned previously, the bank would have to raise more than $1 million in order to cover reserve requirements. Suppose that reserve requirements are 5%. The bank would have to raise $1,052,632 ($1,000,000/0.95 = $1,052,632) in order to lend $1 million.

If the bank views all of its deposits as a "pool" of funds used to finance loans, the answer is still the marginal rate. In theory, the marginal loan (the next loan to be made) should be charged the marginal cost of funds including the cost of equity.

All the examples used here suggest that in order to make a profit, a bank's lending rate should be greater than its cost of funds, including equity.

Performance Pricing

The price of a loan reflects the riskiness of the borrower. When the borrower's riskiness changes, the price of the loan should be changed accordingly. One way to do this is with performance pricing, which allows banks and borrowers to change the price of a loan without renegotiating it. The price can be tied to specific financial ratios, the amount of the loan outstanding, the borrower's debt ratings, or other mutually agreed upon criteria.

Loan Pricing in Practice

Are these models and formulas utilised in practice? This may not always be the case. The market for business loans is highly competitive, so a given bank may find itself in the position of being a price taker. In other words, the price a bank may charge on its loan may be driven by its lowest price competitor. Quite often these low price competitors are new entrants to the particular market and are interested in buying market share.

The bank in question is then faced with a major challenge—whether to make the loan at a lower-than-required rate of return or simply decline the business opportunity. There is no easy answer to this question, which is a trade-off between long-term profitability and business development needs. There is no simple solution to the problem. Nevertheless, a discussion of the following points might be worthwhile.

- Over time, banks must earn a risk-adjusted fully loaded rate of return that compensates their shareholders. If a bank continues to underprice loans against this benchmark, this may have a negative impact—its share price is bound to fall. Sometimes this negative impact may affect an entire industry, if a majority of the industry players continue to misprice.
- Even if underpricing a loan may be justified because of competition, it is important to understand that the overall portfolio needs to earn a risk-adjusted rate of return. Sometimes it is helpful to realise this through a customer profitability approach, as opposed to profitability on a single loan. In any event, a bank that decides to make such a trade-off must be fully aware of all the issues involved.
- Loan pricing in a market would typically find its risk-adjusted level over time. Economic discipline in the market would eventually force the underpricing banks to stop the practice or get out of the business one way or another.
- Banks must keep in mind that it is profits, and not asset size, that matters the most in the final analysis. A profitable small bank will prosper, but a money-losing large bank may not survive. "Managed growth," driven by a minimum rate of return consideration, is a much better management approach than unconstrained growth.
- On a broader level, the banking industry is well known for its "follow the leader" or reactive strategy. Difficult though it may be, it is important for banks to think in terms of proactive, rather than reactive, policy. A risk-based loan pricing approach is the right step in that direction.

Summary

This section summarises the issues and topics discussed in this chapter:

- Banks should always remember that security is never the justification for lending. The objective in a lending transaction is to be repaid in cash for the loan amount plus profit.

Having said that, banks should also obtain when possible a form of security from borrowers to secure their commitment and as a cover for default risk.

- There are various types of security that banks can hold on to, depending on the nature and purpose of the structured facility and the credit worthiness of the customer. The best type of security is one that is durable, highly marketable, stable in value, and easily turned into cash at a value equal to the loan amount. The types of security that banks accept to guarantee the loan include lien, pledge, hypothecation, mortgage, and debenture.

- To reduce default risk and ensure payment in case of default, banks must sign a loan agreement with the borrower that spells out clear conditions and covenants that the borrower has to follow. These conditions and covenants include a subordinated loan agreement, negative pledge and maintenance of stipulated levels of net worth, total liabilities to net worth, interest bearing debts to net worth, and other ratios.

- Banks must price their loans correctly. Overpricing results in some borrowers going elsewhere to obtain loans. Consistent underpricing could adversely affect both the profits and the market value of the banks making such errors. Many banks price commercial loans by using an index rate plus a mark-up of one or more percentage points, while others use the cost of borrowed funds plus a mark-up. The advantage of using mark-ups is that they are simple and easy to understand.

- The disadvantage of using mark-ups is that they may not properly account for risk, the cost of funds and operating expenses. The alternative is to utilise loan pricing models, among them return on net funds, relationship pricing, minimum spread, average cost versus marginal cost, and performance pricing.

Key Terms

assignment	negative pledge
comfort letter	nominal interest rate
constructive title	*pari passu*
debenture	payment accrual basis
effective yield	pledge
guarantees	pricing model
hypothecation	relationship pricing
key man insurance	top-up covenant
lien	trust receipt
loan pricing	unfair preference
mortgage	

Study Guide

1. Why are each of the following considered an "intangible security"?
   a) floating charges
   b) comfort letter
   c) negative pledge
2. In the following arrangements, what role would the bank lender typically play in relation to the borrower?
   a) mortgagor, mortgagee
   b) pledgor, pledgee
   c) lessor, lessee
3. Why should a bank lender be cautious in accepting property as a form of security even if it is a tangible form of security?
4. Which would you consider a more secure form of collateral—computers or sand and gravel? Why?
5. Differentiate between mark-ups and loan-pricing models. Why are mark-ups more prone to loan mispricing?

Further Reading

Basu, Sam N. and Rolfes, Harold L. Jr. 1995, *Strategic Credit Management*. United States: John Wiley & Sons.

Chan Bo-ching, Simon. 2000, *Hong Kong Banking Law and Practice Volume 1*. First Edition. Hong Kong Institute of Bankers, Hong Kong.

———. 2001, *Hong Kong Banking Law and Practice Volume II*. First Edition. Hong Kong: Hong Kong Institute of Bankers.

Gup, Benton E. and Kolari, James W. 2005, *Commercial Banking*. United States: John Wiley & Sons, Third Edition.

Companies Registry website, http://www.cr.gov.hk/.

Appendix 5.1: Sample Loan Agreement (For Illustrative Purposes Only)[2]

This Agreement is entered into as of _____ between a corporation herein referred to as "Borrower" and _____, a corporation herein referred to as "Bank"

---

[2] Sam N. Basu and Harold L. Rolfes, Jr., *Strategic Credit Management* (John Wiley & Sons, 1995), 170–174.

and whereas Borrower has requested a loan as herein specified and Bank has agreed to commit to said loan, subject to the terms and conditions contained herein. The following is hereby agreed:

1. Definitions:

a) "Loan" means the loan as described in section 2 of this Agreement.
b) "Prime Rate" means the rate of interest published from time to time by the Bank as its prime rate.
c) "Interest Payment Date" means _____
d) "Facility Fee" means _____
e) "Agreement" means _____
f) "Events of Default" mean _____

2. The Loan

2.1 From time to time between the date hereof and _____, Bank, upon request of the Borrower, will make available to the Borrower in one or more advances, a loan in the maximum amount of _____dollars ($). Advances made under the loan shall be in a maximum amount of _____ dollars ($) and Borrower shall give Bank a minimum of _____ days notice of each advance made hereunder.

2.2 The Borrower shall pay interest on the outstanding principal balance of the loan at the rate per annum (computed daily on a 365-day year) of _____ percentage points in excess of Bank's prime rate. Interest on the outstanding balance of the loan shall be paid by Borrower on _____ and on the last day of each successive _____ thereafter, until _____, on which date the entire balance of principal outstanding under the loan and interest then unpaid shall be due and payable _____.

2.3 A facility fee equal to percent of the undrawn amount of the loan shall be paid by Borrower. The facility fee shall be payable quarterly, beginning on and thereafter on the last day of each successive quarter until the maturity date of the loan or the commitment to lend by Bank is cancelled.

2.4 Each advance under the loan shall be evidenced by a promissory note in the form as presented in attachment _____executed by Borrower.

2.5. Advances under the loan to Borrower and each payment to Bank under this agreement shall be made at Bank's _____and _____ respectively.

2.6. Borrower may at any time prepay any advance, in full or in part. Borrower, upon thirty days written notice to Bank may cancel the loan commitment provided by the Bank hereunder.

3. Conditions Precedent

The obligation of Bank to provide the loan as provided for in this Agreement is subject to the condition precedent that, on the date of this Agreement and upon the date of each advance under the loan, there shall have been delivered to Bank in form and substance satisfactory to Bank the following:

a) An opinion of Borrower's counsel in form as presented in Exhibit _____ hereto;

b) A copy of a resolution passed by the Borrower's Board of Directors, certified by the Borrower's Secretary authorising the borrowing and the execution, delivery, and performance of this Agreement;

c) A certificate as to the incumbency of the persons authorised to execute and deliver this Agreement and any instrument required hereunder on Borrower's behalf, signed by the Secretary of Borrower;

d) Certified copies of all approvals, consents, and notices to and filings with any government agency or department which, in Bank's opinion, are required in connection with any borrowing hereunder;

e) A certificate, duly signed by an authorised officer of Borrower that there has been no adverse change in Borrower's financial condition sufficient to impair Borrower from performing under this Agreement and no event of default by Borrower under this Agreement has occurred or is continuing;

f) A certificate, duly signed by an authorised officer of Borrower that the representations and warranties as contained in Section _____ and any agreement executed in connection with this Agreement are true and accurate in all material respects.

4. Representations and Warranties

Borrower represents and warrants that:

a) Borrower is a _____ duly organised and existing under the laws of _____, and is properly licensed and in good standing

b) This Agreement and any agreement or instrument required hereunder is a legal and binding agreement, enforceable against Borrower;

c) There is no federal, state, municipal, or other law, regulation, judgment, or decree of any court binding on Borrower, which would be contravened by the signing, performance or enforcement of this Agreement or instrument required hereunder;

d) This Agreement and any agreement or instrument required hereunder is a legal, valid, and binding agreement, enforceable against Borrower;

e) No consent, approval, or action by any federal, state, municipal, or other governmental authority is needed in connection with the signing, performance, or enforcement of this Agreement or any agreement or instrument required hereunder;

f) The execution of this Agreement and any agreement or instrument required hereunder have been duly authorised and are within Borrower's powers;

g) There are no actions, legal suits, or proceedings pending or threatened against or affecting the Borrower, its officers, or directors which might affect Borrower's condition or impair its ability to perform hereunder.

h) It possesses and owns all rights to all patents, permits, licenses, trademarks, and copyrights required to conduct its business and that there are no disputes as to the rights of others relating thereto.

5. Covenants

Borrower covenants and agrees that so long as this Agreement is in effect, and until the full and final payment of all indebtedness incurred by Borrower hereunder, Borrower will, unless such action or omission is expressively waived in writing by Bank:

a) Make all payments of principal and interest on borrowings made under this Agreement promptly and in accordance with the terms of this Agreement; and

b) Maintain adequate accounting and financial books and records and prepare all statements required hereunder in accordance with generally accepted accounting principles and practices, applied on a consistent basis and comply, at all times, with all laws, statutes, regulations, and orders of any governmental authority with jurisdiction over it; and

c) Maintain and preserve its corporate existence and will not liquidate, or merge or consolidate with or into any other corporation or business; and

d) Deliver to Bank in form and substance satisfactory to Bank within _____ days following the close of the first three calendar quarters of each year, Borrower's balance sheet, statement of income, and changes in financial performance for such quarter and certified by an authorised officer of Borrower as being accurate and presenting fairly the financial performance and results of operations; and

e) Deliver to Bank within _____ days following the close of Borrower's fiscal year end, a complete copy of Borrower's fiscal year end audit report, prepared by and containing an unqualified opinion by an independent certified public accountant satisfactory to Bank, which shall include at least a balance sheet, a statement of income and retained earnings, and sources and uses of funds for the fiscal year then ended; and

f) Deliver to Bank in form and substance satisfactory to Bank within _____ days following the end of each calendar quarter, including the last quarter of each calendar year, a certificate signed by an authorised officer of Borrower stating that no condition or event has occurred which constitutes an Event of Default or would constitute an Event of Default upon the passage of time; and

g) Provide prompt notice to Bank of any Event of Default, litigation affecting Borrower in an amount exceeding _____, a material adverse change in Borrower's financial or operating condition,[3] a voluntary or involuntary bankruptcy proceeding or filing, the voluntary or involuntary filing of any liens against Borrower's assets in an amount exceeding _____, any judgment entered into against Borrower which exceeds _____, and a default by Borrower under any other loan or credit agreement if such default is a result of a failure to pay any obligation when due; and

h) Maintain a current ratio of at least _____ to _____, a working capital of at least _____, a debt to worth of _____, and a tangible net worth of at least _____; and

i) Maintain insurance coverage against fire damage, public and product liability, property damage, worker's compensation, and other coverages which are commonly covered by companies engaged in the same business and industry as Borrower; and

j) Not declare or pay dividends to shareholders in anyone fiscal year which exceeds _____% of net income after tax for that fiscal year end.

6. Events of Default

If the occurrence of any of the following events transpires with respect to the Borrower, the Bank's obligation to make advances under the Loan or to be obligated under this Agreement in any manner is immediately terminated and Bank, at its option, may declare all principal and interest outstanding under the Loan immediately due and payable, without notice of any kind:

a) Borrower fails to repay, when due, any interest or principal obligation to Bank in accordance with this Agreement; and

b) Borrower makes false or misleading representations or warranties pursuant to this Agreement, or issues any false or misleading certificate as required herein; and

c) Borrower enters into either voluntary or involuntary bankruptcy proceedings; and

d) Borrower defaults or breaches any provision provided for in Section 5 of this Agreement provided such default or breach is not cured within _____ days; and

e) Borrower defaults under any other loan, credit, or guaranty agreement and the default is not waived by the lender or cured within _____ days; and

f) Borrower shall suspend its business for more than _____ days.

---

[3] The adverse change clause is included to protect the lender in the event of a material adverse change in the borrower's condition not covered in other provisions and which generally are not anticipated. Unfortunately, events defined as materially adverse by one party may not be determined to be material by another party. Therefore, it may prove difficult for the lender to use this clause as the sole basis for declaring an event of default. It may provide, however, a basis for negotiations and discussion between lender and borrower.

7. Miscellaneous

a) Notices or communications between any party hereto are to be delivered in writing to Bank at _____, Attention: _____, and to Borrower at _____, Attention: _____, or to such other addresses or addressees as either party may in writing indicate.

b) This Agreement shall bind and inure to the benefit of the Bank and the Borrower and to their respective successors and assigns; provided, however, that Borrower may not assign this Agreement or any of its duties, obligations, or rights under this Agreement. Bank may assign, sell, or transfer to any corporation all or part of Borrower's indebtedness hereunder and Borrower agrees that any such sale or transfer to a corporation will result in a direct binding obligation of Borrower to said corporation.

c) No delay or omission to exercise any right or remedy available to Bank upon default of Borrower under this Agreement shall impair any such right or remedy of Bank, nor shall it be construed to be a waiver of any such default. No waiver of any single default shall be deemed a waiver of any other default theretofore or thereafter occurring. Waivers or approvals of any kind by Bank of any default by Borrower under this Agreement must be in writing.

d) Borrower promises to reimburse Bank upon demand for all costs and legal fees incurred by Bank in connection with the preparation of this Agreement. In the event of any legal action taken in relation to this Agreement, Borrower will reimburse and pay Bank, on demand, all costs and expenses incurred by Bank in relation to such action.

e) This Agreement and any instrument required hereunder shall be governed by and construed under the laws of _____.

f) Any term or condition under this Agreement may be amended upon mutual written consent of Bank and Borrower.

In Witness Whereof, the parties hereto have executed this Agreement by their duly authorised officers as of the day and year first written above.

Borrower   Bank

By: _____   By: _____
Title: _____   Title: _____

By: _____   By: _____
Title: _____   Title: _____

Address: _____   Address: _____

_____   _____

Appendix 5.2: SME Funding Schemes

To ensure that small and medium size enterprises (SMEs) in Hong Kong remain internationally competitive, the Hong Kong government has devised five funding schemes to nurture their growth in the short and long term. Three of these schemes provide banks that lend to SMEs with a secure government guarantee in case the SME defaults on a loan. The funding schemes are thus potentially an additional way for banks in Hong Kong to earn profits; they typically focus on larger companies to grow their loan business.

To be classified as an SME, a manufacturing company should employ fewer than 100 persons while a non-manufacturing business should have fewer than 50 workers. A business is defined under Hong Kong law as "any form of trade, commerce, craftsmanship, professional, calling or other activity carried on for the purpose of gain."

The risk cover for two of the funding schemes—the Special Loan Guarantee Scheme (SpGS) and the SME Loan Guarantee Scheme (SGS)—is extended to the lending bank, not to the corporate borrower. But the borrower has to qualify for the program. Besides being classified as an SME, it should have its main business operations in Hong Kong.

A third scheme, the SME Export Marketing Fund (EMF), is actually a special grant given directly to SMEs for export promotion activities. The fourth scheme—the SME Development Fund—is solely for support organisations that undertake projects to enhance the competitiveness of SMEs.

The fifth programme, the SME Financing Guarantee Scheme, was launched by the Hong Kong Mortgage Corporation (HKMC) on January 2011 to help SMEs obtain loans from participating lenders. Under the scheme, the HKMC provides guaranteed coverage on 50%, 60%, or 70% of the loans to eligible enterprises.

Special Loan Guarantee Scheme

The Special Loan Guarantee Scheme, or SpGS, was offered starting December 2008 to help cushion SMEs from the then prevailing financial crisis. The scheme is intended to help SMEs obtain bank loans from participating lending institutions (PLIs) for the purpose of "meeting general business needs to tide over the liquidity problem during the global financial crisis with the Government acting as the guarantor." The loan cannot be used to repay, restructure, or repackage other loans.

The bank evaluates the credit risk of the SME borrower by looking at its financial statements, including a certified balance sheet and profit and loss account. Afterwards, the bank endorses the SME for approval by the Trade and Industry Department.

To qualify, the enterprise owner has to issue a personal guarantee; and in the case of a limited company, shareholders owning over 50% equity have to issue the guarantee. In addition, the business should not have any outstanding default in any authorised institution as defined in the Banking Ordinance.

The SME can borrow up to HK$12 million from a bank as a term loan or a revolving credit line (but only up to HK$6 million). The government can guarantee up to 80% of the approved loan for up to 60 months or until December 31, 2015, whichever is earlier. No preferential rate is set by the scheme.

SME Loan Guarantee Scheme

The SME Loan Guarantee Scheme (SGS) provides lending banks with risk protection cover when extending loans to SMEs for the purpose of acquiring business installations and equipment, and meeting working capital needs.

This window is meant to enhance the productivity and competitiveness of SMEs. They can borrow from banks in order to buy:

- machinery
- tools
- computer software and hardware
- communication system
- office equipment
- transport facilities
- furniture
- fixtures (i.e. air-conditioning system, built-in cabinets, and lighting system, but not "decoration works")

These installations and equipment may be bought second-hand and even be located outside Hong Kong. But the loan cannot be used to finance or refinance such items already in the borrower's possession.

The loan has to be either a non-revolving loan or a hire purchase loan. The government guarantee covers only up to 50% of the loan approved by the Trade and Industry Department up to five years from the first drawdown date. The maximum loan amount is $6 million and can be used to buy equipment or for working capital or both.

Any SME can avail of this loan twice provided it has fully repaid the first loan. The same qualifying rules under the SME Loan Guarantee Scheme apply.

SME Export Marketing Fund (EMF)

This fund was set up under the Trade and Industry Department to encourage export-oriented SMEs to promote products in local and international trade fairs. The department extends direct grants to SMEs equivalent to half the cost of their participation as trade exhibitors or HK$50,000 at most. Allowable expenses include travel, hotel, participation fees, printing, and online advertising expenses. Each SME can obtain up to HK$150,000 worth of grants in all.

SME Development Fund

This particular funding scheme can only be tapped by non-profit organisations "operating as support organisations, trade and industrial organisations, professional bodies or research institutes to enhance the competitiveness of Hong Kong's SMEs."

Qualified projects include research studies, award schemes, codes of best practice, conferences, seminars, databases, exhibitions, service centres, support facilities, and technology demonstration projects.

Up to HK$2 million or 90% of total project expenditure, whichever is lower, can be covered, but only for such expenses as manpower, travel, advertising, and patent registration fees. Utilities, entertainment, administrative, rental, and renovation expenses are disallowed expenses.

SME Financing Guarantee Scheme

The HKMC's programme is open to SMEs with business operations in Hong Kong and registered under the Business Registration Ordinance. They must be in operation for at least one year on the date of guarantee application and have a good loan repayment record. Listed companies, lending institutions, and their affiliates are not eligible.

The scheme guarantees both term loan and revolving credit facility, which must be used to provide working capital or acquire equipment or assets in relation to the SME's business. Each enterprise or group of enterprises can borrow not more than HK$12 million for a maximum loan tenor of five years, with interest rate of up to 8% a year. The HKMC will consider extending guarantees for loans exceeding 8% per annum on a case-by-case basis.

6

Meeting Business Needs

After studying this chapter, you should be able to:

1 Understand the business needs of the main types of businesses in Hong Kong

2 Know the types of credit that can be offered to these various types of businesses

3 Examine the trade finance cycle and the various modes of payment available for cross-border transactions

4 Consider the risk factors in structuring trade finance facilities for a business

5 Learn how to calculate and manage the working capital requirements of a business

6 Define the business phenomenon of overtrading and assess its impact on a company

Introduction

Every business is different. Each one has its own business model, operating styles, management capabilities, and foibles, among many others. However, every company operates in an industry sector and is of a certain size in sales and complexity of organisation, and thus shares certain common opportunities and constraints with others in that sector and company size.

In this chapter,[1] we will examine the main types of businesses that are the key drivers of the Hong Kong economy, from the bank lender's point of view. We will then discuss the types of credit that banks make available to these businesses. Since international trading remains a core activity of many Hong Kong companies, we will devote part of this chapter to international trade financing and how bank lending for the purpose of working capital is put in place.

Business Sectors in Hong Kong

We will focus on five broad sector categories and their sub-sectors: retailing, manufacturing and trading, building and construction, professional services and New Economy businesses. We will also take a look at companies in terms of a certain size and mode of operation: multinational corporations and small and medium scale businesses.

Retailing

The sector can be roughly divided into two categories—those that sell goods and those that serve food and beverages. The first category includes shopping centres, department stores, chain specialty stores, supermarkets, groceries, convenience stores, bazaars, and direct sale services. The second category includes some 9,000 restaurants, coffee shops, and fast food outlets that employ more than 200,000 workers in total.

Key Risks

It has been said that one cannot go wrong with selling the basic things that people need to survive, such as food and clothing. The reality is that these are high-volume, low-margin businesses that everyone, it seems, wants to enter. It is difficult for new entrants to survive in such a crowded sector and they face the following risk factors:

- *Retailing is a "low barrier to entry" business.* Many people enter it with little experience in running a business and little true appreciation of the difficulties involved. Most go

---

[1] This chapter uses some material from *Commercial Banking* (2005) by Benton E. Gup and James W. Kolari and *Strategic Credit Management* (1995) by Sam N. Basu and Harold L. Rolfes, Jr., with permission from publisher John Wiley & Sons.

into retailing, thinking they can make a fortune. Unfortunately, this is easier said than done. Large supermarkets and other substantial retail groups render many types of small retailers vulnerable. Their buying power makes it virtually impossible for small businesses to compete on price. Their concept of "one stop" shopping is also disadvantageous to the small retailer.

- *Consumer spending habits are fast changing.* The speedy change in consumer spending habits, caused by fierce competition, has made the operating environment of the retailers increasingly tough.
- *The business environment is increasingly challenging.* Retailers in Hong Kong have been faced with an increasingly tough business environment and financial difficulties following the 1997 and 2008 financial crises. The rapid correction of the stock and property markets eroded the wealth of the consuming public and contracted consumer spending.
- *High overheads and regulations are squeezing profit margins.* High fixed overheads such as rentals and salaries, more stringent government regulations in fire safety and environmental protection such as pollution penalties will continue to exert downward pressure on profit margins.
- *Proposed sales tax could dampen bottom lines.* The launch of a sales tax in Hong Kong has long been proposed. It is expected to have an adverse impact on the performance and profitability of retailers, particularly those with less efficient cost structures.

Bank Lending Strategy

Part of a banker's job is to profile what kind of companies might prove to be successful in any given business environment. A banker has to place a potential borrower within the context of its industry. The tools and approaches we studied in Chapter 3 of this book are useful in this regard, such as the Five Competitive Forces model and the PEST and SWOT analyses.

Applying these models to the retail sector in Hong Kong, we can make one observation: small retailers in Hong Kong must specialise in some way in order to succeed. To win in the market place, they will have to offer something extra in terms of convenience (e.g., location and opening hours), quality, special types of goods, exceptional service, and so on. In short, they will have to become niche players.

Based on their analysis, banks may well conclude that the leaders and survivors in Hong Kong will be supermarkets, specialty chain stores/restaurants with their own labels, and niche retailers/food outlets. The losers, and therefore the businesses to stay away from in terms of lending, are single outlet operators, highly leveraged businesses, and retailers/restaurants with less efficient cost structures.

If a bank agrees with this assessment, its lending strategy for the retail sector would probably be guided by these principles:

- Lending should be focused on short-term working capital needs.
- If long-term financing is requested, it should be restricted to acquisitions of shop premises for the business's own use.

- The relationship should yield cross-selling opportunities for the bank, such as the client maintaining deposits and signing up for treasury and cash management products, utility guarantees, insurance, and credit cards, etc.

Special Observations

Compared with other types of business, the accounts of small retailers can easily be "adjusted" for tax purposes because they primarily operate a cash business. It is relatively easy to take cash out of the business so that it never appears as sales income or reaches the bottom line as profit. Therefore, it is possible that the business is more profitable than the tax returns may indicate.

Another way that small retailers understate profit for tax purposes is by taking goods for sale for their own consumption. For example, the owner of a grocery store can simply take goods off the shelves that he would otherwise have to buy from income. But cash taken out of a business, which forms part of the proprietor's normal income, cannot be regarded as a hidden profit available to repay borrowing unless it has been saved in some way.

Evidence of such savings may be available in bank statements, for example. The movements of the customer's bank account can be an informative source for the lender to determine if a company's performance is really much better than it appears from its tax statements.

That is the upside. The areas of concern include the typical business structure of small retailers. Many are run either as sole traders or partnerships. This means the income which the proprietor takes from the business is accounted for as "drawings" in the financial statements.

From a lender's point of view, the proprietor's income is really a cost to the business, and therefore needs to be taken into account before the cash-generating capacity of the business is established. The "true profit" of small retailers will be the net profit less the proprietor's drawings.

Collateral is another area of concern. With the large degree of uncertainty surrounding the viability of business plans for small retailers, adequate security is usually a key issue in the lending assessment. The security cover must have a sufficient margin to repay the loan if the business fails.

It is also appropriate for the bulk of the borrowing to be by way of loan, with overdrafts being kept to the minimum. And because the success of a small retailing business depends crucially on the proprietor, a suitable amount of life cover should be required, especially if there is no clear succession plan in the business.

Manufacturing and Trading

International trade and OEM (original equipment manufacturing) remain core businesses in Hong Kong. However, the trading environment has become increasingly difficult because of rising competition from other Asian exporters, trade protectionism of export markets in Europe and the United States, and the disruptions caused by major financial crises, which affect export demand and change consumption levels and patterns.

Other problems faced by Hong Kong manufacturers include new labour rules in China that raised minimum wages, among other things, and the growing shortage of factory workers in Shenzhen and the rest of Guangdong province, which borders Hong Kong.

The major traditional trading and manufacturing industries where Hong Kong has established its reputation and which remain the main drivers of growth are textile and garments, toys, electronics, and watches and clocks.

Textiles and Garments

This sector serves not only local clothing manufacturers, but also those with production facilities in China, which account for the bulk of Hong Kong's textile exports, and other offshore production bases in Bangladesh, Cambodia, Indonesia, Vietnam, Sri Lanka, Philippines, Thailand and other countries. Hong Kong has a good reputation as a supplier of quality dyed and printed fabrics. It is also strong in cotton spinning, denim weaving, knit-to-shape panel knitting and fine-gauge cotton knit manufacturing.

Most local manufacturers have relocated their factories to southern China to avail of the low-cost structure there. But since this cost advantage is slowly being eroded by continually rising wages, various other expenses, and the gradual withdrawal of preferential treatments, there is now an increasing trend to move westward and northward in China.

Both textiles and garments are dominated by large manufacturers, which have greater economies of scale and more value-added capabilities through supply chain and information technology competencies. The apparel industry is well known internationally for ODM (original design manufacturing) and OEM production. Many international premium designer labels also source clothes in Hong Kong through their buying offices or other intermediaries.

For banks, one key risk in lending to textile and garment companies is market concentration. Despite the wide availability of customers, the U.S. remains the most important export market for Hong Kong manufacturers. Even when textiles, for example, are technically bound for China, the garments that are made from them are usually shipped to the United States.

This market concentration risk was highlighted in the late 2000s when the U.S. suffered from an economic downturn in the wake of the collapse of subprime mortgages there. The American consumer stopped spending, and the demand for Hong Kong textiles and garments collapsed. Some companies closed operations and the banks that lent to them had to unwind their exposure.

The other major risks include:

- Intensified competition from other Asian exporters, in part because of cheaper currencies.
- Large fluctuations in the price of raw materials, particularly cotton and polyester.
- Long lead times in payment collection.

Toys

Counting re-exports, Hong Kong is the world's second largest toy exporter. A number of OEM companies in Hong Kong make toys for overseas industry giants and licensed holders such as Disney, Hasbro, Mattel, and Warner Brothers. Most local toy manufacturers have relocated production facilities to China. They are particularly strong in plastic toys. The U.S. is their largest export market, accounting for more than half of total toy exports.

Banks should take into account the following vulnerabilities of Hong Kong's toy industry:

- Heavy reliance on the U.S. market;
- Dependence on OEM without owning the brand names;
- Increasingly strong bargaining power of toy giants and retail chains;
- Competition from Mainland Chinese enterprises on stuffed toys and lower-end toys;
- Competition from Internet online games, computer games, and music, which can substitute for toys in entertainment value;
- More stringent safety and environmental laws, which raise production costs;
- Shorter product life cycles, which increase the risk for product development;
- Volatile and rising raw material prices, tight electricity supply, and rising labour costs in China.

Electronics

Hong Kong's electronics industry is divided into three areas of specialisation: AV (audio visual) equipment and parts; IT (information technology) equipment and parts; and IC (integrated circuits). The industry consists mainly of small- and medium-sized manufacturers with low and declining ROCE (return on capital employed, which is computed by dividing earnings before interests and taxes with total assets minus current liabilities).

The electronics firms operate mainly on an OEM and ODM basis, despite the increasing number of Hong Kong brands. The electronics industry is characterised by an increasingly shortened product life cycle with continuous technological innovation and fast changing consumer patterns.

The Hong Kong electronics players enjoy the following advantages:

- Efficient low-cost manufacturing;
- Ability to pick trends;
- Strong capabilities in aesthetic design;
- Continuous improvement in productivity and process re-engineering.

But the electronics industry is plagued by the following weaknesses, which lender banks must take into account when making credit decisions:

- Poor economies of scale;
- Weak capabilities in fundamental R&D and technological innovation;

- Limited capability in marketing and managing brands;
- Narrow product range, largely confined to mature products.

Watches and Clocks

Hong Kong is one of the world's largest exporters of complete watches and complete clocks in quantity and value. The largest export item is the battery-powered wristwatch. Production is largely OEM and ODM, with the labour-intensive processes relocated to China.

However, OBM (original brand manufacturing) is increasingly being adopted as a strategy. A Hong Kong Watch Grading & Certification System has been established to provide manufacturers with quality testing of international standards.

Hong Kong's timepieces industry has been helped by the following trends:

- Wristwatches being worn as a fashion accessory, especially by the youth;
- Consumer preference for fashion timepieces with simple designs;
- Growing demand for fashion brand watches studded with diamonds and precious stones;
- Use of a wide range of materials, other than leather and metal, for casing and wristbands, for example, plastics and wooden materials;
- Rising demand for stainless steel watches requiring no electroplating since use of nickel is restricted there because it has caused skin allergies;
- Demand for digital sports watches and sporty-looking pieces due to a growing health consciousness and promotional campaigns of major sports-related companies;
- Watches that incorporate digital technology such as those capable of data transmission and online game playing and those with built-in MP3 players.

But the industry's growth is threatened by the following risks, which banks must take into account when extending credit to companies in this sector:

- Volatile prices of watch and clock movements, as Hong Kong companies rely heavily on imports of these parts;
- Intensified competition from counterparts in Switzerland (in terms of brands, goodwill, and expertise), Japan (technical reliability and large-scale automation) and China (strong ancillary support);
- Higher risk of accumulating obsolete inventory as watches become more of a fashion item;
- Higher receivable risk as a result of an increasing trend of open account sales;
- Downward price pressure in the face of keen competition from low-cost manufacturers in China and Southeast Asia;
- Over-capacity among local manufacturers;
- Rising wages and tightened tax measures eroding cost advantages of producing in China;

- Gradual phasing out of preferential treatment by the Chinese government;
- Increasing trade protectionism and stringent trading conditions in the West.

Building and Construction

The property and construction industry plays a crucial role in Hong Kong's domestic economy. Property related advances represent over 40% of total facilities made available by banks in Hong Kong.

The industry is characterised by:

- A small number of large local contractors and developers;
- A high level of subcontracting;
- The presence of established overseas contractors;
- A substantial number of companies being both developers and contractors.

Most players are small companies acting as subcontractors for the main contractors. They typically account for less than HK$10 million in gross value of construction work per annum. The industry can be broadly divided into three categories:

- Buildings (residential, commercial and industrial/storage, service);
- Structures and facilities (transport, utilities, plant, environment, sports and recreation);
- Non-site activities (decoration, maintenance and repair).

The civil engineering sub-sector generally employs professionals with higher levels of skill and expertise, which places a high barrier to entry. The sector is in effect an oligopoly, dominated by a small number of players that collectively exert control over the market and supply of services.

Engineering firms involved in construction are multi-disciplinary, including civil, structural, building, electrical, and mechanical services. Those in non-construction related industries cover a broad range of disciplines from electronic, electrical, mechanical, chemical, marine, industrial research laboratory, computer hardware consultancy, and so on.

The risks in Hong Kong's building and construction industry are many and various, which bank lenders must make sure to monitor:

- Long payback period for property developments, which makes developers vulnerable to interest rate hikes during the period of construction;
- Domination of the property market by a handful of big developers, allowing them to dictate prices in the primary market;
- More stringent government regulations on safety, environmental protection, and design as well as rising consumer awareness for better quality, which increase development costs;
- High sensitivity to business cycles;
- Financial difficulties of developer and key contractors;

- Litigation due to disputes over quality of materials or workmanship;
- Low profit margins caused by the competitive bid process and intense competition, especially for sub-contractors;
- Unforeseen technical problems in the construction process causing delays and time overruns.

All that said, there are certain developments that give the industry a positive outlook:

- Continuous large infrastructure works by the Hong Kong government in transport, water mains, and other areas, which provide new opportunities for construction and engineering firms and lending opportunities for banks as well;
- Significant projects such as the redevelopment of the old Kai Tak Airport, Railway Development Strategy, infrastructure integration between Hong Kong and Pearl River Delta, and public and private sector housing;
- Continuing housing reform in China, which is encouraging private urban housing projects and providing opportunities for Hong Kong developers and construction companies with a track record in China;
- Infrastructure projects elsewhere in Asia, particularly in Mainland China and Macau (gaming and entertainment).

Professional Services

From the point of view of bank lenders, professional services companies can be divided into two groups:

- Those that are influential in introducing new business, for example, accounting firms, solicitors, and estate agencies.
- Those that are a source of new business for themselves, such as medical practices, dental clinics, and architectural firms.

Professionals tend to organise themselves into partnerships. This structure has legal implications for the bank. Whereas a contract with a company is an agreement with the "person" which the company is in a legal sense, a contract with a partnership is a contract with all the individuals composing that partnership. Unlike a limited company where directors draw salaries, partners share in the profits, so any money a partner draws is not a debit to the profit and loss account. The banker will be interested in the profit left over after drawings, as this will provide the prime source of repayment for the borrowing.

In the past, professionals had restricted and highly regulated entry qualifications, which enabled them to regulate the supply and quality of services. But increasing competition has caused professionals to act more like ordinary businessmen, with all the implications this has for credit-assessing their businesses.

Hong Kong is an international financial centre. The main drivers of growth for the professional services sector are therefore law firms and accounting firms, among others.

- **Law firms.** According to the Hong Kong Bar Association and the Law Society of Hong Kong, there are more than 7,400 practicing barristers and solicitors in Hong Kong, working in over 130 counsel chambers and 700 solicitor firms. Most are small establishments, with five partners or fewer. China is the most important export market for Hong Kong's legal services industry.
- **Accounting firms.** According to the Hong Kong Institute of Certified Public Accountants, there are more than 3,700 practicing certified public accountants in some 1,470 firms and corporate practices in Hong Kong. Most of them are small establishments with fewer than three partners. CPA (Certified Public Accountant) firms provide statutory audit services, as well as tax advisory, company listing, corporate finance, company secretarial, liquidation, and due diligence services. Non-CPA firms offer services like bookkeeping, general accounting, year-end financial reporting, tax filing and company secretarial work.

Small legal and accountancy firms typically specialise in conveyancing, simple commercial deals, and filing of annual returns. Large firms provide full services from conveyancing, litigation and audit support, corporate finance, intellectual property rights, audit and tax consulting, and restructuring, to merger and acquisition support.

The professional services sector exhibits the following risks:

- Slow collections;
- Single source of income, e.g. conveyancing, filing of annual tax returns;
- Increasing competition from international firms.

The signing of the Closer Economic Partnership Arrangement (CEPA) between Hong Kong and China is opening up more business for Hong Kong law firms. Under Annex 4 of CEPA,[2] Hong Kong law firms with a representative office in China are permitted to operate in association with one domestic law firm located in the same province or municipality or autonomous region as the Hong Kong law firm.

As for accounting firms, consultancy companies established by Hong Kong accountants in China, which satisfy the requirements of China's Provisional Measures for the Administration of the Provision of Bookkeeping Services law, can provide bookkeeping services. Foreign accounting firms can affiliate with Chinese firms and enter into contractual agreements with their affiliated firms in other WTO member countries.

But the same trend could also bring new competition to Hong Kong's professional services companies. For instance, foreigners who have passed the Chinese national CPA examination will receive national treatment (i.e., right to form partnerships or incorporated accounting firms) in China.

---

[2] See Annex 4 (Specific Commitments on Liberalization of Trade in Services) of CEPA at http://www.tid.gov.hk/english/cepa/legaltext/fulltext.html.

New Economy Businesses

This term gained currency in the late 1990s to describe the evolution of the U.S. and other developed countries from an industrial and manufacturing based economy into a high technology-based economy. At the time, the New Economy was widely seen as creating a state of permanent steady growth, low unemployment, and immunity to boom-and-bust macroeconomic cycles. The New Economy was also expected to make many old business practices obsolete.

While many of these views were proven wrong by the recession of 2001 and the failure of a large number of dot.com companies, the heavy investment in information technology did stimulate strong productivity growth. It ushered in a new industry called electronic business or e-business, referring to any business process that is empowered by an information system and uses Web-based technologies.

E-business methods enable companies to link their internal and external processes more efficiently and flexibly, and work more closely with suppliers and partners to better satisfy the needs and expectations of their customers. In practice, this involves the introduction of new revenue streams through the use of e-commerce, the enhancement of relationships between clients and partners, and improvement of efficiency by using knowledge management systems.

E-business can be conducted over the public Internet, through internal intranets, and over secure private extranets. It is more than just e-commerce; e-business covers business processes along the whole value chain, including:

- Electronic purchasing (e-procurement) and supply chain management;
- Processing orders electronically;
- Customer service and cooperation with business partners.

Developments such as the Internet are making markets, products, and services more global. Efficient production is more reliant than ever on information and technology know-how. Goods and services can be developed, bought, sold, and in some cases delivered over electronic networks.

The growth of knowledge-based industries threatens traditional industries in several key respects:

- The advantage of location is diminished in some economic activities. By using appropriate technology and methods, virtual marketplaces and virtual organisations that offer benefits of speed, agility, round the clock operation, and global reach can pose a challenge to traditional businesses, for example, virtual bookstores such as amazon.com vs. national/local bookshops.
- Laws, barriers, and taxes are difficult to apply on a solely national basis. Knowledge and information "leak" to where demand is highest and the barriers are lowest.
- Knowledge-enhanced products or services can command price premiums over comparable products with low embedded knowledge or knowledge intensity.

- Pricing and value depends heavily on context.
- Human capital will be a key component of value in a knowledge-based business to increase competitiveness.

Hong Kong's New Economy companies have wide knowledge of and connections in the Chinese market, so they are regarded as having a competitive edge in offering services from consulting to training to web implementation in China's rapidly developing online market. The country is already the world's largest user of the Internet, with some 384 million people (29% of the total population) online.

Under Annex 4 of CEPA, Hong Kong companies can set up joint ventures in China to provide five types of telecommunications services without geographical restriction:

- Internet data centre services;
- Store and forward services;
- Call centre services;
- Internet access services; and
- Content services.

Multinational Corporations (MNCs)

An MNC is a corporation or enterprise that manages production establishments or delivers services in at least two countries. Multinational corporations are often divided into three broad groups:

- **Horizontally integrated,** which are MNCS with production establishments located in different countries to produce same or similar products
- **Vertically integrated,** which are MNCs that manage production establishments in certain countries to produce products that serve as inputs to its production establishments in other countries
- **Diversified,** which are MNCs that manage production establishments located in different countries that are neither horizontally nor vertically integrated

Very large multinationals may have budgets that exceed those of many countries. Given their international reach and mobility, prospective countries and sometimes provinces within countries compete with each other to entice multinationals to locate their facilities in their countries and/or regions to boost tax revenue, employment, and economic activities.

For bank lenders, doing business with multinationals can bring scale and stability to loan portfolios because of the sheer size of these companies and the potential to cross-sell other bank products, such as cash management and treasury services. However, they will also be under pressure to extend price concessions and guarantee high levels of service, which can cut profit margins and raise costs.

Small and Medium Enterprises (SMEs)

At the other end of the scale from MNCs are SMEs—small and medium enterprises with headcounts or turnover that falls below certain thresholds. SMEs, according to Hong Kong's Trade and Industry Department, are manufacturing enterprises with fewer than 100 employees or non-manufacturing enterprises with fewer than 50 employees.

Government figures show that these enterprises account for over 98% of business establishments in Hong Kong and provide jobs opportunities to around 60% of the total work force, excluding civil servants. As mentioned in Chapter 5, most SMEs are unincorporated companies, i.e., are either sole proprietorships or partnerships. They typically do not maintain proper or detailed accounts and are usually highly leveraged with borrowings largely supported by collateral provided by their owners. Turnover and profits are often understated for tax reasons.

The cash flow of SMEs and that of the owners or the owners' other companies are often mixed together. Inter-company balances show up in the financial statements, which make credit analysis more difficult for banks. SMEs are generally under-capitalised and have irregular patterns of drawings or cash payouts. Balance sheet management is generally weak. The lack of systematic control or records of stocks and accounts receivable usually causes qualifications in audit reports.

Despite these risk factors common to SMEs, they have a reputation for flexibility and innovation. The Hong Kong government has also set up special funds and risk insurance to encourage banks to lend to them (see Chapter 5). Their sheer number also means that banks must lend to some SMEs if they want to fully utilise their loanable funds. After all, there are only a small number of MNCs and large corporations. Banks must take extra care to analyse and monitor the business performance of SMEs, however, given the characteristics and limitations of these companies.

Types of Credit

The most common types of credit that banks offer businesses are the following: line of credit, revolving loan, term loan, bridge loan, asset-based lending, and leases.

Overdraft Facility

An overdraft facility is an agreement between a customer and a bank that the bank will entertain requests from that customer for a loan (or drawings from a current account) up to a predetermined amount. The overdraft facility is established when the bank gives a letter to the customer stating the dollar amount of the facility, the time it is in effect (e.g., one year), the customer's financial condition, and so on.

If the borrower does not meet all the terms and conditions, the bank is not obliged to continue the facility. The loans or drawings are made for periods of one year or less, and they should be used to finance seasonal increases in inventory and accounts receivable. When the inventory is sold and receivables are collected, the funds are used to reduce the loan outstanding, which is usually payable on demand by the bank, or within 90 days.

An overdraft facility is typically made available to established companies with good credit records and strong financial standings. Because banks have little control over the use and source of repayment of an overdraft, collateral will be required if the credit risk of the company is considered high. A higher interest rate will also be charged due to the higher risk, compared to other types of bank finance.

Revolving Loan

Revolving loans are similar to an overdraft facility because they too are used to finance borrowers' temporary and seasonal working capital needs. One difference between a revolving loan and an overdraft facility is that the bank is obligated to make the loans, up to the maximum amount of the loan, if the borrower is in compliance with the terms of the agreement.

Revolving loans commonly specify the minimum amount of the increments that may be borrowed. For example, the loan could be for $30,000 increments up to a maximum limit of $3 million. Another difference is that revolving loans usually have a maturity of two years or more, while overdraft facilities are usually for shorter periods.

Term Loan

A term loan is usually a single loan for a stated period of time, or a series of loans on specified dates. They are used for a specific purpose, such as acquiring machinery, renovating a building, refinancing debt, and so forth. They should not be used to finance day-to-day operations.

Term loans may have an original maturity of five years or more. From the lender's viewpoint, the loan maturity should not exceed the economic life of the asset being financed if that asset is being used as collateral for the loan. Equally important, the value of the asset being financed should always exceed the loan amount.

The difference between the value of the asset and the amount being financed is the borrower's equity. The borrower's equity represents the borrower's investment in the asset being financed. It also provides the bank with a cushion in the event of default. The borrower will lose his or her funds before the bank experiences a loss. Borrowers not wanting to lose their equity investment have an incentive to operate their business so the loan will be repaid. Term loans may be repaid on an amortised basis or in full upon maturity.

Bridge Loan

Bridge loans "bridge a gap" in a borrower's financing until some specific event occurs. For example, a firm wants to acquire a new warehouse facility, but needs funds to finance the transaction until the old warehouse can be sold. Thus, a bridge loan is short-term financing that is made in anticipation of receiving longer-term financing on which an agreement has been reached.

Corporations can also resort to bridge loans not only for acquiring assets but also for shoring up working capital. For instance, a firm needs working capital now, but will only get the funds the following week when it issues commercial papers. A bank can provide temporary financing, meanwhile, with a bridge loan. In this case, the bank loan is being used as a short-term substitute for other debt financing by the firm.

Asset-Based Lending

Asset-based lending is a form of commercial lending where the assets of a company are used to secure the company's obligation to the lender. Most asset-based lenders are finance companies, although some banks do asset-based lending too.

In the broadest sense, all secured loans could be classified as asset-based lending. Asset-based loans have, as their collateral base, accounts receivable, inventory, machinery and equipment, and real estate, single or packaged in various combinations (e.g., receivables and inventory, receivables and machinery, and so forth).

The major distinctions between asset-based loans and other secured loans is that much greater weight is given to the market value of the collateral in asset-based lending than in regular commercial loans. In addition, asset-based lenders place greater emphasis on monitoring than do bank lenders. Moreover, if the borrower defaults, the asset-based lenders are more willing to liquidate the borrower's collateral than is the case for regular commercial loans.

Asset-based loans require a higher level of monitoring than do other "secured" commercial loans. The degree of monitoring to ensure the existence, value, and integrity of the collateral further differentiates asset-based loans from other secured commercial loans. The combination of a higher level of monitoring and a greater willingness to liquidate in the event of default may help explain why asset-based lenders tend to have higher spreads and fees and lower write-offs than other secured lenders.

Leasing

Leasing is a service performed by banks and other companies where assets such as plant and machinery, commercial vehicles, computers, office equipment, etc. are rented or leased out.

A lease is an agreement between two parties: the lessor and the lessee. The lessor is the party to a lease agreement who has legal or tax title to equipment or property, who grants the lessee the right to use the equipment for a fee.

In lease arrangements, banks and financial institutions normally act as lessors to finance the acquisition of assets for business use.

Two basic types of leases are offered:

- Operating leases are rental agreements between a lessor and lessee whereby the lessor owns equipment and leases it to the lessee for an agreed period. The lessor will normally lease the equipment again or sell it after the lease period. As such, the period of an operating lease is fairly short and is less than the economic life of the asset.
- Finance leases are used in connection with financing long-term assets. The lease has a primary period which covers the whole or most of the useful economic life of the asset. For example, a communications satellite may be leased for 12 years. At the end of the primary period, the lessee has the option to continue to lease the asset for an indefinite secondary period at a nominal rent, or the lessee can sell the asset on behalf of the lessor.

Under an operating lease the lessor is responsible for maintaining the leased equipment. In a finance lease, the lessee takes care of the asset.

The lessee has to report in its balance sheet any finance lease under "fixed assets," with the future rentals to the lessor reported out under "liabilities." These liabilities add to the gearing ratio (see Chapter 3). If the lessee has an operating lease, the leased equipment need not be reflected in the balance sheet.

Hire Purchase

Under a hire purchase arrangement, goods are "hired" by the customer who makes a number of hire payments over a certain period. At the end of the hire period, the customer gets to own the goods.

A hire purchase can also be a credit sales agreement, where the customer buys goods and pays on installment.

Hire purchase is similar to leasing, with the exception that ownership of the goods passes to the hire purchase customer either at the start of the hire purchase agreement or on payment of the final instalment. A lessee never becomes the legal owner of the goods. With finance leases, the lessor who purchases the asset can claim the capital allowances for tax purpose while the lessee can claim the lease payments as an allowable expense.

With hire purchase, it is the eventual buyer—the customer—who can claim the capital allowances. But the customer can only claim the interest charges in the instalments paid to the finance company as allowable expenses for tax.

In hire purchase, a customer may require a down-payment for the assets acquired. The lessee under a leasing arrangement does not usually have to pay any deposit.

Factoring

Rapidly growing companies often cannot generate sufficient profits or cashflow to service their debt at their rates of increase. Such companies would benefit from the service of a factoring company, which specialises in managing trade debts and other debts on the client's behalf. Some banks have established their own factoring services or spun this off as subsidiaries.

A factor is defined as "a doer or transactor of business for another." It can offer the following services:

- Administration of the client's invoicing, sales accounting, and debt collection service (i.e., receivables collection and ledger management).
- Credit protection for the client's debts, whereby the factor insures the client against bad debt losses by "debt underwriting" or purchase of a client's debts "without recourse."
- Factor finance by purchasing a client's debts "with recourse" and paying the client in advance of debt collection. When the factoring is done with recourse, the client assumes most or all the risks of non-payment. Because of this, the factoring agent charges a lower fee than when factoring without recourse. In case of the latter arrangement, it is the factoring company that assumes all the risks of default and therefore charges a higher fee.

In the past, companies did not disclose in their balance sheets whether they resorted to factor financing. Unlike conventional banks that tend to lend against audited results, factors can provide financing based on current trading levels of the customer.

The types of businesses that would benefit from a factor's services are those well-managed, medium-sized firms selling a narrow range of products to a fairly small number of customers in a low-risk market, without a single customer accounting for a significant portion of its total turnover and outstanding debts.

In Hong Kong, the demand for factoring companies is growing because:

- Open account trade transactions are increasing, wherein the seller bears much of the risk since the buyer pays only upon possession of the goods.
- The service that factoring companies provide complements traditional trade products.
- There is increasing acceptance and awareness of the service.
- There is wider knowledge of the benefits of factoring.
- The requirements for debtor credit risk coverage have increased and factoring helps cover that risk.

A company can benefit from factoring in the following ways:

- It can pay suppliers promptly, enabling it to avail itself of early payment discounts.
- It can maintain an optimum stock level because the business will have enough cash to pay for the stocks it needs.

- It can finance growth through sales instead of injecting fresh external capital.
- The business gets finance linked to its volume of sales and not to its historical balance sheets, which traditionally are used by banks as base in granting overdraft limits.
- It cuts management time devoted to the problem of slow paying debtors.
- Factoring can help facilitate debtor risk management and improve the collection process.
- Factoring can also protect against buyer insolvency or default risk.
- The business can outsource the receivable ledger management and eliminate the costs of running its own sales ledger department.
- There is no tangible security requirement for factoring.

Banks also benefit from factoring when their clients avail of this service because:

- It provides a more structured form of financing.
- It controls the debtors' factored proceeds.
- It puts in place an in-depth monitoring mechanism.
- It gives credit protection against debtor insolvency/default risk.
- It is one way to package and transfer the risk.

Factors also provide invoice discounting services where they purchase a selection of invoices at a discount. But the invoice discounters do not take over the administration of the client's debtors' ledger. Invoice discounting tends to consist of "one-off" deals which are temporary in nature.

Factoring differs from advances made against account receivables in the following ways:

- Factoring may be on a disclosed or undisclosed basis to the debtor of the borrower. In contrast, in an advance against account receivables the borrower's debtors are not aware of the advance.
- Factoring may be on a recourse or non-recourse basis to the borrower. Lenders will however require recourse to the borrower for the advance against account receivables.
- Under factoring, all receipts from debtors have to be credited to a trust or designated account to settle the factoring advance. In contrast, the documentation and account management of the advance against account receivables are more relaxed and a designated account may not be required.
- Under factoring, the bank may also provide the borrower receivables management and credit insurance services.

Guarantees and Bonds

A *tender guarantee* or *tender bond* is a guarantee given by the bank on behalf of its customer who is trying to win a contract, usually in the building or construction industries. This guarantee is required by the beneficiary (e.g., government and property developers) to safeguard against risk in case a winning bidder backs out of the contract.

A *performance bond* is meant to secure against the non-performance of the bank customer after being awarded the contract.

An *advance payment guarantee* is a guarantee issued by a bank to refund any advance payments made by the beneficiary to the bank customer in case the bank customer does not fulfil the terms and conditions of a contract.

A *warranty* or *retention bond* is usually used in the construction and manufacturing industries. For instance, a sub-contractor takes out a retention bond. This covers both the main contractor and sub-contractor from the risk of the sub-contractor being unable or unwilling to carry out work (such as to repair defects) after the completion of the contract.

In the case of manufactured goods, a warranty bond protects the buyer of the goods in case the contracted goods fail to meet the contractual warranty obligations after the completion of the contract.

Trade Finance

Before books were ever written about trade finance, Hong Kong businessmen were already engaged in it. They bought raw materials from abroad and used these to make their products. Or they bought finished goods overseas and sold these locally or to nearby countries. Somehow, they made their own financial arrangements to complete such cross-border transactions.

Today, banks facilitate the bulk of these buying and selling transactions across national borders being undertaken mostly between total strangers. Foreign buyers are now called importers and foreign sellers are exporters. Oftentimes, a company can be an importer in one transaction and an exporter in another transaction.

Import Finance Cycle

The interest of an importing company is best served by not paying cash in advance and by delaying payment as long as possible (which would help company cash flow) or at least until the goods are in its possession. The least attractive mode of payment for the importer is thus *cash-in-advance*, which means simply that. The importer pays in advance even before getting the goods. If the goods don't arrive, the importer has no recourse.

However, the importer may find another supplier willing to agree to other modes of payment. It can open a *Letter of Credit (LC)* with its own bank for a fee, which obligates the bank to remit payment to the exporter upon the importer's receipt of the goods ordered.

Alternatively, the importer can ask the exporter to arrange a *Documentary Collection (DC)* through the exporter's own bank, for which the exporter pays the bank a fee. A DC is typically cheaper than an LC because the bank does not guarantee payment; its role is limited to assisting the exporter obtain payment from the importer.

The best mode of payment from the importer/buyer's point of view, however, is to get the exporter/seller to agree to an *Open Account* transaction. Here, the importer receives the goods shipped by the exporter without paying for them first.

To understand how the import finance cycle works, let us take a brief look at how an LC transaction works. The importer/buyer goes to a bank and arranges the issue of a letter of credit in favour of the exporter/supplier. The bank charges the importer a fee for this service. The issuing bank sends the LC to the exporter's bank, which forwards the LC to the exporter.

With the assurance that the issuing bank is committed to paying for the goods, the exporter sends the ordered goods to a freight forwarder, which dispatches the goods and submits documents to the exporter's bank. The exporter's bank checks the documents to make sure of compliance with the terms of the LC and pays the exporter. The importer's account at the bank that issued the LC is debited and releases documents to the importer to allow it to claim the goods from the freight forwarder.

Export Finance Cycle

For the exporter, the best mode of payment is cash-in-advance. This mode of payment is usually done through a bank wire transfer or credit card payment. Next to cash-in-advance, other secure modes of payment for the exporter are the LC and the DC. The most risky is an Open Account transaction, although the risk can be mitigated with export credit insurance, which is discussed later in this chapter.

To understand how the export finance cycle works, let us take a brief look at a DC transaction. The exporter/seller sends the ordered goods to the importer and receives documents from the freight forwarder confirming that the shipment has taken place. The exporter presents the documents to its bank, along with instructions for obtaining payment. The exporter's bank sends the documents to the importer's bank, which treats them as *bills receivable (BR)*.

The importer's bank checks the documents for compliance with the terms of the DC. If everything is in order, it releases the documents to the importer when the importer pays it for the goods. The payment instructions could vary. Sometimes it could say the importer has to pay "at sight" (which is called *documents against payment* or *DP*); or by a specified date (which is called *documents against acceptance* or *DA*).

The importer may ask not to make payment for the time being because the retail shops that ordered the goods have yet to pay for them, for example. The importer's bank may agree and for a fee, issues a document called *loans against imports (LAI)* to the importer. The goods will be kept in the bank's approved warehouse for a specified period of time.

It is also possible for the importer to claim the goods ordered without paying the bank first. In this case, the bank will issue a *trust receipt (TR)*, again for a fee, that in effect means the importer is holding the goods in trust for the bank. This situation may arise if the goods in question are raw materials or semi-processed parts that are needed to manufacture finished goods. The TR allows the importer to immediately make the goods without paying the full amount.

Once the importer's bank gets the payment or issues an LAI or TR, it remits what is owed the exporter to the exporter's bank, which credits the exporter's account with the money received.

Trade Finance Cycle

The import finance and export finance cycles come together to form the trade finance cycle. A trade finance transaction obviously cannot be completed without an importer and a corresponding exporter, with the bank in the middle of the trade. Figure 6.1 shows an example of a trade finance cycle.

FIGURE 6.1   Trade finance cycle

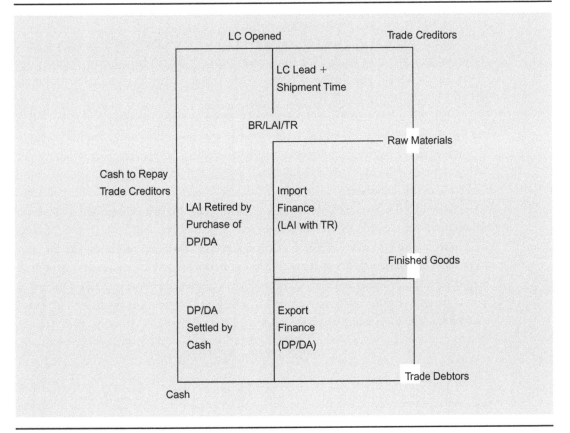

Source: HKIB

Import Facilities

Import finance is made up of two distinct parts: Letters of Credit/Bills Receivable (LC/BR) and Loans Against Imports (LAI). The size of the bank financing is usually based on projected turnover, the anticipated life of the LC, and the period until the goods are sold.

LC/BR Limit

When a company imports under LC, it will need to issue the credit through the bank weeks or even months ahead of the shipment date. This would enable the supplier/exporter to arrange the purchase/manufacture of the ordered goods, knowing that if it complies with the terms of the LC, it can obtain payment from the importer.

The LC is a credit product that obligates the bank to pay the supplier/exporter if it complies with the terms of the LC. There is no direct finance, that is, cash, involved in the LC issuance before the arrival of the documents. For the bank, the financing usually starts when the documents are received, as it will then have to pay the exporter's bank the amount of the bill drawn under the LC if no discrepancies are found and if the importer does not pay in cash but instead takes out an LAI.

The documents received are treated as BR. The bank will usually have security over the underlying goods by controlling the documents of title from LC issuance up to arrival of the BR, by which time the bank will approach the importer for reimbursement or for retirement of the BR into an LAI.

Typically, the customer will open the LC up to an agreed revolving limit, known as the *LC/BR limit*, and pay the bank a fee based on that limit. This limit should be able to accommodate the customer's projected cost of raw material for the year. This is achieved by taking account of the LC lead time, which is the period of time from the LC issuance until the arrival of the documents.

The LC/BR limit is computed by multiplying the total imported raw material required for the year by LC lead time/year. For example, ABC Electronics Trading Co Ltd would like to source 300,000 alarm clocks from suppliers in Taiwan for the next 12 months. The alarm clocks cost about $25 each. The LC has to be opened one month before the shipment and the goods usually arrive in two weeks. What is the LC/BR limit?

To answer this question, we need to calculate the annual amount of the goods sourced by ABC Electronics Trading Co Ltd:

$$300,000 \times \$25 = \$7,500,000$$

As the company needs to open LC one month before shipment and the goods will arrive in two weeks, the LC lead time and the shipment time adds up to a total of 1.5 months. The LC/BR limit is therefore:

$$\$7,500,000 \times 1.5 \text{ month}/12 \text{ months} = \$937,500$$

LC/BR/LAI Period

LAI is granted when the bank still maintains control of the goods via the documents of title, usually the bill of lading. In some cases a warehouse receipt (made out to the bank's order) would be the document of title, in a situation where the goods have arrived but the customer does not require them immediately.

An LAI is effectively an extension of the original LC. As such, the bank's period of risk would be extended and the LC/BR limit must be adjusted to reflect the average outstanding under the LC. The length of time the goods are held under the bank's control would be governed by the length of time the customer needs to make payment. Usually, this reflects the expected arrival of the ship but may also include some warehousing.

This *LC/BR/LAI period* is calculated by multiplying the total imported raw material for the year with the LC lead time and the finance period for shipment, warehousing, and so on. The underlying risks (as distinct from the amount) have not changed with the provision of the LAI. What has changed is that the bank has substituted an obligation to make payment (indirect risk) with making a payment (direct risk).

For example, ABC Electronics Trading Co Ltd estimates that it would need to keep the alarm clocks it ordered for one month in the bank's approved warehouse before taking these out and selling them to buyers. What will the LC/BR/LAI period be?
Including the one-month stockholding period, the LC/BR/LAI period will be 2.5 months. The LC/BR/LAI period is therefore:

$$\$7,500,000 \times 2.5 \text{ months}/12 \text{ months} = \$1,562,500$$

LAI/TR Period

When the importer requires that the goods are released before making payment, the bank may agree to do so against a Trust Receipt (TR). Under a TR, the customer is in essence holding the goods in trust for the bank. The bank's control of the goods is effectively lost and, as a result, the underlying risks increase. The bank will reflect this change in risk by granting a sub-limit for TR, which has a 100% cash risk.

The *LAI/TR period* should be set to reflect the production cycle (for a manufacturer) and this would include the stockholding periods of the raw material, work in progress (WIP), and the finished goods. This should generally not include the period given to debtors.

For example, ABC Electronics Trading Co Ltd has changed its business model. Instead of buying alarm clocks, it now designs its own products, purchases the main components to make the alarm clock so designed, and stamps the clock with its own brand.

The LC lead time and shipment time with suppliers remain unchanged. However, instead of leaving the goods in the warehouse after arrival, ABC Electronics now needs to take them out immediately so it can make its own alarm clocks. It takes 45 days to make the alarm clocks and sell them to buyers. ABC needs to buy 300,000 alarm clock pieces from its Taiwan suppliers at $22 each.

The calculations are:

Annual purchases: $300,000 \times \$22 = \$6,600,000$

$LC/BR = (1 + 0.5)$ month $= 1.5$ months

$LAI/TR = 1.5$ months (i.e., 45 days)

$LC/BR = \$6.6$ million $\times 1.5m/12m = \$825,000$

$LAI/TR = \$6.6$ million $\times 1.5m/12m = \$825,000$

Based on the above, ABC Electronics Trading Co Ltd will need an LC line (total limit adding up LC/BR and LAI/TR) of $1,650,000, within which the LAI/TR sub-limit is $825,000.

Export Facilities

Export finance in the form of LC bills negotiation or DP/DA (documents against payment/documents against acceptance) purchase can be arranged with the bank to fund the working capital of the supplier/exporter until it receives payment from the buyer/importer. The types of export finance range from purchase of the bills of exchange that relates to the export side, to the negotiation of document credit, purchase of documentary collections, and other forms of receivables financing.

The bank provides export finance by purchasing the bills of exchange that relate to the export sale. This will be done when the bank handles the customer's LC. Under this arrangement, the bank in effect finances the customer's debtors.

Pre-Shipment Finance

This type of finance is often given against the security of an export LC, which would be held by the bank, or against a confirmed purchase order in the case of non-LC bills if the customer has a DP line. In effect, this is a "clean advance" and is usually granted for 50%–80% of the value of the goods ordered and normally for a maximum of 90 days. The goods are insured against fire risk.

There are various types of pre-shipment finance that banks can make available to exporter-clients. They include:

- *Packing Credits.* When an exporter is waiting to ship finished goods (e.g., waiting for shipping space, arrival of steamer, or earliest permitted shipping date), the goods are stored in a transit warehouse. The bank may advance this form of bridging loan to help the exporter's cash flow against presentation of the warehouse receipt and retention of the LC. The packing credit advance will be repaid by the proceeds from the negotiation of the export bill under the LC upon shipment. This form of advance has the goods as security.
- *Manufacturers' Advances.* These are loans for the exporter to purchase raw materials, manufacturing, packing of goods, etc.

Post-Shipment Finance

No facilities are required as long as the bank is protected by the LC and the documents tendered comply strictly with the terms of the LC. It is essential that documents be checked thoroughly for any discrepancies. In the event of non-payment by the issuing bank due to discrepancies, the bank only has recourse on the exporter.

The bank may allow negotiation of the LC with discrepancies from the customer against an indemnity. In this case, the risks are similar to those under DP transactions in that the bank loses the security of the LC but still controls the goods.

The bills drawn under the DC (for both DP and DA payment arrangements) do not have the backing of a credit and a bank. If the bank purchases these non-LC bills, it would in effect provide finance against the security of the goods that underlie the transaction and rely on the importer to make payment. In the event of non-payment the bank still retains the right to obtain repayment from its customer even though its first source of payment would be from the importer.

By purchasing *DP bills*, the exporter's bank is in theory financing the transit time of sending the documents to the importer's bank, the period for the latter bank to check the documents, and the transit time for the exporter's bank to receive settlement. There is no cash risk to the exporter's bank when purchasing DP bills, as control is maintained over the documents, and therefore the goods. It has recourse on the drawer of the DP bill (i.e., the exporter) in the event of non-payment. The main risk is that the buyer will refuse the goods due to market or financial reasons.

The DP limit would relate to the customer's projected sales for the year and the length of time taken from purchasing the bill until the exporter's bank receives payment from the importer's bank. This transit time is normally one month, on average.

By purchasing the *DA bills*, the bank is financing the same period as per DP bills, plus a further acceptance period. The exporter's bank controls the goods until the importer accepts the bill. Thereafter, the importer will take up the documents and control of the underlying goods. Since the bank will not have control of the goods after the importer accepts the bill, financing a DA transaction carries a higher degree of risk.

If the importer refuses to pay after accepting the bill, the exporter's bank would not have the goods underlying the bill and would only have recourse to its customer. As a result, the facility for the purchase of export DA bills carries a 100% cash risk to the bank. The DA limit would be based on the exporter's projected sales for the year and the acceptance period (or credit period given to the import plus the transit time).

Example: ABC Electronics

Let us return to the example of ABC Electronics Trading Co Ltd. Now that the company manufactures its own alarm clocks, it needs to purchase other accessory items in cash. These items cost around $1 for each alarm clock made and a stock level of approximately 30 days will have to be maintained, including shipment time after placing the orders with overseas suppliers. The workers' wages and packaging expenses add up another $1.50 for each alarm clock. The alarm clocks are to be sold at $27 each and will be delivered to the buyers upon completion. The buyers pay by 60 days DA.

Assuming it is satisfied with the credit risk profile of ABC Electronics Trading Co Ltd, the bank may offer pre-shipment finance against the purchase orders to help the company buy the accessory items and pay workers' wages and other related costs like packaging expenses.

Annual purchases of the accessory items: 300,000 × $1 = $300,000
Workers' wages and packaging expenses per annum: 300,000 × $1.50 = $450,000

Taking a 30-day stockholding period of the accessory items and a 45-day production cycle, the pre-shipment finance limit is calculated thusly:

$$\$300,000 \times 75 \text{ days}/365 \text{ days} + \$450,000 \times 45 \text{ days}/365 \text{ days}$$

The answer is $117,124, or $120,000 if the figure is rounded up to 75 days ahead of shipment. As the total costs of the accessory items, workers' wages, and packaging expenses account for 9.3% of the sales price, the advance ratio can be up to 10% of each purchase order.

What about post-shipment finance? We can calculate the DA line as follows:

$$300,000 \times \$27 \times 60 \text{ days}/365 \text{ days} = \$1,331,507$$
$$(\text{or } \$1.35 \text{ million if we round up for a 60-day DA line})$$

We can now express the total trade finance facilities required by ABC Electronics Trading Co Ltd:

- Import/Export Facilities of $3,120,000 where the company can use up to:
- $1,650,000 for the import of main components under LC with 45 days TR/LAI sub-limit of $825,000
- $120,000 for the manufacturing advances, up to 45 days ahead of shipment, against a maximum of 10% value of the purchase orders
- $1,350,000 for the purchase of export DA bills up to 60 days

Export Credit Insurance

Hong Kong being an international trade hub, the government has been providing since 1966 a special form of insurance to mitigate risks in international trade. For a fee, the Hong Kong Export Credit Insurance Corporation (ECIC) insures exporters against losses arising from commercial risks—buyer insolvency, bankruptcy, or payment default—and even political risks. This, in turn, lowers the risk for banks that lend to traders.

The ECIC covers risks of non-payment encountered by companies engaged in export trading on credit payment terms, namely Documents against Payment (D/P),

Documents against Acceptance (D/A), and Open Account (O/A). Since the agency is government-owned, all liabilities are government-guaranteed. And because of the protection cover, HK traders can extend more favourable terms to overseas buyers.

ECIC also helps HK traders vet overseas buyers. Its computerised data bank contains detailed information on 55,000 buyers in 150 countries.

For instance, the ECIC states in its website that its Comprehensive Cover Policy (CCP) for Hong Kong exporters and manufacturers "provides cover not only for all your export business on credit terms with goods shipped from Hong Kong, but also those transported directly from suppliers' countries to their destination without passing through Hong Kong."

Both buyer and country risks are covered under the insurance policy for a fee. Covered risks include insolvency or bankruptcy of a buyer; failure of the buyer to pay for goods he has taken delivery of; and failure or refusal of the buyer to take delivery of the goods after shipment. For insolvency, bankruptcy, or nonpayment by the buyer, the maximum ceiling of compensation is 90% of the value of the traded goods.

Country risks include war, revolution, civil disturbances, and natural disasters; blockade or delay in the transfer of foreign exchange to Hong Kong; import bans; or cancellation of import licences already issued.

Risks of Local LCs

A local LC does not usually call for title documents. Only a local transport document is involved. The document does not carry the title of goods. Banks usually have no recourse to and control of goods as they are usually sent directly to the beneficiary against documents such as a cargo receipt or a postal receipt.

If the opening bank is not careful, local LCs can be used for accommodation purposes. There have been cases in the past where local LCs were used to finance fraudulent transactions between related parties, in which there was no actual shipment of goods but only fake transaction documents.

To mitigate the local LC risk, the following can be considered:

- **Know your customer.** Banks should know their customer's line of business and how the business is conducted—their trade patterns and who they are dealing with, such as the names of their buyers and suppliers. Banks should also visit the borrowers' factories or warehouses to understand their trading and inventory situation.
- **Company search and credit checking.** These should be carried out on customers as well as their buyers and suppliers to confirm their relationships and their credit standing. Opening local LCs in favour of the customer's related company or firms related to its directors/shareholders should be avoided.
- **Restricted opening of the local LC.** This should be limited to approved suppliers only. Structured insurance should be required as a condition of the trade finance if the bank is refinancing the local LC issued by an import/merchandise loan against the goods stored in the warehouse with the title transferred to the bank.

- **Storage of the goods.** These should be in a public godown or warehouse, so the bank lender could have a title to the imported goods, not at the beginning but at the end, when the borrower defaults.

Transferable LC vs BBLC

A transferable LC is an irrevocable LC which contains the designation that it can be transferable. This kind of LC is one that can be transferred by the original beneficiary (the first beneficiary or transferor) to another party (the second beneficiary or transferee).

A back-to-back LC (BBLC) is a letter of credit which is issued against the support of another letter of credit, at the request of a middleman, in favour of the supplier of the goods. It is used when the ultimate supplier requires a LC as the term of payment, but the middleman is unable or unwilling to obtain a transferable LC issued by the ultimate buyer's bank.

Both LCs involve a middleman as the driving force behind the transaction. Both will involve the substitution of documents by the middleman. Certain common terms under both types of LC can be altered, for example, amount, price, expiry date, presentation period, shipment date, and insured amount. The availability of both types of LC is restricted to the middleman's bank.

However, there are differences between a transferable LC and a BBLC. The issuing bank of the "baby LC" (i.e., the middleman's bank) is liable to pay when requested documents under the BBLC have been submitted and found in order, while the transferring bank of a transferable LC does not assume any responsibility when transferring such LC.

Under a BBLC, there are two LCs involved, while under a transferable LC, there is only one LC involved. The terms of the BBLC are also more flexible and many of these terms can be changed. In a transferable LC, the terms that can be changed are limited to amount, price, expiry date, presentation period, shipment date, and insured amount, as allowed by Article 38 of the Uniform Customs Practice 600 (UCP600).

There must be a term in the transferable LC that designates the LC to be "transferable," but the terms of a master LC under a BBLC do not specify this. If the first beneficiary of the master LC fails to substitute the documents, the issuing bank of the BBLC can rely upon the power of attorney given by the first beneficiary before the LC is issued to complete the transaction. In comparison, under a transferable LC, the first beneficiary's bank will have to rely upon the provisions of Article 38 of UCP600 to complete the transaction on behalf of the first beneficiary.

Double Financing

In double financing, a borrower is using banking lines from different types of facilities or from different banks to finance the same transaction. One situation may involve the company enjoying both post-import financing (e.g., Trust Receipt loan) and pre-shipment financing (e.g., Packing Credit loan) for the same batch of goods.

The out-of-proportion drawdown of the double facilities could translate into a higher gearing ratio for the company. It may try to disguise the actual level of borrowing by window-dressing the year-end borrowing figures. A common trick is to stretch or delay payment to suppliers so as to free up cash to repay bank borrowings. It is therefore important for the bank to look at the debt/equity ratio (see Chapter 3) as well as the trade creditor turnover period to confirm if the company has been delaying payment to other creditors.

One indication of double financing is if the company requests for an extension of a loan repayment due date. If overdraft is available, a hardcore level of overdraft outstanding is also experienced. This is common to companies abusing working capital facilities to finance other assets and/or investments.

This kind of abuse can be detected in situations where:

- The customer obtains trade finance facilities from a number of banks with size much larger than what it requires.
- LAI and/or DA period is longer than the trade term.
- LAI is used to finance receivable while export factoring is taken.

The cash/liquid funds obtained from double financing are often diverted to acquisition of non-core assets, for example, shares and properties, and sometimes even used by directors for their own purposes.

Accommodation Finance

This occurs when a customer uses the import line to source goods from its related company or supplier on local delivery. No goods are actually delivered and the cash drawn from the finance (LAI/export LC negotiation/DP and DA purchase) will have gone to other purposes unknown.

Other Considerations

- **Seasonal fluctuation.** The working capital requirement may not spread evenly throughout the year but concentrate on several weeks/months, e.g. manufacture of seasonal toys for Easter and Christmas.
- **Multi-banking relationships.** If the customer has several banks, you have to know the trade finance facilities offered by the other banks to accurately assess the size of the facilities the customer requires.
- **Types of goods.** Although banks only handle documents in trade transactions, the goods form an underlying security in trade transactions, especially for documentary collections. Banks have to evaluate the goods a customer imports/exports according to:
  i. Marketability. An awareness of local markets is crucial to guard against the possibility of the customer importing goods for which there is little demand and which may not be saleable on arrival.

ii.   Obsolescence. Unless imported and sold quickly, whether the goods will become obsolete and not saleable, for example, electronic items.

iii. Perishability. Many goods, particularly food, have a limited lifetime. Consider whether the customer is able to sell these goods quickly enough on arrival before they spoil.

iv.   Price. Whether the cost is realistic and reasonable. Check by market knowledge and industry comparison. Bankers also need to beware of goods and commodities that are subject to frequent and often large price fluctuations, for example, oil, copper, and paper.

v.   Insurance. Proper checks should always be made to ensure that adequate insurance has been provided to protect the bank and the customer from loss. It is important that the insurance policy be issued by a sound and reputable company.

Working capital management

In the course of our discussions of trade finance, we sometimes refer to working capital management. This is because trade finance is one of the ways in which banks can help their corporate customers manage their working capital. By extending financing such as import and export facilities, banks assist companies in optimising the use of their short-term finances.

Working capital is the difference between a company's current assets and its current liabilities. It represents a company's investment in net current assets that it expects to convert into cash within a year or less. The more current assets held and the more long-term financing used, the less the risk of illiquidity—but the lower the return. By maintaining a large investment in current assets like cash and inventory, a company reduces the chance of production disruption, sales loss from inventory shortages, and the inability to pay bills on time. The increase in working capital however brings no corresponding increase in profits: as the investment in assets increases, a company's return on investment (ROI) declines, as profits are unchanged.

Banks define working capital more narrowly as stock plus trade debtors minus trade creditors. This is because the other items in current assets and current liabilities, for example, other debtors, other creditors, cash, and overdraft, do not vary in direct proportion to a company's turnover. So a bank's definition of a company's working capital only includes items that necessarily arise from the process of the business itself.

Working capital finance, or normal trade finance, is the most common type of lending by banks to businesses. It can "oil the wheels" of a business. It is called working capital in the sense that it is short-term and is an "in-between funding" to finance a business making payments before the arrival of receipts.

Working Capital Requirements (WCR)

Let us now examine a case study of a fictional basketball manufacturer we shall call NBA Ltd to show how to calculate the working capital requirements (WCR) of a business and

FIGURE 6.2   Extract from financial statements of NBA Ltd

Balance Sheet

HKD (millions)	20XX	20YY
Net Worth	87	93
Long-Term Loans	23	20
Overdraft	44	44
Trade Creditors	46	53
	200	210
Fixed Assets	106	100
Stock	44	51
Trade Debtors	50	59
	200	210

Profit & Loss Account

	20XX	20YY
Sales	351	390
Cost of Sales	300	335
Gross Profit	51	55
Overheads	48	49
Net Profit	3	6

the different ways of financing these requirements. Figure 6.2 shows an extract of the company's balance sheet and profit and loss account.

Additional information about NBA Ltd is as follows:

- The company anticipates an increase of 20% in turnover for the current year (assume the current year to be 20ZZ).
- Any increase in net worth (due to profit) will be used to fund fixed asset purchases or to reduce long-term loans. The company also anticipates no further fixed asset/loan movements.
- The overdraft facility is fully utilised.
- NBA Ltd gives buyers 60 days credit terms on average.
- Suppliers give the company 80 days on average to settle.
- Its stock-holding policy includes the following:
    - i.   Raw materials (RM)—30 days;
    - ii. Work in progress (WIP)—production takes 4 days;
    - iii. Finished Goods (FG)—30 days.
- Its production practices include the following:
    - i.   Raw materials are input on day one of production process;
    - ii. Labour and overhead costs are applied evenly throughout the production process.
- Cost of Sales
    - i.   75%—materials;
    - ii. 25%—labour & overheads.
- Seasonality—sales are spread evenly throughout the year.

Figure 6.2 shows an extract of NBA Ltd's balance sheet and provides more information about the company that can be used to calculate its working capital requirements. Based on the information given, what is the working capital requirement of NBA Ltd for the current year 20ZZ? What are the ways it can finance this working capital requirement if it is increasing? We can calculate the company's working capital requirement (WCR) by using figures from the balance sheet and the terms of trade approach.

Balance Sheet Method

The company's WCR for current year 20ZZ is HK$68 million, as shown by the calculation below. The 20YY figures are multiplied by 120% since the company assumes an increase of 20% in turnover in current year 20ZZ.

		20XX	20YY × 120%	20ZZ
	Stock	44	51	61
	Trade Debtors	50	59	71
		94	110	132
Less:	Trade Creditors	(46)	(53)	(64)
	WCR	48	57	68

Terms of Trade Approach

To calculate WCR using the terms of trade approach, we can start by constructing the working capital cycle based on the information given:

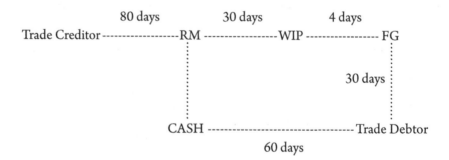

Based on the diagram alone, we cannot determine the company's working capital requirement for current year 20ZZ. We need to compute the estimated monetary value for cost of goods sold for 20ZZ based on information given.

This can be estimated as follows:

	HKD million
Expected sales (20% increase from 20YY)	468
Gross profit (14% of sales)	66
COGS	402

Discounting seasonality, we can estimate trade creditors (TRCR) as follows:

$$\text{Forecast TRCR 20ZZ} = \text{Projected 20ZZ purchases* } \times \frac{\text{Days credit received}}{\text{Days in year}}$$

$$\text{Trade Creditors} = 302m \times 80/365 = 66m$$

$$\text{* Projected purchases} = \text{projected sales} \times (1 - GPM) \times \text{Materials}$$

$$= 468m \times 86\% \times 75\%$$

$$= 302m$$

Discounting seasonality, we can estimate trade debtors (TRDR) as follows:

$$\text{Forecast TRDR 20ZZ} = \text{Projected 20ZZ sales } \times \frac{\text{Days credit given}}{\text{Days in year}}$$

$$= 468m \times \frac{60}{365}$$

$$\text{Trade Debtors} = 77m$$

Discounting seasonality, we can estimate stock (composed of raw materials, work in progress and finished goods) as follows:

- Raw materials

$$\text{Forecast RM 20ZZ} = \text{Projected 20ZZ purchases} \times \frac{\text{Days credit given}}{\text{Days in year}}$$

$$= 302m \times \frac{30}{365}$$

$$= 25m$$

- Work in progress (raw materials and labour and overheads for 4 days)

$$RM = 302m \times \frac{4}{365}$$

$$= 3m$$

$$\text{Labour \& overheads} = 468m \times 86\% \times 25\% \times \frac{4}{365}$$

$$= 1m$$

- Finished goods

$$FG = \text{Projected COGS} \times \frac{\text{Days credit given}}{\text{Days in year}}$$

$$= 402m \times \frac{30}{365}$$

$$= 33m$$

- So stock is:

$$Stock = RM + WIP + FG$$

$$= 25m + 3m + 1m + 33m$$

$$= 62m$$

We can now bring the three main components (stock, trade creditors, and trade debtors) together to determine NBA Ltd's working capital requirement for current year 20ZZ:

$$WCR = Stock + TRDR - TRCR$$

$$= 62m + 77m - 66m$$

$$= 73m$$

The WCR calculated under the terms of trade method is HK$73 million, which is higher than the WCR calculated using the balance sheet method of HK$68 million. The terms of trade approach is arguably the more accurate forecast because it digs deeper into the elements of WCR, rather than simply multiplying the past year's figures by the anticipated increase in turnover for the current year.

Financing WCR

The trade of terms approach shows that NBA Ltd's working capital requirement for current year 20ZZ will be higher by HK$16 million compared with the 20YY WCR. To finance the additional working capital required, NBA Ltd can consider the following ways:

- **Improve working capital management.** This may be the most cost-effective method. Simply by reducing stocks, curtailing buying, and taking steps to exploit the best terms of trade consistent with the company's market credibility, NBA Ltd may be able to bring down the working capital requirement closer to last year's level. Its bank can help in this endeavour by assisting with trade finance arrangements, as discussed previously, and other services such as cash and treasury management.
- **Increase external borrowing.** This can ease the strain on the cash flow in the short-term, but borrowing is a costly method. Many companies, particularly SMEs and fast-growing enterprises, are so sales-driven that an increase in borrowing may simply encourage further sales expansion, leading to overtrading and the need for the company to fall back on financing again. This trend can erode profitability and increase leverage. If the banks decline to continue lending, the company may end up as a corporate failure.

- **Dispose of fixed and other assets.** Where the company has invested in fixed or other assets that are not directly related to the core business, it should sell these assets to improve liquidity. This course of action may however have a short-term negative effect on profitability if these assets can generate higher returns than the assets used in the core business or they have to be disposed of under unfavourable (e.g., forced sale) conditions.
- **Raise additional equity.** This is always the best way to improve a company's capital base and liquidity. However, companies tend to turn to this route when they need huge amounts of money for business expansion, rather than simply to strengthen the capital base.

Overtrading

When a company requests for working capital financing, bank lenders should make sure, first of all, that the business is not overtrading. This is one of the most difficult working propositions that banks can face when extending loans to a corporate customer.

In their book *Accountancy for Banking Students*, J.R. Edwards and H.J. Mellett wrote: "Overtrading occurs when the volume of business activity is excessive in relation to the finance provided by the shareholders, with the result that there is undue reliance on external finance in the form of loan capital, bank overdrafts and trade credit."

The authors continue: "In essence, management has attempted too much too quickly, with the result that the company is left with insufficient resources to meet its currently maturing liabilities, that is, the company will be under severe financial pressure."

Overtrading is frequently cited as a key reason behind a company's liquidity problems, which can happen even to very profitable companies. It is commonly used to describe the situation where a company expands the business excessively in relation to the shareholders' own funds. It results in a company being ultimately unable to generate sufficient funds from its own operations to meet the working capital requirements of the business. The company becomes overly dependent on external finance, either in increased banking facilities or stretched creditor terms.

The following are symptoms of overtrading that bank lenders should be sensitive to when deciding whether or not to lend to companies:

- A general "ballooning" of the balance sheet with particularly large increases in stocks, debtors, creditors, and external finance;
- A large and dramatic increase in sales with a smaller or no increase in gross or operating profit;
- A net outflow of funds combined with a deteriorating capital structure;
- Hardcore overdraft developed in the bank account with little fluctuation in account balance;
- Deteriorating financial ratios:
  - i. Declining operating profit to sales, reflecting deteriorating margin and performance;
  - ii. Rapid increase in sales to operating capital employed suggesting a large increase in turnover from too small a capital base;

iii. Low/declining current and quick ratios;
iv. Falling stock turnover period;
v. Low/declining debtors to creditors ratio;
vi. Lengthening credit payment period;
vii. Low working capital or working capital deficit;
viii. Low/declining ratio of working capital to total assets;
ix. Low/declining ratio of working capital to sales;
x. Increased gearing and debt/equity ratio;
xi. Increased external funding of assets;
xii. Deteriorating interest cover.

Summary

- A bank has to understand the business needs of a client company and the industry it is in, to know what type of facility to offer. Various types of businesses in Hong Kong pose certain risks as well as opportunities for banks that want to service their needs.
- International trade financing is one of the core businesses of banks in Hong Kong because it is a trade hub. They can assist both importers and exporters with trade transactions for a fee through such products as Cash-in-Advance, Letters of Credit, Documentary Collections, and Open Account.
- Trade finance can help companies with their working capital requirements, along with other bank products such as overdrafts and loans. But it is important for businesses and the banks that lend to them to anticipate and calculate the right amount of working capital they need. Before extending financing, banks must make sure the company is not engaged in double financing, accommodation financing, misuse of local LCs, and other irregular activities.
- Sometimes, when sales volume climbs so fast and so high that production cannot meet demand, even a profitable company could fall into the danger of "overtrading." In over-trading, the company seeks out more borrowings to finance expansion. This could lead to liquidity problems, which could affect the company's ability to service its loans.

Key Terms

asset-based lending	drawings
back-to-back letter of credit (BBLC)	letter of credit (LC)
bills receivable (BR)	loans against imports (LAI)
documentary collection (DC)	overdraft facility
documents against acceptance (DA)	overtrading
documents against payment (DP)	packing credit
double financing	revolving loan

term loan

trade finance cycle

transferable letter of credit

trust receipt (TR)

WIP (work in progress)

working capital financing

working capital requirement (WCR)

Study Guide

1. How does asset-based lending differ from other types of lending?
2. What type of facility is most appropriate to use in financing:
   a) Seasonal inventory needs?
   b) Construction of a warehouse?
   c) Refinancing of debt?
   d) Acquisition of equipment?
3. How does the signing of the CEPA affect the business prospects of professional services firms in Hong Kong?
4. Why does financing a DA transaction carry a higher degree of risk for the bank compared with a DP transaction?
5. Why should a bank be wary when sales are outstripping capacity so much so that a business has to tap more loans in order to expand capacity?

Further Reading

Gup, Benton E. and Kolari, James W. 2005, *Commercial Banking*. United States: John Wiley & Sons, Third Edition.

Edwards, J.R. and H.J. Mellett. *Accountancy for Banking Students*. London: Chartered Institute of Bankers, Fourth Edition.

International Chamber of Commerce website, http://www.iccwbo.org/.

Mainland and Hong Kong Closer Economic Partnership Arrangement (CEPA) website, http://www.tid.gov.hk/english/cepa/.

United Nations Economic and Social Commission for Asia and the Pacific (ESCAP) website, http://www.unescap.org/tid/publication/chap8_2224.pdf.

United States Department of Commerce. International Trade Administration website, http://www.trade.gov/publications/pdfs/tfg2008.pdf.

7

Credit Control and Problem Loans

Learning objectives

After studying this chapter, you should be able to:

1 Understand the credit management structure of a bank

2 Know why corporations fail at various stages of their growth

3 Recognise the signs of impending corporate failure

4 Learn what steps to take when a company fails

Introduction

Most banks spend a lot of time, effort, and resources at the time a credit application request is prepared, analysed, and evaluated. The potential borrower's credit risk, financial statements, and other circumstances are carefully examined and weighed against the entire portfolio.

But once the commitment is booked, some banks are not as dedicated to credit management as they should be. The system and level of monitoring of loans vary throughout the banking industry. Yet the fact is that credit control and tracking the performance of borrowers for early detection of problem loans are as important as the decision to lend in the first place.

We discuss the role of credit management in the credit assessment process in this chapter.[1] We also examine the structures that must be in place for effective monitoring, the warning signs that banks should be sensitive to in order to detect problem loans and what should be done in case of corporate failures.

Credit Management Process and Structure

In Hong Kong, the HKMA has issued guidelines on the credit management process in the General Principles of Credit Risk Management module of the Supervisory Policy Manual. Figure 7.1 illustrates how credit functions in an authorized institution should be organised. According to the HKMA, this structure is illustrative only. It is up to the banks to adopt a specific organisational structure that works for them, provided that the general principles of credit risk management in the HKMA guidelines are observed.

The HKMA identifies the functions and components of the credit management process as 1) credit strategy and policy, 2) risk management, 3) credit initiation, 4) credit evaluation, approval, and review, 5) credit administration, 6) credit measurement and monitoring, 7) problem loan management, and 8) independent audits.

- **Credit strategy and policy.** The Board of Directors is ultimately responsible for approving the bank's credit risk strategies and policies. The board ensures that the credit strategy and policy are appropriate to the business and are observed across the organisation. It may delegate all or part of its credit authority to the credit committee or senior management, but the board remains responsible for overseeing credit risk management. The credit committee or senior management is responsible for translating the board's

---

[1] This chapter uses some material from *Commercial Banking* (2005) by Benton E. Gup and James W. Kolari and *Strategic Credit Management* (1995) by Sam N. Basu and Harold L. Rolfes, Jr., with permission from publisher John Wiley & Sons.

FIGURE 7.1   Organisation of credit functions

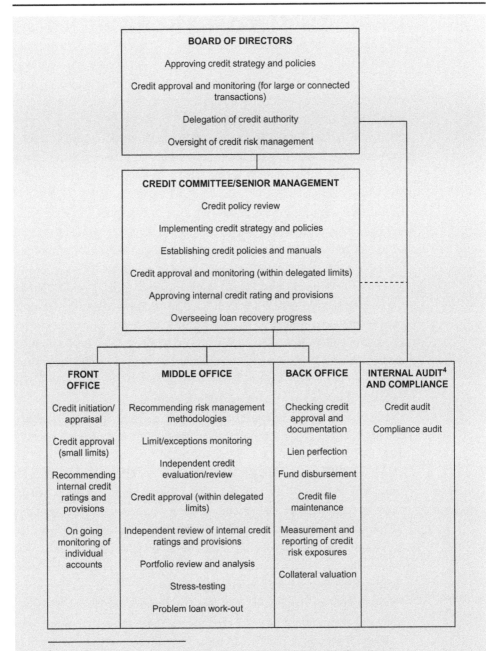

BOARD OF DIRECTORS

Approving credit strategy and policies

Credit approval and monitoring (for large or connected transactions)

Delegation of credit authority

Oversight of credit risk management

CREDIT COMMITTEE/SENIOR MANAGEMENT

Credit policy review

Implementing credit strategy and policies

Establishing credit policies and manuals

Credit approval and monitoring (within delegated limits)

Approving internal credit rating and provisions

Overseeing loan recovery progress

FRONT OFFICE	MIDDLE OFFICE	BACK OFFICE	INTERNAL AUDIT[4] AND COMPLIANCE
Credit initiation/ appraisal	Recommending risk management methodologies	Checking credit approval and documentation	Credit audit
Credit approval (small limits)	Limit/exceptions monitoring	Lien perfection	Compliance audit
Recommending internal credit ratings and provisions	Independent credit evaluation/review	Fund disbursement	
On going monitoring of individual accounts	Credit approval (within delegated limits)	Credit file maintenance	
	Independent review of internal credit ratings and provisions	Measurement and reporting of credit risk exposures	
	Portfolio review and analysis	Collateral valuation	
	Stress-testing		
	Problem loan work-out		

[4]Internal Audit should report directly to the Board of Directors or the Audit Committee.

Source: HKMA

credit strategy into actual practice and ensuring that necessary credit risk management policies and procedures are established.

- **Risk management.** The HKMA recommends that banks establish an independent risk management function in the middle office (see Figure 7.1) to assist the board in managing credit risk. Directly accountable to the board, the credit committee, or senior management, the risk management function is responsible for formulating credit risk management methodologies and strategies and day-to-day measurement, monitoring, and evaluation of credit risk.

- **Credit initiation.** Typically performed by the front office, credit initiation involves account officers soliciting credit business within laid-down policies and managing the relationship with customers. They may also be responsible for preparing credit appraisals for new credit facilities and renewing existing facilities.

- **Credit evaluation, approval, and review.** The middle office (for example, credit control or risk management unit) is responsible for making independent evaluation of credit appraisals and approval of facilities granted by designated credit officers, the credit committee, or the board of directors. The process of credit evaluation, approval, and review covers both extension of new credits and renewal of existing credits. The latter is part of the credit review process, in which the creditworthiness of existing borrowers is periodically updated and evaluated.

- **Credit administration.** The back office undertakes the overall administration of the credit portfolio. Its responsibilities include checking of credit approval and documentation, lien perfection, loan disbursement, collateral valuation, maintenance of credit files, and compilation of management information reports.

- **Credit measurement and monitoring.** These functions are performed at different levels. The board or credit committee oversees credit monitoring on a portfolio basis and may take part in reviewing large or connected exposures. The front office monitors individual accounts on a day-to-day basis and recommends changes in internal credit rating and provisions. The middle office monitors limits and other risk parameters set down by the board, reviews exception reports, and makes sure that problem accounts are properly graded and have provisions made against them. It also performs periodic reviews and analyses the quality of the credit portfolio using stress tests or other techniques. The back office provides support through the measurement and reporting of credit risk exposures for management information.

- **Problem loan management.** This function ensures that problem loans are handled effectively to minimize ultimate credit losses. Less serious cases are usually followed up by the front office. The HKMA recommends that more serious accounts should be transferred to a dedicated workout unit for collection in middle office. The credit committee or senior management is responsible for overseeing the collection process on large non-performing credits and determining the level of provisions for problem accounts.

- **Independent audits.** There should be independent parties, for example Internal Audit and Compliance, that conduct regular independent credit and compliance audits on authorized institutions. These parties should have a direct reporting line to the board or the Audit Committee.

Banks typically rely on various departments and specialists to conduct credit management and monitor credit risks. In the bigger banks, these tasks are often assigned to account executives, line management, credit departments, credit control departments, and loan workout specialists. Smaller organisations may have the same senior credit officer handling both account executive and loan workout functions.

Whatever the structure, it is important that the tasks, controls, and checks and balances in the credit management structure are integrated into the credit review and approval process. It is also important that the sales and marketing aspect of bank lending be kept separate and distinct from credit approval and monitoring, as shown in Figure 7.2, to avoid conflict of interest. When an authorized institution needs to delegate small lending limits to staff in the front office for operational needs, there should be adequate safeguards, for example, an independent review of credits granted, to prevent abuse.

Account Executive

Traditionally, the monitoring function has rested centrally on the account executive or relationship officer. Although credit department managers and line managers support this monitoring function extensively, it is the account executive that has timely and direct access to customer information and intelligence. It is the account executive and his or her

FIGURE 7.2 Separation of duties in credit management

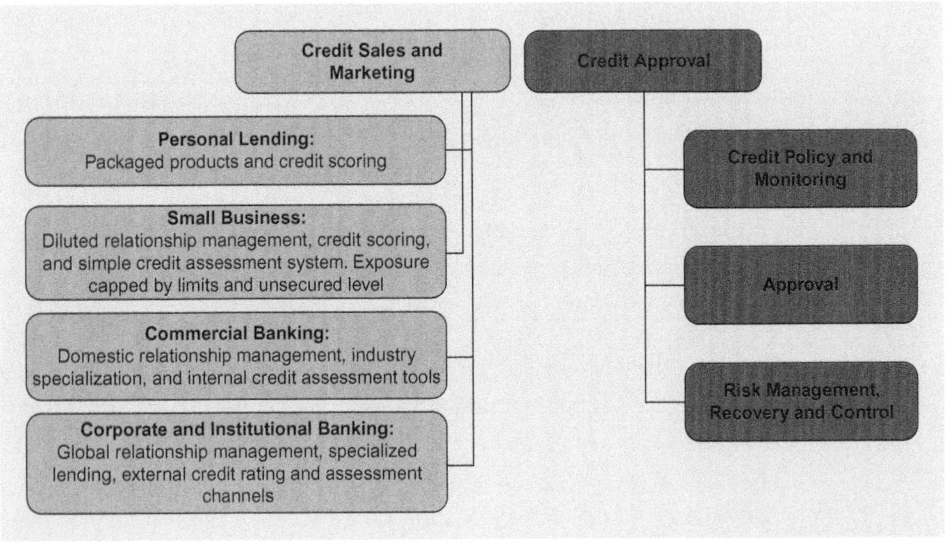

Source: HKIB

superiors who are responsible for customer performance—in practice, they are primarily responsible for initiating changes in client credit risk ratings.

This traditional approach for monitoring client risk has had mixed success in the past and it is doubtful this will be effective in the future. Because of new and expanded banking products, banks are compelled to become more sales-driven and account executives are likely to be involved more extensively and exclusively in sales and marketing roles.

Credit departments may have to assume more responsibility for monitoring and managing customer credit risk. This approach has both drawbacks and benefits. On the one hand, credit analysts usually have limited contact with the clients. On the other hand, they are not constrained by sales and revenue considerations.

Account executives in many banks report to line management and have both marketing and credit responsibilities. As the officer recommending customer credits and/or sale of financial products, the account executive is responsible for the performance of customer credits and their recovery. The account executive performs the following credit-related functions:

- Maintains primary contact with the customer. Evaluates customer needs and capabilities and then structures and negotiates credit and corporate finance solutions to satisfy these needs.
- Structures credits including pricing, repayment terms, collateral conditions, and documentation.
- Performs credit and financial analysis, prepares and recommends credit applications, and submits these to credit authority for action/approval.
- Establishes and maintains customer credit risk ratings.
- Prepares and processes documents for the credits approved by the credit authority. Maintains responsibility for credit agreements and ensures all conditions are met as required in the applications.
- Monitors and evaluates customer performance. Alerts line management on any deteriorating trends.

Line Management

Line managers are the bank managers who manage and support those engaged in the structuring and sale of bank products or services. They exercise the following credit-related responsibilities:

- Supervise the account executives in credit and corporate finance matters and review and affirm their credit recommendations. Their endorsement and/or approval should always be necessary whenever a loan request breaches a certain ceiling set by the bank's board of directors or senior management.
- Assign customer accounts to appropriate account executives, manage their performance and make changes as appropriate.
- Manage portfolio risk and are responsible for the credit performance of risk assets of the business function.

- Manage the risk/return component of the loan portfolio.
- Direct the development and training of account executives.
- Manage the growth and sale of portfolio assets and the portfolio mix.

Risk Management Department

The risk management department reports directly to the senior/chief credit officer or risk director. This unit's functions, objectives, and credit support functions may vary depending on the degree of responsibility and authority it is granted. The risk management department:

- Reviews credit applications and financial analyses prepared by account executives.
- Approves credit applications within the delegated limits set up by the bank's board of directors.
- Monitors client financial performance, periodically prepares reports, and alerts account officers and line management to deteriorating trends, etc.
- Supports the account executive's compliance function.
- Maintains credit files and supports the account officer in booking and documenting new credits and monitoring repayment performance.

Credit Control Department

The credit control department reports to the senior/chief credit officer of the bank. Key committees within this department may include the credit policy committee, the credit committee, and the country limit committee. The credit control department:

- Establishes credit policy and procedures.
- Monitors and manages portfolio concentrations or mix. Evaluates portfolio risk and reserve levels, and recommends or implements change as appropriate.
- Establishes the credit risk rating system and monitors its application and effectiveness.
- Delegates credit authority to credit and line officers.
- Establishes country cross-border limits, industry limits, product limits, etc.
- Oversees credit training and the establishment of credit training programs.
- Evaluates the account executives' credit portfolio performance and communicates results to line managers for inclusion in performance results.

Loan Workout Specialist

The loan workout specialist is the account officer for problem assets. The specialist reports directly to the bank's senior/chief credit officer and undertakes the following tasks:

- Reclassifies problem credits.
- Pursues debt recovery actions even after an account has been written off.

- Manages the portfolio of problem assets and assumes responsibility for their collection.
- Negotiates credit restructures, workouts, legal actions and so on.
- Performs the functions of an account executive but only for the problem assets assigned to him or her.
- Manages the collateral, including their disposal and maintenance.
- Reports periodically on the progress of recovery efforts to the credit committee or senior management to facilitate their monitoring and review.

Characteristics of a Sound Credit Monitoring System

Just because a bank has an independent credit management structure in place does not automatically mean it has a sound credit monitoring system. One of the key objectives of a good credit monitoring process is the accurate and early warning of changes in risk or the identification of problem assets. Traditional credit procedures usually require a borrower risk evaluation to be updated at least yearly. More frequent evaluations, both formal and informal, may be required for problem or classified credits.

Sound credit monitoring processes and procedures provide an overall and updated risk profile of the customer from a variety of sources within and without the authorized institution, as well as track a variety of other factors that could have an impact on a loan or portfolio. Sound credit monitoring processes and procedures share the following common characteristics:

- The credit risk policy specifies, among other things, the types of facilities to be offered, along with ceilings, pricing, profitability, maximum maturities, and maximum debt-servicing ratios for each type of lending.
- Responsibility for customer credit risk rating and its monitoring is clearly identified and understood.
- Customer financial and operational information is obtained on a timely and regular basis. Sources of information include:
    i.   Current quarterly and annual financial reports provided by the customer
    ii. Information acquired by account executives during customer calls
    iii. Third-party financial databases, securities reports and business periodicals
- Timely communication is made among the account executive, line management, credit officer, and credit control officer on the customer's financial performance, repayment records, and trend analysis of the business.
- Periodic review of customer credit relationship and risk evaluations are conducted and reported to appropriate authority.
- The bank's internal auditors perform credit audits of all line units on a regular and scheduled basis.

- Country, industry, portfolio, and large exposure risks are controlled and monitored centrally by senior-level credit managers, with regular reports to appropriate risk committees.
- A ceiling for the total loan portfolio is identified, in terms of the loan-deposit ratio, undrawn commitment ratio, maximum dollar, or percentage of capital base.
- Portfolio limits are made for maximum aggregate exposures by country, industry, category of borrower/counterparty, product, groups of related parties, and single borrowers.
- Limits, terms and conditions, approval, and review procedures and records are kept on connected lending, which is governed by a formal policy statement endorsed by the board.
- The types of acceptable collateral, loan-to-value ratios, and the criteria for accepting guarantees are made explicit, along with the minimum information required from loan applicants.
- A policy endorsed by the board is in place to control and monitor large exposures and other risk concentrations of various kinds.
- Interdependencies in portfolios are identified and dealt with to avoid contagion effects that a substantial decline in property prices, for example, may have on the default rate of commercial and industrial loans that rely heavily on property as collateral.
- Large exposures exceeding 10% of the capital base are carefully monitored, notwithstanding that the limit on such large exposures under the Banking Ordinance is 25%.
- Prudent mismatch limits are established in cases where long-term domestic lending is financed by short-term external borrowing, to control the risk of a reversal of capital flows leading to a liquidity squeeze and exposure of the bank to adverse exchange rate movements.

Credit Risk Mitigation

A company may not make big profits or may even lose money in some bad years, but this should not matter much to the bank so long as the company continues to service its loans. In the long run, of course, the continued health of the borrower does matter, since the chances of making new loans would be curtailed if the business is not growing or if it is deteriorating. However, the bank's immediate concern is the risk that the bank borrower will fail to meet its obligations in accordance with the agreed loan terms.

In theory, credit risk could be mitigated if the bank has been judicious in examining the borrower's financial and other circumstances, as outlined in the previous chapters, during the credit assessment and approval process. In practice, however, not all contingencies can be provided for. There are many sources of credit risk, including suppliers, customers, and the bank itself, and counterparties have a two-way relationship with each other, as Figure 7.3 shows.

FIGURE 7.3   The two-way nature of credit risk

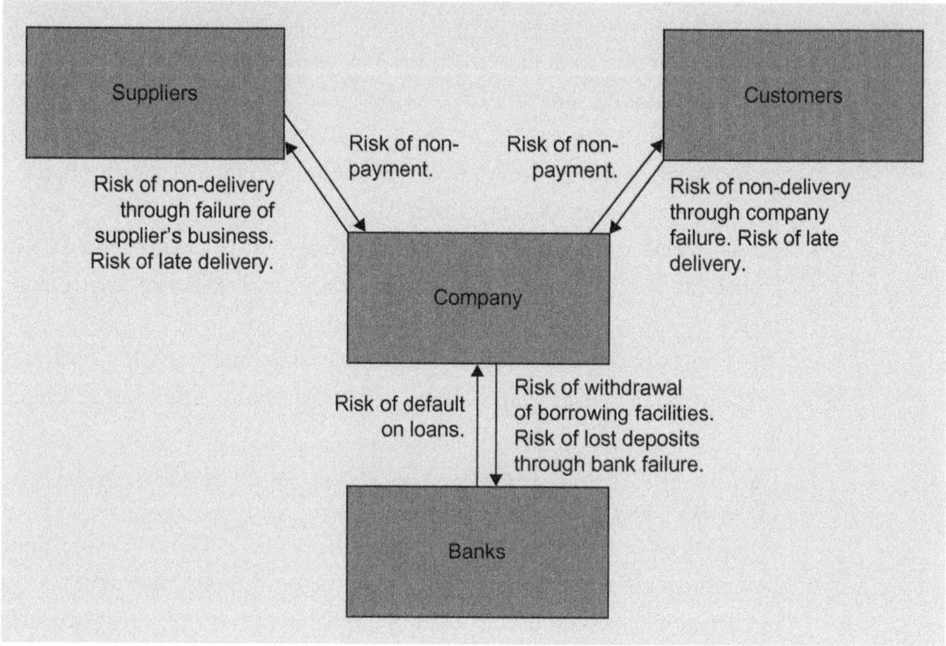

Source: HKIB

The inter-related nature of credit risk underscores the need for comprehensive credit management structures and a sound credit monitoring system within the bank, as discussed in the previous sections. It also strengthens the case for the bank to also examine the ecosystem in which the borrower operates, including its major suppliers, buyers, and operating locations, to flag sources of credit risk. The deficiencies or problem areas it may discover need not automatically lead to the loan application being declined, but they could serve as important inputs for:

- Additional loan covenants;
- Additional collateral;
- Higher pricing of the loan to reflect heightened credit risk;
- More frequent interim reviews;
- More onsite visits by account executives and/or credit officers.

Corporate Failure

There is a distinction between a company defaulting on its loans, which may entail a temporary inability to repay, and a company that has gone out of business, and therefore will not repay the loans at all. Long before a business fails, however, there are usually tell-tale signs that should have alerted bank lenders of impending trouble.

The challenge is to recognise these red flags as soon as possible. Towards this end, it is helpful to remember the main reasons why companies collapse, which include poor management and structural defects, misdirected strategy, poor financial and accounting information, inadequate response to change and constraints, overtrading, undertaking "the big project," and overgearing.

The size and the company's stage of development are also factors in corporate collapses. Studies have shown, for example, that small- and medium-sized enterprises account for 50% to 60% of business failures. Many start-ups also fail to mature into viable enterprises.

Poor Management

Many businesses run into trouble and fail to repay their bank loans due to poor corporate management and structural defects, such as:

- An autocratic "one man rule" style of management by the CEO/owner, who believes in dominating rather than leading.
- A shallow management bench, with a shortage of skilled managers at various levels of the company.
- An imbalance in the top management team, showing an inadequate spectrum of skills.
- A non-participating board of directors weighed down by parochial views instead of the long-term and broad interests of the corporation.
- A lack of financial controls.
- A leadership vacuum at the top, due to one person performing the combined functions of CEO and chairman of the board.

Misdirected Strategy

Companies also fail due to the following wrong strategies:

- They concentrate more on avoiding taxes rather than expanding the business and putting it firmly on a sustainable growth path.
- They focus on generating sales even at the expense of costs going out of control and falling profits, on the theory that gaining market share will eventually mean higher earnings.
- They invest in prestigious high-profile ventures rather than less prominent but profitable projects.
- They devote time and resources to short-term "fire-fighting" and forget about crafting and implementing long-term strategy.
- They resort to window-dressing their financial statements to make their company look healthy.
- They complicate their group organisational structure unnecessarily, which results in vague, duplicative, or confusing functions.

Poor Financial Information

Failing businesses often issue vague financial statements, particularly in the areas of budget control, cash control, and cost control. As a result, top management and the bank lender are kept in the dark as to the actual financial state of the company.

The first line of defence for the bank lender is the examination of the borrower's financial statements and financial ratios, as discussed in the previous chapters. During the credit assessment stage, the bank should not focus only on the actual numbers reported, but also on the systems that generated those figures. The existence and strength of the financial reporting and internal control systems are preferably certified by a reputable external auditor.

However, things can change, particularly when times are bad, such as a recession. A bank lender would do well to carefully compare the company's actual revenues to what had been budgeted. The same comparison should be done with costs, profits, and other financial measures. Cash and cost controls are important as well—the actual cash on hand, level of borrowings, investment spending, direct and indirect costs, and other expenditures should be compared with what had been programmed.

Inadequate Response to Change

As we learned in Chapter 3, successful companies are those able to adapt quickly to changes in their external environment, their market, and industry. Many corporations fail because they are unable to cope with these changes.

For instance, in many countries, the political situation is volatile and could lead to legal and regulatory adjustments that would affect businesses. An election of a new head of state could relax or tighten trade quotas, raise or lower taxes, or open up new investment opportunities.

Social changes also affect companies in terms of consumer attitudes, demography, ethnic mixes, lifestyles, and the extent of political consciousness of citizens. For instance, countries with young populations tend to go for certain products and services, compared to those with ageing populations. Countries with active trade unions would have a different level of labour protection compared to those that do not have unions. Or countries where citizens are vocal about consumer rights would have tougher regulations regarding products, especially food, drugs, and cosmetics.

Changes in a nation's macro-economic environment and even the state of the global economy could also have profound effects on businesses, especially the heavily leveraged ones, in times of recession, high inflation, interest rate increases, and volatile currency exchange rates and commodity prices.

Even if the socio economic and political environments do not change, an external threat to a company could come from within its market or industry. For instance, new technology may deliver the same product at a lower cost or a new product that could render the current goods in the market unappealing or obsolete. Or mergers could produce new threats or cheaper foreign imports could edge out higher priced local goods.

Overtrading

As we discussed in the previous chapter, overtrading could harm even profitable companies. It occurs when sales rise so quickly and so high that a company may respond by expanding production and operations quickly. At that point, it does not yet internally generate enough funds for its working capital but must borrow in order to meet its working capital requirements and at the same time service its creditor payments.

An external threat such as a sudden change in the socio economic or political environment or in the industry or market could heighten default risk and lead to company failure.

Aggressive Projects

Sometimes even a well-established business could falter when going into an undertaking or obligation that is too large compared to its resources. There are many examples where companies fail after aggressively launching new products, diversifying outside their core business, or undertaking a series of mergers and acquisitions in a short period of time.

Overgearing

In Chapter 3, we learned about the financial ratio to measure debt, which is called gearing. Gearing is calculated using the following formula:

$$\text{Gearing} = \frac{\text{Total external borrowing}}{\text{Tangible net worth}}$$

A company practices overgearing when it has debt in excess of its tangible net worth (e.g., 200% and above). It then becomes highly vulnerable during a recession and in a rising interest rate environment.

Beaver's Univariate Model

One particular framework called Beaver's Univariate Model continues to be in use today as a way of forecasting financial failures. The model was proposed by William Beaver, an American professor emeritus of accounting at Stanford University, in a 1968 study entitled "Information Content of Annual Earnings Announcements," which was published in the *Journal of Accounting Research*.

Beaver obtained the financial statements of 79 failed companies and 79 successful firms. Each collapsed firm was paired off with a successful corporation in the same industry. He then applied the same financial ratios we studied in Chapter 3 and came to the conclusion that three ratios in particular stood out as the best indicators for predicting financial failure. In the order of their usefulness to forecast failure, these are:

- Cash flow/total debt;
- Net income/total assets (return on assets);
- Total debt/total assets (debt ratio).

Beaver concluded that "the cash flow, net income and debt positions cannot be altered and represent permanent aspects of the firm. Because failure is too costly to all involved, the permanent, rather than the short-term factors, largely determine whether or not a firm will declare bankruptcy or default on a loan payment." On further examination of the financial statements the year before the firms' collapse, he developed a theory that posits that failed firms have less cash and inventory but more accounts receivable before going under.

Beaver's Univariate Model can be a useful tool for credit monitoring in that account executives and credit officers can focus first on the financial ratios and other elements that the model predicts are among the most reliable in forecasting a corporate failure. Given the big number of accounts that have to be looked after and the various elements to be examined, this approach can help banks prioritise which borrowers should receive special attention in terms of the likelihood that their loans may turn problematic.

Other Warning Signals

Table 7.1 summarises the warning signals for problematic credits and corporate failures that we have discussed, and presents other signs of looming corporate trouble, such as:

- Rapid increase/decrease of turnover in bank accounts;
- The practice of multi-banking and exits by other banks;
- Key management changes, shareholder disputes, and/or departures;
- Sudden share price falls or increased trade volumes;
- Issuance of court writs;
- Accounting problems such as auditor qualifications, frequent change of auditors, delay in completion of audited accounts, emergence of unknown but substantial amounts in management accounts, and large variance in budget and actual figures.

Remedial Actions

When these warning signs are detected and further investigation shows there is reason for serious concern, what should the bank do? The following remedial actions can be considered:

TABLE 7.1   Warning signals of loan or corporate troubles

Structural/Strategic	Financial	Managerial
No product differentiation in conjunction with a high cost structure.	Weak financial controls and inconsistency in reporting.	Management dominated by one person (founder, etc.).
Material regulatory changes which affect competitiveness.	Late or incomplete reporting of financial information.	Board of directors dominated by management and/ or is ineffective in the performance of its duties and responsibilities.
Ineffective delivery/distribution system in a changing market environment.	Change in auditors. Declining financial trends. Debt equity ratios	
Strategic plan and planning inconsistencies.	Liquidity Cash flow Margins	Excessive board of directors or senior management turnover.
Major acquisitions or disposition.	Expense ratios	
Change in market demand/share brought on by technology or regulation/deregulation.	Change in account procedures/ practices. Consistently fails to meet plan.	Sudden change in the CEO or in the company's senior management.
Introduction or cancellation of key products/services.	Delinquency or late payment of obligations.	Insufficient depth of management.
Major restructure, expansion, or contraction of the company.	Occurrence of judgments or liens against customer assets.	Unusual management behavior.

Source: Sam N. Basu and Harold L. Rolfes, Jr., *Strategic Credit Management* (John Wiley & Sons, 1995), 152.

- Designate the loan as a problem asset and manage it separately from the rest of the loan portfolio. The bank may allow the relationship officer or account executive to retain management responsibility for the workout effort with the support of the legal, accounting, and tax departments. Alternatively, responsibility can be shifted to the bank's special loan workout team or officer.
- Complete a review of the borrower's credit file and all loan documentation. The value of the collateral should be reassessed. The bank should also examine the options available to it under the terms and conditions of the loan agreement. The actual and imminent violations of the loan agreement should be identified.
- Determine if immediate action is required to protect the bank's interest and minimise the downside risk. This requires the ability to differentiate between problem loans that can still be fixed and those that can no longer be fixed. Meeting the borrower's senior executives and the company's other creditors, as appropriate, can help the bank come to a decision on the approach.
- Depending on the assessment of the viability of the problem loan, the bank can then embark on any or a combination of the following courses of action:
  i. Form a creditors' group to address common interests and develop a joint course of action.
  ii. Renegotiate loan terms and conditions, including requiring collateral (if the loan is unsecured) or asking for additional collateral. The loan can also be restructured to give the borrower breathing space, such as lengthening the loan period and forgiving part of the penalties.

iii. Establish new key objectives/targets/milestones for the borrower to follow. The bank must recognise, however, that circumstances have changed from the time when the loan was first negotiated, and so it must be firm but realistic in negotiating with the borrower. The objective is to help the borrower stay current on its loans because delayed payments are better than outright default.

iv. Obtain a commitment from the borrower to observe financial transparency. The company may have hidden its problems before, but now that the bank is aware of the problems, the company should be obliged to keep the bank appraised of all relevant information and developments as they happen. A schedule of regular reports is a useful way to turn this commitment into reality.

v. Call in the loan.

vi. Foreclose on the collateral and recover any shortfall.

Business Review Specialists

When it becomes clear that the borrower's problems are far more serious than what the bank's internal staff can deal with, accountants and other outside experts should be appointed to review the business's viability. They should be asked to start with a review of the financial position of the company at a recent date, probably the latest management accounts review. The priority is to do a financial forecast of the company, instead of concentrating on a backward review of what went wrong. The forward picture should cover a period of six months to two years since the future of many troubled companies could be determined within that period.

Accountants should review management accounts and at suitable intervals, track a troubled company's progress in achieving its corporate strategy and report the progress (or non-progress) to the creditors. There should be continuous and intensive monitoring, especially of interest payments.

With sizeable accounts, which could justify the costs and time involved, a senior member of the bank's credit monitoring team should sit alongside the company's senior executives. Such expensive hand-holding may only work with major cases and as a short-term measure.

Turnaround Specialists

The bank can sometimes persuade an ailing company to hire turnaround specialists to help restructure the company. Most of the major accounting and consultancy firms offer such advisory services. This is only justified if there is a fair chance of success because "company doctors" do not come cheap. The borrower may decide to follow the bank's suggestion if the alternative is foreclosure on its loans and the consequent damage to its reputation and even its financial viability.

The turnaround specialist may make the following recommendations:

- Improve cash flow and balance sheet through faster debt collection, stock reduction, and control, sale of surplus or unproductive assets, new sources of finance such as equity, sale, and leaseback, resort to factoring and sale of non-core peripheral activities.
- Undertake changes in management, products, methods of operation, value re-engineering, marketing, pricing policy, and refinancing methods.
- Renegotiate with banks and other creditors to restructure debts.
- Close down the business entirely in an orderly manner.

Winding Up

If all else fails, the business may be sold or liquidated, and the loan file transferred to the bank's legal department or loan workout department. If possible, the bank should try to participate in deciding how to end the company's life in order to protect its interests. For example, a company with a solvent balance sheet but no likelihood of future profits may be able to wind down its affairs in an orderly way and end up with a surplus.

If the decision is to sell the company, the bank should help ensure that it is properly valued as a going concern and that a competitive bidding is held to get the highest possible price. The new owners may be persuaded to honour all the sold company's obligations and so it is possible that the bank's loan could still be repaid. The sale should be organised in a methodical and orderly way.

Winding up a company in Hong Kong can be a complicated procedure that can take months or even years to complete, which is a typical situation in other jurisdictions. There are two ways to liquidate a company: through a voluntary winding up or a compulsory winding up. Most liquidations in Hong Kong are of the voluntary type because there are fewer formalities to be complied with, compared with a compulsory winding up.

In both cases, a company winding up typically involves:

- Transfering the management of the company to an outside independent insolvency practitioner, usually a certified public accountant.
- Providing for the early realisation of assets and meeting of claims, and for that purpose to suspend the individual pursuit of claims by creditors.
- Prescribing an equitable ranking of claims by unsecured creditors and distribution of the proceeds of realisations among creditors according to a statutory order of priorities under the Companies Ordinance.
- Setting aside transactions made by the company in the run-up to winding up that are prejudicial to the interests of the general body of creditors or which unfairly give preference to one creditor over another.

- Investigating the conduct of those concerned in the management of the company, with a view to the filing of criminal or civil proceedings for culpable behaviour causing loss to the creditors[2]

The bank's main interest would be to make sure its claims are properly ranked according to the law, that it is paid properly from the proceeds of realisations, and that none of the creditors are given unfair preference.

Summary

- Banks often concentrate on attracting loan customers but do not devote as much time and effort to monitoring their financial health once the loans are booked.
- Banks should assign sufficiently experienced personnel to perform the various independent functions needed for credit approval and control.
- Banks should have a well-defined and transparent credit risk management structure, and a comprehensive set of credit policies and guidelines in place to monitor credit risk as part of its normal routine.
- Bank personnel, assigned to do credit monitoring, should be familiar with the warning signs of a business going under, and take immediate steps to avert or mitigate such an event. However, if failure is inevitable, the bank should ensure that the process of winding up the business is orderly and that all its claims are properly ranked and repaid as provided by law.

Key Terms

account executive	loan workout specialist
compulsory winding up	overgearing
corporate failure	overtrading
credit control	remedial and recovery actions
credit department	voluntary winding up
credit risk management structure	warning signals
line management	

Study Guide

1. Why do some banks fail to detect when a corporate borrower is failing until it is nearly too late? Give two examples.

---

[2] Simon Chan Bo-ching, *Hong Kong Banking Law and Practice Volume Two* (Hong Kong: Hong Kong Institute of Bankers, 2000), 269–270.

2. What can a bank do to monitor possible loan defaults by a company?

3. Why is it "important that the sales and marketing aspect of bank lending is separate and distinct from credit approval and monitoring?" Give an example of what may happen if this is not the case.

4. What would justify sending a Mr. Fix-it or "company doctor" to an ailing business?

5. As an account executive in your bank, you read in the news that an established company that has long been a part of your credit portfolio is embarking on an ambitious project outside its core competence. Since the company has a good track record of debt repayment, would you advise your bank to extend the loan for this new project? If the bank does extend the loan, what steps should it take after booking the loan?

Further Reading

Basu, Sam N. and Rolfes, Harold L. Jr. 1995, *Strategic Credit Management*. United States: John Wiley & Sons.

Beaver, William H. 1968, "The information content of annual earnings announcements" in *Journal of Accounting Research*, Supplement, 67–92.

Chan Bo-ching, Simon. 2000, *Hong Kong Banking Law and Practice Volume Two*. Hong Kong: Hong Kong Institute of Bankers.

Hong Kong Monetary Authority, "General Principles of Credit Risk Management" in *Supervisory Policy Manual*, http://www.info.gov.hk/hkma/eng/bank/spma/attach/CR-G-1.pdf.

_____. "Problem Credit Management" in *Supervisory Policy Manual*, http://www.info.gov.hk/hkma/eng/bank/spma/attach/CR-G-10.pdf.

Index